The Emerging Mind

The Emerging Mind

CO-WRITTEN AND EDITED BY

KAREN NESBITT SHANOR, PH.D.

RENAISSANCE BOOKS
Los Angeles

To my mother, Irene, and my son, Daniel.

Note to reader: Several of the articles contained in this book have more than one author. It can be assumed that when the word "I" is used, it is in reference to the primary author.

Library of Congress Catalog Card Number: 99-068854
ISBN: 1-58063-057-X
10 9 8 7 6 5 4 3 2

Design by Tanya Maiboroda
Author photo on jacket by Richard Millstein/David's

Published by Renaissance Books
Distributed by St. Martin's Press
Manufactured in the United States of America
First Edition

ACKNOWLEDGMENTS

I am forever indebted to the contributors to The Emerging Mind: Drs. Frank Putnam, Jayne Gackenbach, Deepak Chopra, John Spencer, and Karl Pribram, for sharing their extraordinary expertise and cutting-edge visions. I can't think of a more dedicated group of scientists.

Dr. John Spencer would like to acknowledge the research done by Dr. Phuong T. K. Pham for the Mind-Body Medicine chapter, and Dr. Jayne Gackenbach would like to dedicate her chapter to the memory of Dr. Charles Alexander.

I would like to thank my wonderful agent, Muriel Nellis, for believing in this book, Jane Roberts, for her valuable assistance, and the talented team at Renaissance Books, especially editors Robin Cantor Cooke, Joe McNeely, Arthur Morey, and Matthew Daley, who cared enough to make this the best book possible!

Philosophy professor Roger Paden and N.I.H. scientist, Valerie Barr, were exceptionally helpful in a number of ways. In addition to their intellectual contributions, they have been loyal friends (as well as my patient instructors at the Capital Aikikai Aikido dojo here in the Washington area). Thanks so much to my understanding clients who have shared their psychotherapy sessions with piles of books and papers and have eagerly awaited what one patient referred to as "the emerging book." Others who have been so very helpful along the way include: Anne Conover Carson, Judith Milon, Coach Nick Zoulias, Juris Jurjevics, Srimati Kamala and the wonderful people at the Ghandhi Center in Washington, William and Lorraine Dorgan, Ian and Connie Falconer, Dudley and Larry Doan, Kathy Kogok, Carlos Rivas, Tomasa Ruiz, Tshanda Tshimanga, Eric Pringle, Edi Ramirez, Rigo Cruz, Robyn and James Graney, Kenneth and Kim

Cohen, Stacy and James Brennan, Mirna and Rogelio Molina, Lilian Kew, Sam Leven, and Stephen Chang.

While writing this book, I have been privileged to meet and work with Georgetown University professors George Farre, Josef Rauschecker, and Jag Kanwal in the development of the Cognitive Science Programs' 1999 international conference on "The Brain and Communication," honoring Dr. Pribram. I thank them for their help and inspiration. In the academic realm I would also like to acknowledge those who have guided me over the years, including Drs. Richard Atkinson and Melvin Gravitz, and to remember Drs. Harold and Ruth Greenwald. Finally and most importantly, my mother Irene Van Horn and my son Daniel Perry deserve medals for their patience and constant understanding, as I have had to take valuable time from being with them to complete this book. I'd like to thank David Cohen for being so very supportive during the writing of the book. I would also like to remember with love my brother Daniel Nesbitt and my father George Nesbitt.

Contents

Introduction

"Perhaps the only limits to the human mind are those we believe in."

—WILLIS HARMAN

RIDING ON A LIGHT BEAM

It is said that in developing his theory of relativity, Albert Einstein imagined himself riding on a beam of light. Is this just a quaint anecdote about the creative process or is the mind truly capable of such a feat? There is scientific evidence from researchers at renowned universities that the mind can do even more than this. For example, studies at Stanford have shown that through our thoughts we can affect a distant person's blood pressure or heart rate.[1] And scientists at Princeton have documented the mental communication of information from one person to another over distances of thousands of miles.[2]

Moreover, the speed of light[3] doesn't approach the superluminal speeds of many subatomic waves and particles, the entities smaller than atoms that are the stuff of cosmic intelligence and information. Our thoughts therefore could defy limits of time and space. What we think does matter. In fact, many scientists believe our thoughts are capable of creating matter. And why not? When we move beyond physical, material limitations, a thought—consisting of certain frequencies of energy and mind waves, which will be explained later—can affect subatomic particles or even create them. Someday soon the adage, "Be careful what you ask for, you just might get it" may be expanded to include the warning, "Be careful what you think of, it just might happen." At the forefront of discovery, *The Emerging Mind* endeavors to:

- explore the fascinating "layers" and components of the human mind;
- examine the quantum nature of the mind; and
- show how to use some of the latest research to improve our lives.

The 1990s were referred to as the decade of the brain. Discoveries in a variety of disciplines coupled with advanced information technology have resulted in an exponential growth in our understanding of the mind (which as you will see is not simply the activities of thought). The latest research in physics, mathematics, biology, chemistry, and psychology tells us that the brain itself is in reality only one small part of the mind, the physical transmitter and receiver, if you will, of something much more comprehensive and profound.

Several years ago I developed a lecture series for the Smithsonian entitled "The Brain and Consciousness: Previews of the Twenty-first Century," the overwhelming success and popularity of which inspired this book. Renowned experts on different areas of the mind shared their knowledge with a lay audience—hundreds of people curious about and enthusiastic for information that could affect their lives. Something extraordinary occurred during this eight-week series as we all, speakers and participants alike, were educated, enchanted, enthralled, and sometimes confounded by the lectures and thought provoking exchange of information and ideas.

Before presenting the first lecture of the series on the "Evolution of the Brain and Consciousness," I introduced the program in a rather unusual way. As the auditorium lights dimmed, I asked the audience to relax and close their eyes as they listened to a short story by Caldecott Medal winner Ed Young in which seven blind mice went one at a time to explore a mysterious phenomenon by their pond. The first six mice vehemently disagreed about the Something, since each had explored a different part. Then the seventh mouse went to investigate. She ran up one side of the Something and down the other, across the top, and from end to end. "Ah," she said, "now I see. The Something is as sturdy as a pillar, supple as a snake, wide as a cliff, sharp as a spear, breezy as a fan, stringy as a rope. But altogether, the Something is...an elephant!"[4]

The moral of the story is that while knowing in part may make a fine tale, wisdom comes from understanding the whole. The story, of course, was adapted from the classic tale of the blind men and the elephant. While I wanted to make the point that we were going to hear various lectures presenting different parts of the elephant of consciousness, I also wanted to create an experience and metaphor that would involve the audience more deeply than a simple allusion to the well-known classic. Later, a psychologist in the audience asked me if I had tried to "entrain" the group with the exercise. While I had not thought in terms of the actual process of entrainment, in which minds are synchronized in some manner, I had very much wanted to create a mind-set of openness to each speaker, and to encourage active thinking and consideration of new concepts.

I was also able to help the audience relax a little and realize that while they would be listening to lectures from top scientists, they should not feel intimidated, for the brain and consciousness is a subject in which we all have a degree of expertise because of our personal, intimate involvement. And, of course, such is the aim of this book. Much of our continued individual growth is mental. A number of scientific visionaries believe that we are not only learning more about our mental capabilities, but that the human mind is evolving to a higher level of intelligence and awareness. Our scientific sophistication no longer demands that we experience the world and ourselves in fragments. Body, mind, and spirit can again be integrated and understood as a comprehensive whole.

THE IMPORTANCE OF THE WHOLE

As a young girl, I would sometimes race home to tell my family an exciting bit of news. As my story unfolded, my father would ask critical and perceptive questions. If I couldn't respond to his satisfaction, he would remind me to "get the whole story" the next time. A sense of wholeness is important to us all. When we haven't done a task completely, we tend to feel restless and irritable. When we do finish, we feel good—even energized. Some theorists suggest there is an actual release of potential energy when we reach a desired goal.

Using the big picture to frame a current problem generally makes the problem seem smaller, and at the same time more solvable. Drawing upon both hemispheres of the brain gives us more resources to work with and makes us feel stronger as well, like using two hands instead of one to carry a heavy load.

Humans have long looked at the vast sky in awe and reverence. Such a sense of wonder and curiosity about who we are and the universe around us stirs many scientists and philosophers to work toward and reach new levels of understanding. This is what a young child does naturally, if its development isn't impeded. When we stop reaching ever and ever more to learn, to understand, and to grow, something dies inside. In this book, we're reaching for increased understanding of the whole. Each contributor brings a significant piece of the puzzle and the expansive design unfolds with each chapter.

WINDOW OF PERCEPTION, MIRROR OF THE SOUL

Although "the mind" is a noun, it should be a verb, for it is ever dynamic, seeking to grow, understand, and in some way touch the profound and eternal. Modern science offers exciting tools for understanding the mind as our innate urge to grow stirs us to evolve—to emerge. Meditation, mind waves of varying frequencies, unified energy fields, quantum jumps, and fourth and fifth dimensional communication are examples of important areas of exploration in the twenty-first century. Our largely linear ways of looking at and experiencing the world will be shaken up, challenged, and greatly enhanced as we understand more on the very tiniest and at the very grandest levels. Knocking on our door are theories about what happens at subatomic levels, challenging what most of us learned years ago in science. You probably learned, as I did, that material things broke down into molecules, which broke down into individual atoms. The average atom had a nucleus with a proton and a neutron, and then far, far away from the center were some orbiting bits of energy called electrons. Although these energetic blips couldn't be seen by even the most advanced microscope in those days, we were assured that the electrons did indeed exist—because we had electricity, didn't we? And, according to the teaching of the time, we could pretty much predict where those electrons were at any set interval based on the type of element we were observing.

The vast space comprising more than 99% of each atom was virtually written off as nothing—certainly nothing of significance. However, some modern scientists believe that that space, which we in the western world thought of as a bunch of nothing, is very much something. It is energy, intelligence, quite possibly, in fact, the essence of consciousness. This new concept is not how I was taught to think of things.

We know that energy and matter are constantly changing back and forth, one into the other; and that energy comes in many forms and frequencies. Moreover, quantum physics (more precisely "quantum mechanics") tells us that at the subatomic level change occurs in jumps. Particles and waves can get pretty wild. It's hard to predict what they'll do. And just by observing these minute entities, we can change—or even create them.

Each contributor to this book spoke at the Brain and Consciousness series at the Smithsonian, as did Stanford University psychiatrist David Spiegel, whose part in "The Power of Hypnosis" chapter derives from that series. After a look at the evolution of our understanding of the brain, N.I.H. psychiatrist Frank Putnam and I explore the "States of Consciousness from Infancy to Nirvana," explaining how a child develops a sense of self, what the study of multiple personalities can tell us about normal states of mind, and delving into such diverse issues as memory, sex, sports, the effects of drugs on our states of consciousness, and how television and computers affect our minds. We show how everyone experiences many different consciousness states throughout the day, and how we can better create and use these states for health and well-being. Next, dream and sleep expert Jayne Gackenbach introduces us to the various levels of consciousness states in sleep, ranging from lucid dreaming, where we can control our dreams, to much deeper, profound levels of awareness. Deepak Chopra endeavors to explain these depths of consciousness as he draws upon modern science as well as ancient Vedic wisdom. And since the deep part of the mind has been shown to be a reservoir for healing, John Spencer, one of the originators of the Office of Alternative Medicine at the National Institutes of Health, and I explore the mind-body connection—

consciousness and medicine. Hypnosis, one way of accessing the deep levels of consciousness, is studied in the following chapter. Next, renowned scientist Karl Pribram interweaves the latest findings of neuroscience with human spiritual yearnings in "The Reality of Conscious Experience." Finally, we conclude with a fresh synthesis toward understanding and using the mind in the dawn of the twenty-first century.

Throughout this book we explore the power of deep consciousness and how to tap into this enormous wellspring of power, love, and wisdom. Deep consciousness is the deepest all-knowing part of the mind. It has been given many names: hidden observer, thinker behind the thoughts, executive mind, conductor, witness, the space between our thoughts, "lights on, nobody home," the void, supermonad, higher mind, Consciousness, Self, inner wisdom, even the soul.

SCIENCE AND SPIRIT IN HARMONY

These are challenging and thoroughly thrilling times. And when we feel overwhelmed by the latest research, it is important to remember that the finest scientists and mathematicians in the world do, too. I was privileged to attend several of the international gatherings that Karl Pribram sponsored between 1991 and 1996, where top scientists from all over the world gathered to talk, think, and share information about the mind. These gatherings included Nobel laureate in chemistry Ilya Prigogine, physicist Basil Hiley, who worked for many years with the late physicist David Bohm, mathematical physicist Roger Penrose, scientific philosopher John Searle, and Mortimer Mishkin, an expert on memory at the National Institute of Mental Health, to name a few. In one lecture about fuzzy logic and neural networks, I was straining to understand; my own neural networks at that point were feeling extremely fuzzy and illogical. Then I looked over to see Sir Roger Penrose at the next table straining, too, looking almost like a first grader, poised on the edge of his chair and running the fingers of one hand through his hair, as he frantically took notes with the other. I've seen Karl Pribram looking confused at times, although he's been in the vanguard of mind research for over half a century. So, as you read this book don't feel that anyone truly has it figured out. We are all stretching our minds and trying to answer the eternal questions that humans have always asked and that are now being debated in the halls of science, questions such as: Who am I? Why am I here? Is there a God? What happens around those stars that I see every night? Is there life on other planets? Does some part of us go on after our physical bodies give out? How far does the mind reach? What can the mind really do?

In defining the scientific optimism and possibility of our day, Karl Pribram reminds us that:

There is…in the making a real revolution in Western thought. The scientific and esoteric traditions have been clearly at odds since the time of Galileo. Each new scientific discovery and the theory developed from it has, up until now, resulted in the widening of the rift between objective science and the subjective spiritual aspects of man's nature. The rift reached a maximum toward the end of the nineteenth century: mankind was asked to choose between God and Darwin; heaven and hell were shown by Freud to reside within us and not in our relationship to the natural universe. The discoveries of twentieth century science…do not fit this mold. For once, the recent findings of science and the spiritual experiences of mankind are consonant. This augurs well for the new millennium—a science which comes to terms with the spiritual nature of mankind may well outstrip the technological science of the immediate past in its contribution to human welfare.

CHAPTER ONE

The Brain
and Consciousness

Karen Shanor, Ph.D.

"An interest in the brain requires no justification other
than a curiosity to know why we are here, what we are
doing here, and where we are going."

— NEUROSCIENTIST PAUL MACLEAN

STARTING WITH THE BRAIN

The human brain, often called the last frontier, will dominate scientific investigation in the twenty-first century. As we probe further into its functioning, we will bridge the chasm between the physical and the ethereal; already, brain researchers have clues to the link between mind and matter. Ongoing studies of how our thinking affects the world around us and beyond will very likely confirm that our thoughts not only interpret but actually can create our physical reality.

Although the adult brain weighs only three or four pounds, it contains over one hundred billion neurons—which, if we could line them up, might extend from New York to Boston. They engage in such magnificent complexity that Santiago Ramon y Cajal, a pioneer of modern brain science, reverently referred to these pulsing vital neural networks as the "beating wings of the mysterious butterflies of the soul."[1]

Until recently it was thought that we were born with almost all the brain cells we could ever have, but scientists now know that we can increase our neurons throughout our lives if we continue to learn and to use our minds vigorously.

The more we understand about the brain—the material part of the mind—the more it appears to function like a physical transmitter and receiver, decoding and encoding information between our bodies and the outer world.

SETTING THE STAGE: CLASSICAL AND QUANTUM PERSPECTIVES

Historically, views of the brain and consciousness have paralleled our views of the universe and ourselves. In the Western world in particular, such views changed from traditional religious and mystical explanations to a decidedly material focus at around the time of Descartes and Galileo in the seventeenth century. These two men made a sharp distinction between the physical world that could be seen and described by the science of that time and the more elusive mental and spiritual realms. Over the years the scope of scientific explanation centered on what could actually be seen and deduced from the five senses. Anything beyond was discarded as non-scientific and therefore in a larger sense not "true." The universe and life itself were investigated under Newtonian laws of material objects and cause and effect, such as the effect of one billiard ball hitting another. (Classical physics, as we refer to it today, was built on the brilliant findings and deductions of Sir Isaac Newton.) But Newtonian physics, as useful as it is in many types of scientific investigations,

is only part of the story. Even Newton himself alluded to this at the
end of his life when he wrote:

> I do not know what I may appear to the world; but to myself I
> seem to have been only like a boy playing on the seashore, and
> diverting myself in now and then finding a smoother pebble or a
> prettier shell than ordinary, whilst the great ocean of truth lay all
> undiscovered before me.[2]

In physics, that "ocean of truth" has been further understood in
the last three hundred years with theories and research in areas of
subatomic and quantum physics which have very different activities
and "laws" than the classical (Newtonian) arena. "Quantum leap"
has become a popular term and does in fact express what science
has found—that much of the change in nature does not happen in
a smooth, continuous process, but rather in jumps.

Most of our present day Western scientific method is still based on
classical physics, studying only that which we can confine, control, and
measure in the material realm of the five senses. This is a specific and
verifiable method, and important discoveries have come to us through
this approach. However, if we limit our investigations to one methodology (as we presently tend to do in biology, for example), do we not
also limit our understanding of the increasing complexities and intricacies of our universe? Many times, I'm reminded of an analogy I read
as a teenager in a popular science book which compared what we as
humans understood about the universe to the experience of a tiny ant
walking on a table, encountering a human finger and, with head
down—seeing only a small part of the nail and finger— defining that
as all of reality. Limiting ourselves to only Newtonian explanations of
the universe and of the mind seems equally myopic.

Furthermore, much of the research centering on molecular and
cellular levels is what is referred to as reductionistic—examining

specific parts in isolation from knowledge of a whole system. Examining parts of a system is necessary and very important, but if we draw conclusions about a system by reducing everything to some of its fragments, we are likely to miss something. A careful examination of moon dust, for example, yields only a portion of the information needed to understand gravity or the workings of our solar system. And very often a whole system takes on attributes which are not evident in its individual parts—the whole is more than the sum of its parts. Take H_2O, which means that two hydrogen atoms are bonded with one oxygen atom to create a water molecule. Yet separated, these individual hydrogen and oxygen atoms are *not wet*.

Still, some scientists steadfastly define the entire world by measuring material fragments, and all of the mind by examining a portion of it. Biologist Francis Crick does that when he asserts that the physical functioning of the brain neurons themselves are the sole basis of consciousness and perhaps even the human soul. Crick does not include ideas of God or the human spirit in his consideration of brain function. Nor does he include scientific knowledge about subatomic interactions. According to him, experiences felt by some people to be mystical in nature are no more than sensations produced by the physical functioning of our neurons that trick us into thinking there is something beyond our physical bodies. Crick's explicitly materialistic approach is summed up in his words:

"You, your joys and sorrows, your memories and ambitions, your sense of personal identity, and free will, are in fact, no more than the behavior of a vast assembly of nerve cells . . . . As Lewis Carroll's Alice might have phrased it: 'You're nothing but a pack of neurons.'"[3]

In his 1994 book, *The Astonishing Hypothesis*, which develops the above assertion, Crick says there is little reason to even consider quantum physics in the study of the brain, since according to him most of the information we need is explained by classical Newtonian physics.

In contrast, many scientists believe that we must go beyond the limitations of our five senses to the quantum level in order to understand the brain and consciousness. Scientific panels (including those convened at the National Institutes of Health) continue to work on developing methodologies that surpass the classical Newtonian framework. A vast array of interdisciplinary research is confirming that in addition to the more material Newtonian cellular and molecular processes that occur in the brain and throughout the body, there are wave oscillations, vibrations, and subatomic activity that can be explained only by quantum physics. Examples of these have been shown to occur in the retina of the eye, in the hearing mechanism, and in a number of functions in the brain itself. Many of these will be explained in later chapters.

The classical processes of chemical changes and associated electrical charges within and across the spaces (synapses) between neurons can be compared to wire circuits—passing on information within a controlled area. We could compare this circuitry to that of a radio which we plug into an electric wall socket. A radio also picks up waves and frequencies of various programs from the air. Each neuron does something similar—just as the physical part of the radio receives the radio frequencies; this process happens at a holistic quantum level (therefore not confined to a wire circuit or a physical neuronal pathway). In a groundbreaking 1999 study on perception at the National Center for Scientific Research in Paris, Francisco Varela showed that the instant we are aware of a concept our *whole* brain is energized, which is probably a quantum event. (This reminds me of the "light bulb" lighting up over a cartoon character's head to represent an idea!)

As will be explained in more detail in his chapter, Dr. Pribram believes one place where the neurons receive and process this holistic quantum information is the dendritic weblike area located near the border of the synapse—the gap between two neurons. Analogous to a delicate spider web that is vulnerable to the slightest breeze, the dendritic web has been shown to tune into the most subtle subatomic vibrations and changes in energy. Another way to understand the difference between the circuits of the neurons and the web which catches quantum level vibrations is what happens when we talk on the telephone. The vibrations caused by one's voice (quantum in nature) are transformed into electrical currents which in turn travel within a wire in a linear fashion such as the communication from neuron to neuron.

Roger Penrose and Stuart Hameroff suggest that a likely site for interaction between quantum and classical levels of activity among the cells is within the microtubules, minute tubelike structures in the neurons in the area of the dendrites. These tiny insulated tubes which seem to guide much of what takes place intracellularly, are thought to possess quartzlike qualities—similar to the idea of a radio receiver.

Newtonian and quantum processes complement and interact with each other. Quantum information, which forms the basis of consciousness, changes into physical properties at the level of molecules and larger, and the reverse occurs as well: Information is brought in from the environment and quantum soup of the universe, transformed and encoded in some way in our brain and the rest of our body, then used or stored. Conversely, our thoughts and emotions are coded in subatomic information which is broadcast (cast broadly) into the environment, like a radio wave, both locally and at great distances depending on the frequency and power of the transmitter. Scientists are just beginning to understand how this might happen by investigating various transformations, spectral domains, and the phases of waves—using cutting edge technology to explore age old theories and questions about the mind.

HISTORIC MODELS OF THE MIND

One could say that Rene Descartes invented the concept of the mind in the early seventeenth century. Before him, philosophers spoke instead of the soul (which often incorporated workings of the body, especially the autonomic nervous system), or reason (which in some theories was thought to survive a person's physical death), intellect, spirit, and other concepts, attempting to explain the world and our part in it. The ancient Greeks, for example, divided the world into animate and inanimate objects. Each form of life, in their way of viewing the world, possessed a soul. But it was Descartes who reified, named as a thing, the mind as our awareness and our consciousness. His famous "cogito, ergo sum" (I think [more precisely: I know, I am aware], therefore I am) can be seen as an explanation of self-awareness, our individual separateness, our human uniqueness.[4]

Descartes believed that the mind was extracorporeal, outside our body. The physical brain was certainly not the thinking part of us, for how could something as exquisite as our thoughts and awareness be centered in the crude enfolding tissues and fissures inside the skull? In fact, he thought of the physical brain as a type of radiator, which cooled the blood that was heated in steamcooker fashion in other areas of the body.

Descartes believed there was a distinct difference between the mind and the body. And his distinction continues even today when, for example, we see mental health as separate from physical health. According to Descartes, the mind communicated with bodily parts through the pineal gland, located in the brain and referred to in Eastern cultures as the "third eye." Descartes believed this gland to be like a round ball with holes in it that somehow could connect the mind with the physical, mechanical body.[5] It was not until scientists were able to dissect the body that the brain's more direct connection to thinking was acknowledged.

EIGHTEENTH-CENTURY LESSONS IN BRAIN ANATOMY

In the West such a connection was stimulated by the work of German physician Franz Joseph Gall, who at the end of the eighteenth century studied in great detail the functioning of the human brain. Gall found that gray matter was the essential active portion of the brain and that what he described as white matter served largely as connective tissue; he also correctly identified various regions of the brain responsible for specific functions. However, Gall's theory that some cranium shapes correlate with personality traits was misunderstood by the public and resulted in the birth of phrenology, a popular and controversial fad of reading bumps on the skull. As a favorite parlor game of the German emperor and aristocratic society, phrenology played an important role in spurring interest and funding for brain research. Although Gall's reputation as a distinguished scientist was tarnished because he was wrongly associated with phrenology, his research and the resulting focus on the mind gave rise to a renaissance of study and theories surrounding the brain and mind.

Over the years, such theories proceeded along the lines of the ever-changing cultural views of reality. For example, early diagrams and thinking about the workings of the brain actually showed cogs and wheels in our heads. These mechanical conceptualizations of the brain, originating from Descartes' designation of the mechanical workings of the body, took the shapes of and reflected our great fascination with machines, especially during the industrial age.

ELECTRICITY AND THE BRAIN

When electricity was discovered, the brain-mind began to be perceived as an electrical phenomenon. We learned that nerve impulses are carried along nerve fibers and jump across the gaps, or synapses, between the fibers as a wave of electrical activity. This electrical charge is coupled with chemical changes in the nerve cell and around the fibers, and a reversal in polarity occurs. We then learned that these changes in polarity and the electrical current they generated could be measured by electrodes placed on the scalp. An electroencephalograph (EEG) would then record on a sheet of paper the brain waves or changing electrical potentials of the nerve impulses in the brain. Certain abnormal brain wave patterns associated with such conditions as epilepsy, brain tumors, or stroke, or actual death of the brain usually can be picked up by the EEG. (General references to "brain waves"—in contrast to other frequencies and vibrations which involve other mental activities or "mind waves"—usually infer this electrical process and frequency.) However, the complexity of the brain and the inability of an EEG to detect the direction of nerve impulses leaves many important questions unanswered.

BIOELECTRICITY AND ELECTROMAGNETIC FORCES

Around the time that Gall was focusing on the anatomy of the brain in Germany, Italian Luigi Galvani (1737–1798) was discovering the forces of bioelectricity, the phenomenon of electrical activity in plants and animals. Electrical theories had already been proposed in the practical clinic, but were regarded by many scholars (mainly physicists) with great suspicion, and sometimes denounced as quackery. Galvani, a skilled practicing physician as well as professor of anatomy at the University of Bologna, identified the electrical composition of muscles and nerves, which he called "animal electricity." In Biology I, most of us simulated some of Galvani's experiments as we dissected frogs and observed their legs twitching due to the electrical impulses racing through them.

Galvani's discoveries opened the door to one of the more interesting debates in the history of science. His principal opponent was Italian physicist Alessandro Volta (1745–1827), inventor of the voltaic pile, the first electric battery, and from whose name the term volt is derived. Volta came up with a different interpretation of Galvani's findings, arguing that electricity was not inherent in a living organism, but was a product of the contact between two different metals.

Unfortunately Galvani's important work was derailed for almost forty years because the majority of scientists at the time took Volta's side.

Another area of inquiry and debate was that of magnetism itself. Newton's seventeenth-century theories about gravity and magnetic forces were investigated and experimented with by many of the great minds of his and later times. The fascinating idea that something or someone could be influenced from a distance provoked scientific work as well as "experimental" parlor games among the aristocracy of Europe. The concept of "animal magnetism" was popularized in the eighteenth century by Franz Mesmer, who was also known for his pioneering work in hypnosis. Increased scientific knowledge eventually reinstated much of what Galvani, Mesmer, and others were postulating about the electromagnetic properties of living tissue, as well as the mind.

For decades, heart pacemakers have been used to regulate the electrical currents in the heart. And in the 1970s, when advances in medical technology brought in nuclear magnetic resonance (NMR)—called MRI in medical circles—consideration turned to the intricate interplay within a fluctuating ongoing three-dimensional electromagnetic field. This field combined our knowledge of the electrical components of the brain with the holistic, three-dimensional hologram-type model and brought in a definitive recognition of the effects of the magnetic forces surrounding the brain.

An example of these forces was shown recently when researchers found unique particles with magnetic qualities in the pineal gland, the same gland, you may remember, Descartes thought served as the connection between the body and the mind. This small important organ, attached to the back wall of the third ventricle or cavity of the brain and located in the forehead region between the eyes, produces the hormone melatonin which is associated in varying ways with a number of biorhythms, including daily bodily vacillations and seasonal changes, as well as long-term processes such as the onset and progression of puberty. Melatonin is also known to modulate a variety of biological processes that are involved in the regulation of retinal physiology, sleep, vascular tone, metabolism, free radical scavenging, and the immune system.

In addition to documenting how the pineal gland is affected by the electromagnetic fields around us, scientists are continuing intricate studies of exactly how this tiny gland regulates the brain and nervous system, how it controls so many essential bodily functions, and how our thoughts intervene with, and possibly even guide this process.

Scientists are also renewing their focus on understanding how our thoughts and moods actually influence the electromagnetic

Because of its effects on sleep patterns and circadian rhythms, melatonin supplements are used to positively enhance our sleep patterns, and prevent or combat jet lag. And a number of scientific studies have validated melatonin's growing reputation as an anticancer molecule.[6]

At the June 1997 World Congress for Electricity and Magnetism in Biology and Medicine held in Bologna, Italy, a number of speakers expressed concern that the natural melatonin in our systems is being strongly decreased by effects of electrical power itself, including frequencies of the electromagnetic fields (EMFs) and artificial light interfering with our sleep.

It appears that Benjamin Franklin was right when he asserted that "early to bed and early to rise makes a man healthy, wealthy and wise." Although most people's schedules don't allow for going to bed at sundown and waking up with the birds, we can try to create the best possible sleep environment, which includes minimizing the sources of eletromagnetic waves — of which television is an example—and keeping the room as dark as possible. Interestingly, meditation has been shown to be a way to stimulate the pineal gland and the creation of much-needed melatonin.

forces within and around us. For example, in August 1998, at an international physics and neuroscience conference in Helsinki, it was reported that while the direct electrical current (DC) coming from the brain of a person in deep non–rapid eye movement sleep is very low, there is a high electrical charge coming from the brains of persons practicing yoga or meditating. Such findings may substantiate the claim long made by practitioners of meditation and yoga that these disciplines do indeed revitalize us and give us more energy.

COMPUTERS AND ARTIFICIAL INTELLIGENCE

The invention of computers in the 1950s offered other ways to think about specific functions of the brain. Scientists tried to correlate some computer models with the workings of the brain. Binary theory, in which all operations are broken down into two simple components, has been used as a basis for many computers and offers some explanation of thinking models. However, the multidimensional nature of the brain was shown to transcend the limitations of the binary system.

In the last two decades of the twentieth century, exciting advances were made in computer simulations of neural networks in the brain, parallel processing, components of the visual system, and a vast number of biological and chemical systems. Buoyed by the technological and information explosion, proponents of strong AI (artificial intelligence) are insisting that in a century or less (some say it will be more like thirty or forty years) computers will be doing everything a human mind can do. One well known computer scientist has described our minds as merely "computers made of meat."

Sir Roger Penrose vehemently disagrees. In his best-selling book, *The Emperor's New Mind*, described by the *New York Times* as "among the most innovative and exciting science books to have been published in the last forty years,"[7] Penrose builds a strong case against the possibility that the mind could ever be duplicated by a computer.

One of the arguments he makes is based on Godel's Theorem, devised in 1931 by Austrian mathematician Kurt Godel, who argued that one must have a way of evaluating an algorithm or correcting it if it is inaccurate. An algorithm, as many may remember from their math classes, is a mechanical rule or procedure used to solve problems. Long division is a simple example. If people carry out long division according to a rule that is slightly wrong, they may go on indefinitely without realizing they are proceeding incorrectly. There has to be something beyond a mechanical rule, something to monitor and keep the process on track. Penrose argues similarly that if the mind is just a very complicated, self-enclosed machine for doing calculations, in other words, a computer, it has no way of going outside of itself and judging the truth. To state this argument in a slightly different way, Penrose is quoted as saying that "Godel's Theorem... implies that . . . if the mind or the brain is working according to preset rules . . . as a computer does . . . you can always leap outside of those rules, and this gives you a contradiction." [8]

Presently, even the smartest computerized robot can't figure out how to stack blocks as well as your two-year-old can. This is just *one* task. Seems pretty simple to a seasoned adult, and even to most children beyond the toddler stage. Yet many life lessons must be learned to stack those blocks. Most robots try to build from the top down. It doesn't work. So, obviously one life lesson is an understanding of gravity.

And if we're so smart, why haven't we invented a robot to do the housework? Because it's considered a mindless job? Seriously, the work a computer can do still relies on how a human being constructs the computer and what information a human being puts into it. Could a computer ever really feel love? Appreciate a beautiful painting? Have free will? Despite our affection for R2D2 and the humanlike qualities possessed by it, how cuddly could a computerized robot be? How much could a computer truly empathize with us? In fact, psychologists have shown that people who spend a lot of time on the Internet are becoming increasingly lonely and depressed.

Speaking of feelings, one strong dismissal of the idea that computers could ever be able to think like humans is that computers could never have feelings, or sentience. Nor could they be equipped to explain the "qualia" of something—the individual perception of the redness of red, or the painfulness of pain. Subash Kak, a professor in the Department of Electrical and Computer Engineering at Louisiana State University, argues that machines could never duplicate the human mind and be conscious because they do not and could not be hardwired to use inner representations (pictures such as humans have in their minds) to solve problems. Nor can they participate in what is associated more and more with quantum intelligence processing in the human mind—the essence of intelligence. According to Kak:

> Quantum mechanics is a theory of "wholes" and in light of the fact that the eye responds to single photons—a quantum mechanical response—and that the mind perceives itself to be a unity, one would expect that its ideas would be applied to examine the nature of mind and of intelligence.[9]

Kak goes on to say that it would be impossible to make machines capable of holistic processing, self-organizing, or binding patterns.

To summarize: Continued work in the field of computers and artificial intelligence augments our understanding of a variety of mental components but cannot begin to replicate the holistic and expansive nature of our thinking and consciousness. And ultimately, how do you create a computer that reflects upon itself?

LASERS AND HOLOGRAMS

Scientific advances in laser technology and holographic capability in the 1970s gave us another logical model for the holistic workings of the brain. In a hologram, each piece actually contains information of the whole. Created by splitting laser beams, a hologram, or three-dimensional photograph of an object, has fascinating qualities. A hologram of an apple, for example, looks exactly like an apple; but a hologram is only a visual representation composed of light and having no physical substance. You could pass your hand right through the realistic-looking apple. And, most intriguing of all, if the hologram of the apple were cut in half, two complete apples would result. Cutting the picture in quarters would result in four apples, and so on, with each fractional representation of the whole apple diminishing in detail from the original. This holographic view of the brain reflected Karl Pribram's findings of decades ago, the essence of which is as follows: A number of brain processes are three dimensional and holistic rather than linear, incorporating wave interference patterns and certain phases of waves and energy, which in turn incorporate quantum information. At such a level information is distributed throughout the system and processed much more rapidly than if it took the physical circuit route from neuron to neuron. Today, some scientists assert that the human brain is not limited to the gray matter in our heads; every cell in our bodies, every functional combination contains properties of the whole. Even our big toes do some thinking and may have emotions too—as the following findings regarding neuropeptides, the molecules of emotions, suggest.

MOLECULAR ADVANCES CONFIRMING THE HOLISTIC, QUANTUM NATURE OF THE BRAIN

The last decade has brought significant advances in the molecular area, with scientists identifying the chemical transmitters that mediate communication between the neurons of the brain and the central nervous system and other cells in the body. Since the first neuronal messenger or neurotransmitter was identified in 1921, more than seventy have been analyzed. Subsequently, numerous drugs have been manufactured to enhance, block, or in other ways modify these natural chemicals of the brain. At the same time, we are once again realizing we can't separate the mind from the body. Our immune system is affected by and affects these biochemicals.

Neuropeptides, another group of amino acid–based substances, are considered to be evidence of the biochemical basis for awareness and consciousness. Dr. Candace Pert, pioneer researcher in the area of neuropeptides and their receptors while at the National Institutes of Health, explains in her groundbreaking book, *Molecules of Emotion*, how our thoughts and feelings (whether we're happy, sad, or angry) mobilize certain chemicals in our bodies. Biochemical messengers "intelligently" communicate information throughout our bodies to orchestrate countless conscious and unconscious activities. It is as if we each possess a "mobile brain" that instantaneously guides and directs information that in turn affects the immune system, our sense of well being, and how we interact with the world. Since many of these neurotransmitters and peptides are common amino acids found throughout the body, we can safely say that our brains and our thinking are not confined to the gray matter in our heads.

Every cell in the body does some type of thinking. Every cell in the body in some way processes feelings. And every cell in the body responds to internal and external stimuli. A concentration of neuropeptides, for example, has been found in the intestines, so our "gut" reactions do have some scientific validity. The more we learn, the better we will understand the forces of cohesion at work throughout the body, even on the molecular level.

Within this biochemical realm, a startling phenomenon has been discovered which serves to confirm the quantum theory of change and communication, and has direct relevance to understanding forces in the brain and the neurological system. In the older mechanistic models, changes—especially fluctuations and disturbances of natural phenomena—were viewed as signs of trouble. After all, in classical physics the second law of thermodynamics, the law of entropy, states that pressures and disruptions in a system inevitably bring on decay and degeneration of that system. However, Belgium chemical physicist Ilya Prigogine, Nobel Prize winner in 1977, dramatically demonstrated that the pressures of change can in fact create more advanced and adaptable phenomena. In his work with amines (part of the amino acids which make up all parts of our bodies), Prigogine proved that "dissipative," or scattered chemical systems, can actually regenerate to higher levels of self organization in response to environmental demands. Living systems have the capacity to respond to disorder (non-equilibrium) with renewed life, progressing to new, higher forms of order.

Prigogine showed that communication occurs even in non-living chemical solutions, generating order. In the chemical clocks (timed chemical reactions) Prigogine studied, the random mix of molecules managed to become coordinated. For example, at a certain point a murky gray solution would begin pulsating, changing to black, and then to white. In chemical clocks, all molecules act in total unison, changing their chemical identity simultaneously. Amazingly, each molecule seems to know what the other molecules will do at exactly the same time, over relatively great distances.[10]

The amino acids respond and communicate at a quantum level, illustrating an example of a quantum leap as the dissipative structure communicates over vast distances and changes at a speed faster than the speed of light (considerably faster than could occur over the mechanistic route of brain neuronal communication). A lot is clearly happening at levels much smaller than the neuronal connections in the brain, and organizing and responding to the environment at speeds and frequencies astronomically beyond those in reductionistic neural theories. (These amino acids from primordial soup at some level have even provided a framework for the origin of life.) The amines with which Prigogine worked are similar to the brain amines that regulate our emotions and drive our thinking. In a dissipative structure, phenomena in the environment that disturb the equilibrium of the systems play a crucial role in creating new forms of order.

Chaos, for example, usually precedes creativity. An ally in this thinking is Frank Putnam, co-author of the next chapter, who has concluded from his own and other studies on various consciousness states that there often is a direct correlation between chaos and creativity. Prigogine's findings certainly lay out the framework for new possibilities in responding to environmental pressures, and provide more evidence of quantum level activity in biochemical realms.

INFORMATION: SCIENCE, THEORY, AND PROCESSING (A POSSIBLE HOOK ON WHICH TO HANG THE UNIVERSE)

Much of the effect of certain systems on one another and communication in general is now being explained by information theory. Psychological anthropologist Gregory Bateson defined information as "the difference that makes a difference."[11] I remember my amazement at hearing that the information recorded between 1961 and 1981 exceeded all of the prior recorded information *throughout the history of man.* Imagine how much we've added since 1981!! Most of us have felt harassed by the information explosion. If the papers on your desk, or the news media's intrusion in your life, or the seemingly limitless possibilities of the Internet don't convince you of the overwhelming amount of information to which you are exposed, just wait until your daily delivery of junk mail!

At the same time, the term "information" has given us, in the last several decades, a common thread with which to communicate across disciplines as disparate as psychology, physics, biology, chemistry, language, sociology, systems analysis, business, the humanities, and library and computer sciences, to name a few. The science of information endeavors to increase understanding of how information is generated, stored, and made available. And we talk about "information theory" which has certain established laws and theories (such as the concept of "feedback") which are useful to just about any profession or discipline.

Information is not constrained by the Cartesian division of matter or non-matter, for it is both. For instance, drawing upon Bateson's definition of information as that difference that makes a difference, information can be the difference between a person and the cup of hot steaming tea which may be on the table before her. And the difference between the cup (a solid), the tea (a liquid), and the steam (a gas). So the form—matter or non-matter, solid, liquid, or gas—is not the essential criterion in information theory, the *difference* is. It also follows that information is not limited by time or space. There is a difference between the woman and the teacup on Wednesday as well as on Monday (time) and the difference ostensibly is the same whether they are in Hawaii or Alaska (space). Therefore it can be said that information is a quantum rather than a classical concept because it is not material in nature and is not confined to time/space distinctions. Furthermore, just as in quantum physics, information can change depending on the observer.

Candace Pert applies the concepts of information science to her research on neuropeptides and their receptors when she writes:

> The emotions are the informational content that is exchanged via the psychosomatic network, with the many systems, organs, and cells participating in the process. Like information, the emotions travel between the two realms of mind and body, as the peptides and their receptors in the physical realm, and as the feelings we

experience and call emotions in the nonmaterial realm .... Information...is the missing piece that allows us to transcend the
body-mind split of the Cartesian view, because by definition,
information belongs to neither mind nor body, although it
touches both ....

Information theory [takes us beyond many of our old, Newtonian and reductionistic ways of looking at things, providing
instead] a new...rich language of relatedness, cooperation, inter-
dependence, and synergy rather than simple force and response.[12]

In contrast to those who suggest that physical neurons and the
functioning of other material parts of our brain create what we experience as consciousness and even mystical sensations, it can be
argued that information theory seems to be converging with Eastern
philosophy to suggest that the mind, our consciousness which consists of information, exists first and the physical realm is merely an
out-picturing of consciousness.

MODERN METAPHORS AND "LAYERS" OF THE MIND

Various analogies have been used to explain the intricacies of the
mind. One metaphor is an onion with its many layers of skin repre-
senting the numerous mental levels each person possesses. We also
know that these layers of the mind are often contradictory. In a
smoker, for example, one layer and state of consciousness may want
to hold on to the smoking habit while other layers are very much
ready to quit. The many contradictions that exist at various levels
influence how hypnotherapy works to help someone stop smoking.
Hypnosis usually is most effective when combined with psychotherapy to help a smoker realize and do away with the resistant
thoughts (and contradictory layers) of the mind. For example, when
a client is made aware that her belief that a cigarette relaxes her is

an erroneous one as nicotine is a stimulant, she can do away with the thought, "But, I need a cigarette to relax me when I'm stressed out," which interferes with the contradictory thought, "I want to quit smoking."

Another popular metaphor of the mind is a symphony orchestra, with its various instruments and sounds, its creative and harmonious possibilities. Psychiatrist John Beahrs, author of *Unity and Multiplicity*, writes:

> ...like the overall self, the orchestra is a complex whole with a personality of its own. Like any multicellular organism or a social group, it is composed of many component parts, or orchestra members, each one with it's own sense of identity and unique personality, but all of which function together to the advantage not only of the whole, but of all the parts. While the music is made entirely by the composite parts, which transcend being a mere algebraic sum, it is held together and organized by the leadership. In this orchestra of the mind, we all have a simultaneous co-consciousness existing within and perhaps even contributing to the essence of our cohesive self, with the conductor—who makes none of the music—in charge.[13]

A less familiar analogy is suggested by neurologist Richard Restak in his book *The Brain: The Last Frontier*. A Washington, D.C., resident, Restak (not surprisingly) compares the brain to the government—pervasive in decision and effect, with no central power base, rather a fine interworking of a variety of stimuli and responses. Priority, selectivity, discrimination, and memory input all have constant interplay, with no tangible, material indications of how this occurs.

In considering the updated theories and research of the mind-brain, we might conclude that the brain is primordial quantum soup—subatomic particles waiting to be potentialized in and out of physical form. And our mind, vibrating energy—potentiality too—waiting for our thoughts and input from a higher force, as well, to coalesce into meaning, direction, and even physical events!! In twenty years the average person may conceive of the human brain and mind in this quantum way, realizing the limitations of the "bunch of neurons" analogy, just as today we are amused by a nineteenth century picture of the brain depicted as cogs and wheels.

The evolution of technology has certainly helped us better understand the brain and thinking processes. Over recent years we've supplemented exploration with electrodes on the brain (the popular EEG or electroencephalograph, for example) with noninvasive imaging techniques such as positron emission tomography (PET) and functional magnetic resonance imaging (fMRI) which depend on close interaction between neuronal activity, energy consumption, and regional blood flow. In PET scans, for example, we can see which areas of the brain are involved in certain processes, such as specific tasks in memory or when we speak. Colors become the indicators. The areas of the brain responsible for thinking of a word might appear bright red, revealing increased blood flow and activity in that area of the brain, or yellow indicating lesser activity as the subject speaks the word. Such exploration and revelation is indeed astonishing. Once considered to be incomprehensible, the brain and the human mind are now the focus of scientific attention in the Western world, forcing us to consider the concept of consciousness itself.

GRASPING CONSCIOUSNESS

What in the world do we even mean by consciousness? The term is bandied about, often with a variety of nuances for even the most precise user. Just as Restak's governmental analogy of the brain presumes an effusive, non-localized, inherently intangible system, consciousness stretches us much further conceptually. In fact, many

Eastern traditions view Consciousness (with a capital C) as the source of all intelligence and power.

In the West traditional scientists have tended to define consciousness as awareness. A hundred years ago psychologist William James brought in even more specifically the attention factor: that on which we focus attention is that of which we are conscious at a specific time. And of course Freud's psychoanalytic view of consciousness suggests an iceberg, with the conscious mind above the water and the deep profound unconscious or subconscious submerged. If we use a simple definition of awareness to get a grip on what we mean by consciousness, then obvious questions arise. Awareness of what? Who or what is experiencing the awareness? And as we look at the concepts of quantum physics, awareness itself may even beget more to be aware of, or, at the very least, in some way modify the object of our awareness. So the more we learn, the more we investigate, the more we enhance our understanding and definition of consciousness. Each contributor to this book offers a definition of consciousness based on his or her particular research and experience. No matter how precise we try to be in developing a working definition of consciousness, the process is continually evolving.

The evolution of our thoughts about the brain and consciousness is not a linear event. Many past explanations still have a certain validity and should not be discarded like yesterday's fashions; instead in a Hegelian mode a synthesis can be created from these seemingly disparate views. The brain does indeed have a mechanical aspect; it does indeed have a pervasive energy system; it is affected and guided by neurons and is a masterful system of chemical interactions and creations; it has been proven to have holographic tendencies; it is in many ways analogous to the computer and to information processing. It even compares in some ways to a government, an onion, and a symphony orchestra. And it is still

George Wilhelm Friedrich Hegel (1770-1831), a German Idealist philosopher, greatly influenced modern philosophy, especially in the areas of the
mind and reason. His system rejected the notion of humanity as separate
beings and minds existing in time and space in favor of the idea of an all
encompassing unity. In his famous dialectic on concept, the thesis is followed by its opposite, the antithesis; the ensuing conflict between the two
is brought together at a higher level as a new concept, the synthesis.

(Source: *Barnes and Noble New American Encyclopedia*)

more. In probing the various components of the brain and "layers"
of the mind, scientists are encountering fascinating phenomena—
including what has been called the "hidden observer."

THE HIDDEN OBSERVER

In 1975 psychologists Ernest and Josephine Hilgard conducted a
landmark scientific study in their laboratory at Stanford University in which they demonstrated the existence of what they were
later to term the "hidden observer." The Hilgards were trying to
determine whether a person who had been hypnotized to not feel
pain, and who had demonstrated through objective tests that he
didn't feel pain, was still able, in some part of himself to feel pain.
They asked the subject to allow a finger to rise if he did indeed
feel pain. A finger rose. When they asked to speak to that part of
him that raised the finger, that part was able to describe what was
actually happening, even though the subject was hypnotized and
aware neither of any pain nor of the part which did feel pain.[14]
This part that responded, now commonly referred to as the hidden observer, was able to show reality testing as an objective sci-

entist would—far more than was customary for the subject—even in his non-hypnotic waking state.

The Hilgards' research, followed up by later studies, shows that the easiest way to converse with a hidden observer is simply to ask to speak to it, as one might call upon a particular person in a group. That part then comes out and talks. It also can be accessed in other ways, such as through a hypnotic signal, and even can refer to situations in the past when the subject was hypnotized. It seems that while the hidden observer knows both of its own experience and that of the hypnotized observer, the hypnotized subject knows nothing of the hidden observer. There appears to be a one-way amnesic barrier, like the one often seen in multiple personalities. Thus, the hidden observer seems to have a consciousness, which is in a very real sense all its own.

Another example of some hidden knowing part of the mind is the uncanny ability called "blindsight." Lawrence Weiskrantz, one of several psychologists who have studied this phenomenon, writes of his patient D.B., who was rendered blind in his left visual field after having a tumor removed. In visual tests, D.B. said he was unable to see the stimuli (such as vertical or horizontal lines) presented to that eye, yet when asked to guess whether the line was horizontal or vertical, D.B. made almost no mistakes. Weiskrantz tells how, after many trials, D.B. was told how well he had performed:

"Did you know how well you had done?" he was asked. "No," he replied, "I didn't—because I couldn't see anything. I couldn't see a darn thing." "Can you say how you guessed—what was it that allowed you to say whether it was vertical or horizontal?" "No, I could not because I did not see anything; I just don't know." Finally he was asked, "So you really did not know you were getting them right?" "No," he replied, still with something of an air of incredulity. [15]

Back to my earlier question, "Where is the awareness?" And where or what is aware? Each of us has a variety of levels of awareness, different at different times. Sometimes boundaries between the levels are permeable, information and awareness may be shared by some of the compartments, or not. Over the years these divisions have been given various names, such as ego, states, hidden observers, cognitive structural systems, and multiple personalities. Children have been shown to be more facile than adults in accessing these various levels. As a child matures and develops a sense of self, natural inhibition of some of these levels begins to occur. What we easily brought to conscious awareness when we were children, we may find difficult to bring to the surface as adults. We will examine this next as we look at states of consciousness and development of the self.

Frank Putnam, M.D.

I have been privileged to know Dr. Frank Putnam for almost two decades. I first heard of Dr. Putnam in relation to his groundbreaking research in the areas of trauma and multiple personality disorder at the National Institute of Mental Health, and it was gratifying to see that such an eminent scientist is also a very caring person.

Trained as a psychiatrist at Yale and George Washington universities, Dr. Putnam is the author of scores of professional papers and journal articles, author of the books *Diagnosis and Treatment of Multiple Personality Disorder* and *Dissociation in Children and Adolescents: A Developmental Perspective*, and is considered an international authority on consciousness states.

He lives with his wife, Karen, and their two sons in Bethesda, Maryland.

CHAPTER TWO

States of Consciousness from Infancy to Nirvana

FRANK PUTNAM, M.D. AND
KAREN SHANOR, PH.D.

OH, WHAT A STATE I'M IN: DEFINING STATES

Has this ever happened to you? You're driving along the highway, perhaps humming a little tune, thinking about what happened at the office during the day when suddenly some jerk pulls right in front of you in the fast lane, almost causing an accident. Your heart starts beating rapidly, your breathing changes, and the incident and subsequent adrenaline rush leave you upset and extremely alert. An instantaneous change! You are still "you," but you are feeling and thinking and probably acting quite differently. You have made an abrupt transition in your state of consciousness.

"State" is a concept and term we use often in psychology and everyday life; we speak of a state of mind, a state of consciousness. But what exactly do we mean by a state of consciousness, or an altered state of consciousness, or, as some have referred to them, alternate states of consciousness?

The word state comes from the Latin *status*, which means a condition of being. While there are many sources of information and theories about states in diverse areas of study such as biology, chemistry, psychology, and physics, these sources and theories have not yet been well integrated. Perhaps as we move into the next century, we can begin to integrate data from various scientific disciplines to create a more comprehensive understanding of consciousness states.

For a start, there is a series of what are called pathological states. These are the province of psychiatry and include states of mania, panic attacks, and anxiety attacks. Catatonia also fits into this category, where people go into rigid, trance-like states and are basically unresponsive and immovable. People in a catatonic state have a waxy flexibility and may actually assume the same position for hours and hours. And yet they're there, taking in and processing a great deal of information. Generally, they can be brought out of catatonia through the use of medication, but recede when the medication wears off. A number of cultures actually provoke catatonic states through the ritual use of music and dance.

Then there are dissociative states, forms of consciousness in which events that should be connected are somehow divided from one another. We all engage in dissociation in small ways every day. Daydreaming is a prime example. As one student aptly described a dissociative state, "You're there, but your mind's somewhere else." Hypnotic trance is a specific type of dissociative state. Deep meditation is another. Dissociation often occurs during a traumatic event, serving as a kind of mental protector, and in severe and special cases can result in multiple personality disorder.

Meditative states, hypnotic states, and states of deep relaxation are of interest to many of us in terms of what they can tell us about higher consciousness and the ability to go deeply within our minds and volitionally achieve states that are transcendental. These states also may be associated with healing properties.

Yet another set of states can be pharmacologically induced through the use of legal and illegal drugs. Drug induced states are very interesting because they can become a conditioned response. It's possible, for example, to fool cocaine addicts and get them to have a cocaine high without their actually having taken any cocaine. We think this happens because the drug creates its own pathway of neurons in the brain and central nervous system, and once drug users understand how to enter that state, it's possible for them to manifest the "high" and enter that state without the actual drug. Hypnosis has also been used to facilitate this process.

We think of a state of consciousness as an ensemble of self-organizing variables, existing in multidimensional psychological space. The variables that combine to form a particular state have measurable physical components such as muscle tone, levels of motor activities, eye movements, vocalization, respiration, heart rate, and electrical activity emanating from the brain at various times (which is measured by an electroencephalograph, or EEG). By looking at the patterning of these variables, we can identify discrete, discontinuous states of behavior. Typically, scientists work with about five or six variables at a time, as working with more than that yields results that are too complex to accurately measure and interpret. Five dimensions seem to be sufficient to define discrete, or specific states.

One of the important things we have learned is that variables do not shift gradually as you move along a continuum of states. It is not a matter of your heart going from sixty-seven beats per minute to sixty-nine beats per minute to maybe seventy-two beats per minute. Your heart rate doesn't move gradually between these different levels, it *jumps*. It jumps as you move from one state to another. So during a typical day, your heart rate does not move up and down smoothly; it actually makes some fairly abrupt, discontinuous transitions. And the same is true of many of the other variables. Respiration, for instance, often changes abruptly. Just check to see how many times during the day—especially when you're under stress—you actually stop breathing.

One of the remarkable things about different states of consciousness is that they have the intrinsic property of organizing themselves, of being resistant to destabilization, and of being able to recover from outside interference; but they are not indefinite. They are time-limited. States last an average of twenty or thirty minutes, and then a person moves on to the next state. Some states are very short-lived and others can last for hours or even longer. And changes between states are not linear; they jump. There's a skipping process.

Transient, short-lived states that occupy the pathway between two stable states are called "switches." Lasting only a few seconds to a few minutes, switches are brief compared to the time spent in a state. If, as you're intently reading this sentence, someone were to call your name, you would probably go through a brief switch of consciousness as you drew your attention from this book to the person calling you. The next state you got into would depend on who was calling and why and how you would react to the interruption. If you were being called to dinner, you might suddenly remember that you're hungry. You might even salivate. On the other hand, if your child had fallen, you might rush out of the chair to help—your adrenaline level, heart rate, and breathing changing drastically and instantaneously.

In exploring these states of consciousness we will start where it all begins by looking at normal child development and the role that states of consciousness play in infants and small children. Then we'll jump across developmental lines to look at a particular dissociative state manifested in the group of psychiatric patients who have what we call multiple personality disorder, or MPD. As we examine these two very different models, we will see principles that link the behavior of both groups with an emphasis on the properties of states of consciousness.

THE CHILD'S MIND

As children, most of us were able to do things with our minds that we can no longer do. David, an artist and businessman in his fifties, remembers how, as a four-year-old, he would become totally absorbed in play, especially while waging war with marbles on his bed quilt. The marbles took on life as the solders he imagined them to be, and the quilt became a grassy field of battle. Then one day when he was six, try as he might, the marbles would not become soldiers and the bedcover remained a quilt. David still vividly recalls his frustration and sadness at no longer being able to recreate his favorite battle scene.

Can you remember being able to envision things as a child in a way you no longer can? Many adults remember fantasy friends who seemed utterly real, and how entranced they could become in play: Sand piles became castles; playhouses, forts, and train sets all seemed imbued with lives of their own. Isaac, who has a Ph.D. in economics, remembers how as a child in Ghana he could "become" the stick floating down the stream or the air he gently breathed in and out again. According to him, adults in his culture can still stretch their minds in such ways, but his Western academic training altered his ability to do so. Scientist Jacobo Grinberg-Zylberbaum has shown that children can be trained through meditation and other mental exercises to consciously access and utilize their hidden observers, and to "know" what is around them even though they are blindfolded.[1] Children over fifteen years of age cannot be taught this skill.

This flexibility of young minds is consistent with the findings of Franco Lapore, George Deutch, and others researching the hemispheres of the brain. Lapore and Deutch for years have studied split brain patients—persons in whom the left and right brain sections are separated, usually because the corpus callosum, the fibrous connection between the hemispheres, is severed due to disease or head trauma. These persons, who can be said to have almost two distinct brains because of the disconnected hemispheres, are believed to actually experience two different and distinct consciousnesses. Lapore and Deutch believe in the possibility that a fully integrated consciousness—whatever *that* is—does not develop until the child is several years old. Such a belief corresponds with findings that the fibers of the corpus callosum do not begin to mature until one year after birth, and do not reach maturity until age ten or older. (Interestingly, this fibrous connection between the hemispheres has been found to be about eleven percent larger in left-handed and ambidextrous people than in right-handed ones.)[2] Most younger children gradually take on more integrated thinking patterns as they mature. It seems that the younger we are, the more separate are our states of consciousness.

NORMAL CHILD DEVELOPMENT AND THE ROLE OF STATES OF CONSCIOUSNESS

Visiting a maternity ward can be awe-inspiring. Rows of newborns tucked into their tiny beds, some with ruddy little faces, some with china-smooth skin as new as can be imagined. Some glow with otherworldly light while others seem wrinkled and dented with skin two sizes too big. If asleep, their serene demeanors suggest dreams about some other world, so new are they to ours. A sound disturbs one infant and her body jerks, just slightly. A cherub in the corner wrinkles his face into a grimace and, with eyes in a wrinkled slit, stirs, stirs some more, then cries out but briefly as a nurse hurries to pick him up. As if in synchrony, a delicate doll close by follows in kind, stirring, clenching every muscle in her face (and others besides), not crying, but instead looking up and around, bedazzled, it seems, and certainly hungry.

Only a few hours, or maybe days, after birth. What could they possibly be dreaming about? What are they thinking? Scientists wonder as well. And since newborns can't answer us, we learn what we can by studying their physiology and behavior.

DISCRETE BEHAVIORAL STATES OF YOUNG CHILDREN

An examination of young children's behavioral states must begin with what they do most, at least when they're born: sleep. Sleep is a set of states. We tend to refer to stages of sleep, but these are really a set of states through which we cycle repeatedly during the night. In the laboratory, discrete markers for these stages manifest themselves as differing EEG wave forms in the brain and distinct varieties of body movement (or their absence—in certain states of sleep, the body is actually paralyzed except for the muscles of the face).

Jayne Gackenbach has shown children's sleep patterns to be very different from those of adults, with a progressive shifting as the child matures. Young children not only sleep more than adults do, they must spend more time experiencing different kinds of sleep, such as the delta and rapid eye movement (REM) varieties, in order to develop properly.

A newborn's states of consciousness are closely tied to its sleep patterns. All parents have lovingly observed their newborn at rest, enjoying non-REM, or regular, sleep. This state is characterized by passive muscle tone; the baby's limbs are loose and move easily, its face is relaxed, and it's breathing at a leisurely pace—about thirty-six breaths per minute. You can maneuver this child out of her car seat, carry her inside, change her diaper, place her in her crib, and she won't wake up.

But this state doesn't last long; REM, or irregular sleep, comes soon after: Muscle tone increases and the baby's arms and legs resist if you try to move them and jerk intermittently on their own; the eyelids are closed with the eyes moving from time to time, back and forth, up and down; the baby's breathing has become more vigorous and accelerated to a rate of about forty-eight breaths per minute. If you try to maneuver the baby out of her car seat in this state, she'll awaken with the click of a seat belt, and changing her diaper will be a two-party adventure.

From here the child often proceeds to a drowsy state and then on to the fussy or crying state, then back to a state of alert inactivity, then back to a drowsy state, and possibly back again to irregular sleep, and then regular sleep. A one-month-old baby goes through this cycle many times each day, confirming that its sleep patterns form the foundation of its behavioral states.

The importance of sleep does not end in infancy. We know that constant disruption of critical phases of sleep can severely impede a child's development. And Dr. William Dement of Stanford, who has been researching sleep for more than four decades, asserts that many behavior problems we see today are at least partly due to poor sleeping habits and sleep deprivation. Teenagers, for example, need at least nine hours of sleep a night.[3]

Other studies have shown that brain wave patterns of preadolescent children feature an abundance of theta waves throughout the day as well as at night. Theta waves are much rarer in adults and occur most frequently during what is referred to as the hypnogogic state—a kind of twilight zone we inhabit before we drift off to sleep—a time when dreams and reality seem to merge. Consequently, a child's waking consciousness seems comparable to a consciousness most adults associate with drifting off to sleep. No wonder children are more open to fantasy and broadened perceptions! Their creative possibilities seem limitless. This changes during puberty, when the older child's thinking becomes more like that of adults as the prevalence of theta waves decreases significantly.

Some people try to tap into theta states, usually to enhance their creative abilities. Thomas Edison is said to have done this in an interesting manner. He would doze off in a chair with his hands dangling over the sides of the armrests. In each hand he held a ball bearing, and on the floor below each hand was a tin pie plate. As Edison would drift into the theta state, his hands would relax and the ball bearings would drop into the pie plates. The resulting clatter would awaken him and he would write down any thoughts—usually creative ones—that came to him.

THE INTERACTIVE BRAIN

While it would be hard to overemphasize the importance of sleep in the development of human thinking patterns, even children have to wake up sometime. And the way children grow mentally and integrate their thinking patterns is largely due to how they interact with the environment. The actual neural development of the brain—the development of neurons and the pathways they form as the child develops—is molded by the child's interactions with parents, caretakers, siblings, and friends, as well as other environmental influences. While our individual genetic codes determine whether our eyes will be blue, brown, or green, our interactions with the environment decide to a great extent how these eyes will perceive the world, and how we will use our inheritance to act upon it.

Much of what we inherit are predispositions toward certain characteristics. We could have "tall" genes but grow up short if we aren't fed, exercised, or treated properly. Similarly, those of us who are predisposed toward diabetes might not get the disease if we maintain a healthy lifestyle, particularly in terms of nutrition. And while some of us may be predisposed toward depression, we can often avoid it by changing our cognitive patterns, exercising, eating well, and meditating.

Environment can also have profound effects on the most fundamental elements of identity, including sexual orientation and the ability to see.

Most babies are born genetically equipped to have clear, accurate eyesight, but we now know that visual acuity requires certain conditions to develop. This was demonstrated in the early 1970s to a group of clinical psychology interns who were given an unusual assignment at San Diego's Mercy Hospital: to hold a tiny baby for at least thirty minutes a day while maintaining constant and expressive eye contact with her.

A former intern recalls, "When I first held Kelly, she didn't seem able to see me. I thought she was blind. Her eyeballs and pupils even looked as if they were not totally formed. But as we worked with Kelly, she changed dramatically. Eventually she was

According to neurologist Richard Restak, in certain cases a person's ultimate sexual identification can be significantly affected if not determined by his or her interactions with the environment. For example, there is a condition known as testicular feminization in which a male chromosome pattern exists within a female body type, causing persons with the condition to appear female although they are genetically male. Although the debate continues as to the "real sex" of persons with testicular feminization, Restak says that "studies of the brain functions of such persons support the view that they can grow up to be either sex, depending on how they are raised." D.N. Masica of the Johns Hopkins Medical School found that persons with testicular feminization who were raised as females had what our society considers a predominantly feminine cognitive style (their verbal abilities exceeded their spatial abilities) while those raised as males developed a masculine cognitive style (their spatial abilities exceeded their verbal abilities).[4]

The Brain: The Last Frontier, Richard Restak, M.D.

able to look back into our eyes with interest and emotion. In a matter of weeks, this baby, who first appeared sick and unresponsive, was laughing and relating to us in intelligent and loving ways."[5]

What was wrong with Kelly to begin with? She was born to blind parents who, although they held her, cuddled her, and loved her, could not gaze lovingly into her eyes. Because Kelly had no meaningful eye contact with her parents, her visual development was stunted. For her brain and visual system to develop normally, she needed eye contact with other seeing persons, as well as to see the facial expressions, hear the sounds, and feel the touches that corresponded to the eye contact. And all this had to occur during a few critical weeks at the beginning of her life.

It is now common knowledge that a child's interactions with its caretakers have a profound effect on the way the child will eventually perceive and interact with the world. Part of the story lies in the myelin sheath that surrounds the nerves in the spinal cord. This sheath is not fully developed at birth, and a baby actually needs to be lovingly stimulated in order for the sheath to continue growing and for healthy nerve and brain development to occur. In his work at the National Institute of Mental Health in the 1970s, James Prescott concluded that gently rocking a baby back and forth actually stimulated the creation of neuronal pathways, which in turn led to peaceful, serene feelings within the developing child. Deprivation of this kind of interaction, Dr. Prescott felt, could result in violent behavior later in the child's life.[6]

CONTROLLING BEHAVIORAL STATES—INTERACTION BETWEEN CHILD AND CARETAKERS

As the child gets older, she develops enormous repertoires of states, and architectures for each state. She also begins to have more volitional control over them. An infant, for example, is generally driven by some sort of internal clock and is seen as cycling through states. A newborn's behavioral states move in a fundamentally orderly fashion, with about twenty to thirty minutes for each state. Even at this early time of life the child is very responsive to environmental input. States can certainly be affected by caretakers, who may pick up the child while she's asleep or make a loud noise that causes her to wake. And it is quite possible, particularly as the child gets to be about six or eight months old, for the caretaker to manipulate and modulate her states. That has a lot to do with what we as parents do in terms of trying to get that child in the right place at the right time: trying to help her through difficult periods, trying to get her to sustain the appropriate state or bring out the state that's appropriate to the context. For example, if you want to see some great work at state modulation, go to a restaurant and watch parents try to get a tired toddler through dinner! A great deal of distraction generally goes on, including all sorts of parenting tricks for trying to help the child recover from crying or to sit quietly. And that says a lot about the mutuality of states—that states are shared processes. We induce states in others and in turn respond to other people's states. Often, one of the issues that exists between parents and children is whose state is going to rule.

As the child develops, caretakers may use many methods for changing or controlling a child's behavioral states. For example, instead of slapping a child or saying no to a toddler when he carries out natural exploration in learning about the world, maybe reaching for a prized crystal vase which shouldn't be within his reach in the first place, a wise parent will practice the art of distraction. The parent might hug or play with the child, or position a brightly colored dancing toy to catch the child's attention. An ideal caretaker is always aware of the child's behavioral state and knows how to guide it at any time. While none of us is perfect, the more we do correctly to understand and guide our children in the early years, the less corrective and heartbreaking time we will have to spend with them later on.

States are contagious. They can be transmitted from parent to child and, of course, from child to parent. When our child is cranky or unhappy, we are concerned and not as joyful as we are when all is well. Sharing of states—whether positive or negative—is a powerful part of bonding between individuals.

Not only are our moods affected by the states or moods of those around us, it appears that what we learn and how we remember things are also dependent to some extent on the situation, as well as our own mood at the time. This seems to be even more true of very young children as their brains are developing. Part of a child's healthy development means she is learning how to integrate information and behavior across different states, and she needs to be helped by her caretakers to learn to do this.

Let's take an example. One of a baby's favorite games is Drop The Toy. It usually helps a parent frustrated by picking up the toy only to have baby drop it again and again (often laughing while doing so) to understand that the baby is learning an important lesson about gravity: what you drop goes down (and so does Mom or Dad, which makes it even more fun). Often baby is also learning a good way to get attention. Through many, many drops of many things over time and in different situations, from the crib, the high-chair, the stroller, and Dad's arms, the young child learns that there is a consistent lesson—even across moods. The dropped rattle goes down whether the child is laughing or crying. As silly or frustrating as this "dropping" behavior may seem to a weary parent, the child is learning some very important developmental lessons.

Typically, young children must be helped to generalize information acquired in one behavioral state or social context to other behavioral states. At the same time, the child is learning that there are specific contexts where certain behaviors or information are used. If family members limit their household eating to the kitchen and dining room, a baby learns this quickly. It is also fascinating to observe children learning to speak in a bilingual environment. They learn rapidly to keep Spanish and English words separate when speaking; they know who can communicate in Spanish and whom they may speak to in English. This is not a simple process. Yet toddlers learn this along with a myriad of other complicated lessons.

The development of behavioral-state integrative processes overlaps with many general mental functions, such as telling the difference between appearance and reality, visual perception, identifying the sources of various stimuli (where the music is coming from, who is touching my arm), cause and effect, in what order things occur, what certain things are used for (a spoon to eat cereal, a coat to keep warm), and endless others. Most of these capacities appear between the ages of one and five years, although they take many more years to refine and mature.

Throughout a child's very complex learning process, during which time pathways are actually developed in the brain, parents and other primary caretakers are instrumental in helping him or her integrate information and behavior across behavioral states and social contexts. Caretakers remind the child of what she or he has already learned in other states and situations, and help the child generalize this learning to the ever-enlarging world. A mother might say to her two-year-old, who is examining a daisy during their walk through the woods, "See that's a flower, too. Just like the red flowers we have on our table in the dining room, and the pretty, bright yellow flower in your big picture book." These lessons usually include logical connections between situations and things, an understanding of time, an ability to distinguish events in the past, present, and future, as well as cause and effect. Effective parents are professors at the most essential level. Continual, informative, and loving interaction is necessary for the development of intelligent, caring, happy, and well-functioning children. Every interaction between children and their environment and caretakers helps them develop a sense of self.

DEVELOPMENT AND INTEGRATION OF SENSE OF SELF

"Who Am I? We all ask this philosophical and personal question at various times throughout our lives. Yet most of us have a sense of being uniquely "me"—different from anyone else, a separate, insulated entity. In our culture, such a feeling might be even stronger than in other places in the world. In fact, a number of cultures don't have a corresponding word for "self." While the group, family, or clan is considered more important than the individual in many societies (especially non-Western ones) most human beings feel a general uniqueness and separation as well as an integration of their various moods, roles, and experiences into a unified self.

It's a long journey to the adult, integrated self, and in a child's development of self, the challenging twos stand out. From birth, a child is in the process of separating from the mother. Harvard psychiatrist Alvin Poussaint says, "Being a parent means going through a continual series of losses."[7] Raising a child in a healthy way means helping a life unfold and become more separate and autonomous with every step.

At around one-and-a-half years of age the sense of self is forming prominently. The child is learning to trust those around him at the same time that his physical mobility accentuates his separation from his mother. The utter excitement and freedom of being able to crawl away from Mom to that object which is so tantalizing! And at two, to run and express one's self through words. To understand the headiness of a two-year-old's experience of wanting to move on his own and control his environment, just imagine what it would be like if you awoke one morning to find you had wings. Would you want to be confined?

Every day a healthy child becomes more autonomous. The teenage years and beyond are critical times for defining one's uniqueness, one's capacities, one's particular likes and dislikes, and preparing to go off into the world as a self-sufficient adult. This process of development and defining of self can be exciting, scary, and disjointed in the best of situations. In fact, if we are healthy, throughout our lives we continue to expand, mature, and integrate the physical, mental, and spiritual parts of the self. When he was in his eighties, psychologist Carl Rogers used to say that instead of growing older, he was older and growing.[8]

THE AUTHORIAL SELF

Roughly between the ages of two and four years, children develop an "authorial self." The authorial self is sufficiently independent of context states to enable a child to begin selecting modes and aspects of self to emphasize in given situations. As developmental researcher Dennis Palmer Wolf notes, "It...is a new kind of self, one who can speak as object or subject, as observer or participant."[9]

This authorial self represents the child's efforts to internalize the sense of self as well as to integrate the state-dependent aspects of self and control them. The child emphasizes different aspects of self according to what he or she desires or needs. Beginning at about two-and-a-half to three years of age, this developing capacity expresses itself wonderfully in fantasy play. Children pretend to have different selves. They may have fantasy friends or want to be called by different names at different times. They immerse themselves so deeply in play with toys that for moments, the toys seem to take on life. Then the child can come back to who she or he is. With such play, children begin the larger process of uncoupling the sense of self from the immediate situation.

If those around us are pessimistic, angry, or upset, we feel it. Young children are even more pliable and vulnerable to the states of others, especially their significant caretakers. If parents, for example are always complaining and negative, the child will pick up their unhappiness and integrate it into the self they are forming. The child will learn to see the world through "dark-colored glasses," focusing on negative and possibly threatening situations, with little awareness of the beauty or possibilities life has to offer. This is a very intense learning process, since a child's natural development is a positive one. If a parent tends to be unhappy and negative most of the time, the child may also blame him- or herself for a parent's bad mood, since children in developing their sense of self can be quite egocentric.

ALTERED STATES OF CONSCIOUSNESS IN A CHILD'S NORMAL DEVELOPMENT

In the process of developing a sense of self, the child also experiments with and creates altered states. One way is through fantasy, as described above. As the child matures into a teenager, he or she might experiment more with various moods as a way of defining an individual sense of identity. That's one reason most teenagers seem so moody.

In normal people, mood also has a significant impact on how they act or feel about themselves. All of us have a range of selves, each of which is in some way state-dependent. We may have a business self, a childlike self that is open to play and spontaneous interaction with the world; we may have a parent-like, super-responsible self, as well as a private self that wants to be alone and quiet; there is the more social self, the wise advisor self, and also the more frightened, fragile self that emerges every so often. We all play different roles and have numerous behavioral states in our repertoire. However, in a normal person, specific state-dependent senses of self are sufficiently integrated with one another so that a continuity of self is maintained across state and situation. This is one of the critical differences between the self of a normal person and the dissociated selves of persons with multiple personality disorder.

A young child's sense of self is especially dependent on the state she or he happens to be in. Scientists who study the development of self have found that young children have multiple senses of self, depending on their internal states and what is happening around them. As children mature, they develop selves that bridge different contexts and learn to activate different selves at will. They learn to modulate their behavioral states and integrate them to form an internal stabilizing system. A baby can go from laughter to tears or vice versa in a matter of seconds because a baby reacts so strongly to what is happening outside himself, such as a parent walking away, which makes the baby cry, or a caretaker making faces and silly sounds, which brings a burst of laughter. A five-year-old probably would not change moods so quickly; certainly not a thirty-year-old.

As we mature, the bridging of states also includes a stabilizing internal state or sense of inner, real, and continual self which is aware of, monitors, and has some control over our reactions to external happenings and influences. A mentally healthy, integrated person might get angry at a salesperson for trying to overcharge him, but at the same time retain perspective and not lose control of his emotions. He would be momentarily angry on the outside with an inner awareness of and healthy perspective on that specific event and life in general.

Altered states of consciousness are part of everyday life. Most aren't considered dissociative because they don't involve significant alterations to a person's identity. The person still retains a general sense of self, and can go back to that anchored sense of who she or he is. A man may be deeply affected by a religious conversion and change many of his former behaviors and attitudes about life; yet he still has a basic sense of self. A young woman may leave her hometown of seven hundred people to attend college in Chicago and find herself experimenting with new ideas and values. Her brain will prune old neuronal pathways and sprout new ones according to the self she is defining, yet she too will retain her fundamental sense of self.

ALTERED STATES OF CONSCIOUSNESS IN EVERYDAY ACTIVITIES

Some of the different states of consciousness we experience during the day are associated with certain activities. Sometimes we focus on an activity and may dissociate a bit, as when we're driving home from work after an argument with a coworker and reliving the event so vividly we miss the exit. More often, we go in and out of such states, as when we read the newspaper intently for a few minutes and then suddenly look up and ask the waiter for the check. Sometimes an activity we especially enjoy, such as playing the piano, painting, sewing, or fishing will transport us to an altered mental state. For many people, this is achieved through sex and athletics, which generate a series of alternative states of consciousness. Both activities create states in which physiological changes occur, pleasurable sensations are experienced, attention is focused intensely in the moment, and sense of time is altered. And, as folk wisdom knew long before science confirmed it, both activities can provoke strong emotional responses in their participants, sometimes to the exclusion of reason.

This process of evolving a sense of self while remaining anchored in an established identity is part of a healthy child's development. For some children, however, healthy development does not occur.

TRAUMATIC ALTERATIONS TO THE ARCHITECTURE OF BEHAVIORAL STATES

Two basic processes occur in early childhood: One, the child builds a complex repertoire of behavioral states, and two, the child learns to monitor and control these states. If a child is traumatized or maltreated or both, both processes may be seriously derailed at critical stages so that the child does not integrate behavioral states and experiences into a distinct sense of self.

From birth, the child is constantly adding more complex behavioral states and architectures of states. The healthy child is guided by caretakers to learn to monitor these states, and eventually learns how to create certain moods and behavioral states on his own without being affected only by what is happening around him. When little Johnny is one month old, he cries out for food when he is hungry. This is important for him to do if his caretaker hasn't anticipated his hunger and fed him. But when he is five years old, Johnny should be able to tell his mom or dad that he is hungry and ask politely when dinner will be ready. And he should be able to control his behavioral state to wait fifteen minutes or so for dinner if it is not yet on the table. Johnny has learned to recognize his feeling of hunger, to articulate it constructively, and to monitor his emotions in a reasonable way. By doing so, he develops an understanding of his own internal needs and emotions, and how to appropriately interact with his environment. The physical sensation of hunger and the need to eat to sustain himself are innate, while much of his other behavior and expectations are the result of his experiences with and instruction from his caretakers. Johnny has developed a sense of himself as "Johnny"—a self apart from Mommy and Daddy and his siblings and playmates. Johnny also has learned to trust that when his mom says dinner will be on the table soon, this will happen. A child is constantly learning trust from infancy. If he can depend on his caregivers to take care of his needs and follow through with what they say they will do, the child learns a sense of order and trust. This is healthy. This is how a child develops a sense of self and learns how to interact with the world in a constructive way.

But what if a child has not been treated as lovingly and wisely as Johnny has? What if she is not loved? What if she is left alone as an infant when she cries out to be fed? What if she finds that she cannot depend on the adults around to love her and keep her safe? Even worse, what if she is maltreated by one or more of them in a severe way—for instance, sexually or physically abused? What if,

TRAUMA AND THE NERVOUS SYSTEM

Just like a veteran who has flashbacks of a terrible battle when he hears a firecracker explode, a child can reexperience a terror of the past by hearing someone yell or by being touched in a certain way. Brain researchers suspect there are physical pathways in the brain that unleash stress reactions when a triggering stimulus from the past occurs. This is consistent with modern brain research that confirms that, as we learn certain things, we develop corresponding neural pathways in the brain and central nervous system. Furthermore, traumatic events as well as repetitive activities not only develop such neural pathways, but may actually short-circuit or override others. This would be logical, as the first task of any form of life is to do what it must to survive a life-threatening attack. Inner resources become directed and prioritized to survive, and other areas such as learning, physical growth, and social development may become retarded.

instead of feeling safe and valued, she feels frightened, or even terrorized? The degree of trauma as well as the stage of the child's development in which such trauma occurs are determining factors in the physical and mental health of the child.

What happens to a young child who does not receive nurturing care, but instead is severely abused or neglected? What kind of behavioral states develop? How do these trauma-associated behavioral states influence fundamental developmental tasks, such as the consolidation of a unified sense of self?

MULTIPLE PERSONALITY DISORDER

One of the most extreme consequences of severe childhood abuse is a psychiatric condition popularly known as multiple personality disorder (MPD) and officially designated as dissociative identity disorder.

MPD belongs to a larger class of psychiatric conditions known as dissociative disorders, the essential features of which are severe discontinuities in the unification or integration of consciousness, identity, and memory. Individuals with MPD experience themselves as more of an "us" than an "I." They have a sense of possessing multiple separate identities each with a unique sense of self, and sometimes including self-perceived differences in age, gender, and race. These alter personalities often have different ways of speaking, acting, and relating to the world. One alter personality may be right-handed, another left-handed. One may require reading glasses, while another has no difficulty with fine print.

Multiple personality disorder has fascinated psychiatrists and psychologists for over two centuries. Benjamin Rush, the father of American psychiatry, taught medical students about this condition shortly after the American Revolution. In the late nineteenth century, the great psychologist William James wrote and lectured at length about MPD and related dissociative disorders; Morton Prince, considered the father of psychosomatic medicine, founded the *Journal of Abnormal Psychology* in part to facilitate publication of medical cases of dissociation. At the same time in France, Pierre Janet, a friend of James and Prince, established that dissociative disorders are linked to experiences of overwhelming trauma.

At the beginning of the twentieth century, however, the diagnosis of multiple personality fell into disuse, as many of these patients were incorrectly subsumed under the newly coined and then quite faddish diagnosis of schizophrenia. A few notable cases, such as the one described in the book *The Three Faces of Eve* in 1954, continued to attract attention, but by and large, MPD was forgotten or diagnosed as a form of schizophrenia.

In the late 1970s and early 1980s a new psychiatric diagnostic system, developed and adopted by clinicians, highlighted the many important differences between MPD and other psychiatric conditions, particularly schizophrenia. Once again, relatively large numbers of cases were identified and the first modern research on MPD was initiated.

JANE

We shall now turn to the case example of Jane (a pseudonym) who had been hospitalized for suicide attempts over twenty times in a decade. Neither her business partners nor her employees would have guessed that she had tried to kill herself numerous times. Given her legendary efficiency as CEO of a software firm that she cofounded, it would also have surprised them to know that she had repeatedly failed to accomplish what she set out to do. On the job she was known for the meticulous care with which she planned projects and the tenacity with which she tackled every obstacle. True, she was considered odd, often alternating between wearing conservative business attire and more flashy makeup and outfits. When it came to relationships, she was considered distant and distracted, often forgetting people's names or the circumstances of their last meeting. But overall, she was regarded with awe by her staff and colleagues, and considered a model of professional drive and success.

Jane diagnosed herself as suffering from multiple personality disorder (MPD) after reading an autobiographical account written by a former MPD patient. Jane's psychiatrist, whom she had been seeing for five years, was highly skeptical about the existence of MPD, let alone her self-diagnosis.

The psychiatrist had diagnosed her as suffering from major depression with features of borderline personality disorder, although he was admittedly puzzled that her depression and suicidal behavior were largely confined to her private life and rarely manifested themselves in her work. Concerned that he might contribute to her mistaken belief that she had MPD, he initially refused to talk with her about the other parts of herself of which she was becoming increasingly aware. He changed his opinion following a therapy session in which he met Janice and Liz, two of Jane's alter personalities.

When Janice appeared for the session, she described in a detached and businesslike manner how Liz was planning to commit suicide by tricking Jane into taking an overdose of antidepressant medication. Janice said it was she who called 911 after the most recent suicide attempt. (The psychiatrist considered this an attempt at attention-seeking because Jane called for help immediately after taking a potentially fatal overdose of medication. He recalled that when he had seen her in the intensive care unit, she denied taking the overdose but could not otherwise explain what had happened.) Janice then said that together with Beth, another alter personality, she was responsible for handling Jane's professional life. Janice went on to say that Liz as well as several child alter personalities often emerged at home, where Janice had less control. Janice described Liz as an angry teenager who hated Jane and wished to kill her.

At this point, Janice dropped her head and became unresponsive for several minutes. When she raised her head once again, she appeared quite different; her face had a peculiar angry look which the psychiatrist recalled seeing on several prior occasions. She introduced herself as Liz, saying that she hated Jane and Janice and that she was going to kill both of them so that she could have control of the body. Amazed and a little frightened by this strange departure from Jane's usual depressed and passive behavior, the psychiatrist attempted to engage Liz in a discussion about her wish to kill herself. Liz insisted that she could kill Jane and Janice but that she herself would not die. Later in the conversation, Liz appeared to fade away, and with a confused look, the psychiatrist's patient asked how she had come to be in his office and what was going on. (She now identified herself as Jane.)

Convinced that he had done nothing to encourage her behavior, the psychiatrist sought out information on MPD and consulted with an expert. He learned that many MPD patients have alter identities that regard themselves as so separate from the others, they believe they will not die even if the other personalities do. This is referred to as the delusion of separateness and illustrates how autonomous many alter personalities believe they are. Apparent suicide attempts by MPD patients often turn out to be cases in which one alter personality attempts to kill another in the belief that this will give him or her control. (This process is referred to as an internal homicide and has been described in medical accounts of MPD for over a century.) Fortunately, other personalities often intervene to save the individual's life, although this process of making and then reporting a suicide attempt may appear to others as manipulative behavior. Many MPD patients have alter personalities similar to Jane, who was depressed and depleted; Liz, who was fraught with anger and self-hatred; and Janice, who was highly functional professionally but largely without emotion or interpersonal relatedness. Child alter personalities are common and one or more usually contain memories of severe abuse or other early traumas. Such memories are reported by virtually all MPD patients who participate in medical studies.

UNDERSTANDING ALTER PERSONALITIES

How are we to understand the alter personalities of MPD? Are they really as different as separate people? Research indicates that they are unique and highly discrete behavioral states, each organized around a differentiated and individualized sense of self (often including a distinct body image), an affect (for example, depression, anger, or fear), with a limited repertoire of behaviors and a set of memories that are most easily recalled while the individual is in that alter personality state.

When the alter personalities of MPD are conceptualized as discrete behavioral states, they become less mysterious and easier to understand. In the typical MPD patient, there are between three and twenty distinct alter personality states. We sometimes hear of a patient with more, perhaps as many as a hundred, but in such a case most of the personalities are transient versions of a core group of personality states. In a person with MPD, these alter personality states embody very different modes of thinking and functioning, different moral values and belief systems, and different sets of memories—particularly emotionally charged autobiographical memories. Authorities on MPD agree that these alter personalities are not as separate as different people; rather, they usually share many underlying characteristics. In fact, it is a serious mistake to relate to the alter personalities of an MPD patient as if they are separate people.

How aware of one another are the alter personalities? In the vast majority of cases, MPD patients report a mixture of different levels of awareness among alter personalities. For example, alter A reports no awareness of alter B; but alter B describes being able to "look over A's shoulder" and see and hear all of A's experiences. As treatment progresses, MPD patients usually report a growing awareness among the alter personalities of one another's existence, which is part of the larger therapeutic process of integration.

It is difficult to test in the laboratory this subjective experience of awareness or lack of awareness across alter personality states. What we can investigate is how well newly learned information is later recalled across alter personality states within a given MPD patient.

There are two general types of new information processing tasks that researchers use for these kinds of experiments. The first is called *explicit* information processing and involves conscious, deliberate recall of learned information, such as memorizing words from a list, together with an awareness of how and when that information was acquired. The second is called *implicit* information processing and involves presenting new information to a subject in such a way that he or she is not aware of learning it. Often the subject is casually exposed to the implicit information while working on another task.

Researchers draw a distinction between explicit and implicit information processing because they involve different systems in the brain. Experiments with patients who have certain kinds of memory disorders (perhaps elderly persons with Alzheimer's disease or alcoholics with Korsakoff's psychosis) show that one information processing/memory system may be relatively intact while the other is profoundly impaired. A simple explanation is that explicit information processing is a conscious process and implicit information processing is an unconscious one.

Scientists around the world have conducted experiments to determine if explicit and/or implicit information learned by one MPD alter personality is available to another alter personality, particularly an alter that denies awareness of the personality that learned the information. Such experiments go something like this: Two alter personalities are identified (for familiarity's sake, let's call them Janice and Liz). In the first session, Janice engages in explicit information processing, first memorizing words from a list and then looking at a set of pictures (the contents of which will be tested for implicit processing later). Later in the session, Liz emerges and also engages in explicit processing, but she memorizes a different word list and looks at a different set of pictures.

In the next session, which usually takes place several hours to several days later, Janice and Liz are each tested to see how much of the information is available; in other words, how many items each can recall from the word lists (explicit), and how quickly each can recognize an object embedded in a fragmented line drawing seen earlier in the sets of pictures (implicit). Janice is tested on the information she learned while she was in the Janice state as well as what she was exposed to in the Liz state; likewise, Liz is tested on the information she learned while she was in the Liz state as well as what she was exposed to in the Janice state. By comparing the number of words Janice retained from her list to the number of words she retained from Liz's list (and vice versa), scientists can calculate how much information is actually shared by the alternate personality states, despite their denial of knowing of the other's existence.

Although the results of such studies sometimes differ because of variations in how the experiments are performed, many common findings have emerged. One is that even when two alter personalities report that they have no awareness of each other, information learned by one is available to the other. Aha!, you may be thinking—doesn't this indicate that persons who claim they have multiple personalities are actually faking these personalities, even if they sincerely believe they have them?

Well, scientists wondered about this, too. And so they decided to determine whether or not MPD patients were pretending to have alternate personalities by including in their experiments a group of "normal" or simulating control subjects—actors, in other words—along with the patients. Each actor was told to create an alter personality for him- or herself and practice thinking and being within that personality, much the way an actor does when preparing a role. Then the actors underwent the same activities as did the MPD patients. Using the Janice-Liz experiment as an example, the actors—as themselves—would memorize lists of words and look at sets of pictures; they would then switch to their created personalities and memorize new lists of words and look at new sets of pictures.

The results were revealing. The amount of information shared among the alter personalities of the MPD patients *was much smaller* than the amount of information available to the actors' alter personalities, indicating that there are discontinuities in learning and memory among MPD alter personalities. These findings support MPD patients' reports of amnesia regarding the experiences and behaviors of some of their alter personalities. That being said, however, there is always some sharing of information among these alter personalities, indicating that they are not utterly separate identities, and that they do share a common memory system.

Another common finding is that MPD patients have trouble retaining explicit information when the information is emotionally charged, as when they are asked to memorize a list of words that includes such terms as slap, burn, abuse, scream, rape, and bite—words that evoke painful memories. This research fits in with our clinical experience that MPD patients have the most problems recalling painful memories. These patients often compartmentalize memories of extremely distressing events within a few alter personalities, rendering the memories unavailable to the person as a whole. By dissociating painful and frightening memories into a few specific alter personality states, badly abused children may be relatively unaffected by such memories when they are in alter states that are not privy to these memories. Compartmentalizing in this way seems to enable these children to relate to the abusive adult or adults in their lives and secure whatever nurturing they may have to offer, however meager it may be. (It also enables them to relate to nurturing adults who may be present and able to provide some comfort.)

But pragmatic as this compartmentalization of memory may be, it exacts a terrible price. The child cannot continue the developmental process of integrating its different behavioral states into a unified, continuous self. The discrete behavioral states are kept apart by the power of the painful memories they are sequestering. It is these early, trauma-related behavioral states in an abused child that come to form the developmental basis of the alter personalities in MPD patients. Working with adult MPD patients, the therapist's task is to identify the painful, often hidden, memories, perceptions, and beliefs that produced the sense of separateness and to help the whole person work through them to a more fully aware and integrated sense of self.

PHYSIOLOGICAL EFFECTS OF MULTIPLE PERSONALITY

Many people find reports of physical differences between alter personalities even more amazing than the psychological differences. For more than two centuries, physicians have described differences between alter personality states in dominant handedness, physical abilities, speech, allergic sensitivity to foods, and physical symptoms. Sensory processes such as vision, taste, hearing, and touch are frequently reported to change with switches in alter personalities. More than a century ago, Alfred Binet, the inventor of the intelligence test, described his clinical experience:

> All patients having 'second states' . . . have peripheral sensory modifications which signalize the transition to a new state. This is logically necessary. From the moment the character is modified and the span of memory is changed, it is natural to expect that the ability to perceive sensation should be equally affected.[10]

Modern researchers have sought to document these long-observed physiological differences using brain imaging and other techniques. In an experiment, we mapped the electrical brain activity of an MPD patient and her three alter personalities, Penny, Prissy, and Gladys. All three of these alters were doing the same thing: sitting quietly in a darkened room with their eyes open. When we examined the differences in the amount of electrical activity for a set of frequencies (8–13 Hz) that are called Alpha waves, in each case most of the Alpha activity was located at the back of the head, where we would normally expect it, but the amount varied across the alter personalities. When we looked at higher brain wave frequencies, such as Beta 2 waves, which are about 40 Hz, we found even greater differences in the amount of activity. Indeed, most researchers have found that the greatest differences in brain electrical activity across alter personalities occurs in Beta-wave and higher frequencies. Other research with normal individuals has shown that these higher brain wave frequencies can be associated with specific states of consciousness.

When we ask normal control subjects to simulate different alter personalities and take the same test, they do not produce significant differences in the patterning of their brain waves. In one experiment, we compared ten MPD patients with ten simulating controls, who were given ample opportunity to create and practice an alter personality. The MPD patients showed statistically significant differences across alter personalities on about eighty percent of the variables that we were measuring. The controls were able to change fewer than five percent of these variables, despite some excellent performances in their alter egos. Other researchers have found similar impressive differences using different brain activity mapping technologies.

In another study we asked, How stable are the physiological differences among alter personalities over time? Using the same group of patients and simulating controls (who had ample opportunity to rehearse their performances as they were used in four different experiments), we measured heart rate, blood pressure, respiration, reaction time, and electrodermal activity in each of three alter personalities on a weekly basis for one month or longer. In addition to the alter personality each control subject had created, each control was given a choice of a third discrete behavioral state, either hypnosis or deep relaxation. The alter personalities of the MPD patients and the controls were measured in a different order each week to control for order effects. Nine out of ten of the MPD patients showed statistically significant differences among their three alter personalities that were able to be replicated from week to week. Only two of the controls were able to produce a similar degree of difference. In the controls, these changes involved differences between the hypnotic state and the other two states (the controls as themselves and in their created alter personalities) examined in the study. When we looked at the pattern of physiological changes, we found that in the hypnotic state, the controls were going into a deeply relaxed state with slowing of heart rate and a decrease in autonomic nervous system activity. In contrast, the MPD patients showed many other physiological differences that are not associated with relaxation so that they were producing different kinds of physiological changes from the simulating controls.

These experiments show that the alter personalities of MPD patients are capable of changes in physiological function that are significantly different from each other and that are stable at least over a period of a month or more. Clinically, we know that the unique features of MPD alter personalities can be remarkably consistent over periods of years, although with successful treatment these differences disappear as the alter personalities merge with the larger personality of the individual. We also see that under certain conditions, control subjects can produce discretely different stable states, although they may require interventions such as hypnosis to assist them.

Normal control subjects cannot, however, duplicate the physiological changes found across the alter personalities of MPD patients simply by pretending to have another personality. These kinds of differences between MPD patients and simulating controls have been found by a number of different investigators using different tests. They prove that MPD patients are not people who are simply faking the disorder.

THE SWITCH

Indeed, anyone who has witnessed someone with MPD change from one alter personality state to another—a process that we refer to as a "switch"—is struck by the profound shifts that may occur in the person's face, tone of voice, manner of speech, body posture, and language. Jane's psychiatrist in the case study mentioned earlier said he was absolutely amazed by the transition in her face as Liz faded away and was replaced by a confused Jane, who denied any awareness of coming to his office. This process of state change, or switch, has also drawn attention from researchers.

Different kinds of switches, of which there are many, have been studied in a number of psychiatric disorders, most frequently in bipolar disorder, or manic depression. One kind, called a rapid switch, takes place in just a few seconds. It is a very abrupt, almost instantaneous change, and sometimes quite dramatic. We can videotape these switches and look at them frame by frame, sequence by sequence. There are often startling changes involving the facial muscles, which may rearrange the shape of the face so that it appears quite different. Once I was having lunch with an MPD patient who was also a medical professional. The waiter took our order while she was in one of her female alters. When the waiter returned with the food, I was talking with one of the male alters. The baffled waiter asked if the gentleman would like to order, and where should he set the lady's food?

Sometimes patients transition from one state to another by passing through an intermediate mixed state, which appears to be a combination of the state they are leaving and the state they are entering. The person then gradually stabilizes him- or herself in the new state. That is, when the person goes from state A to state B, for a moment he or she seems to be in a sort of combination AB state. Another form of switch that looks similar to the mixed state is a transition from state A into state B through a set of unstable intermediate states that may oscillate and finally settle into a stable B state. These transitions are not unique to multiple personality patients, but also appear dramatically in manic-depressive illness where people move back and forth between manic and depressed states, often passing through a relatively normal state. We also see these transitions in anxiety attacks, when people go in and out of panic states, and in periodic catatonia.

Indeed, there are a number of psychiatric disorders that are characterized by these sorts of behavioral state transitions.

Another form of switch that we see involves passing from state A through a void or trance-like state before emerging into state B. This may have been what Jane's psychiatrist saw when he observed her switching from Janice to Liz. This can be a very spooky thing to observe. We call it "lights on, but nobody's home." There seems to be no consciousness that you can reach. The person appears zombie-like, sometimes staring blankly at you for minutes.

Finally, another form of transition involves passing from state A through a period of sleep before waking up in state B. This is one of the reasons why eighteenth- and nineteenth-century reports often refer to persons with MPD as somnambulists—sleepwalkers—as this also describes the trance-like states frequently observed in these cases. This sleeping switch is common in bipolar disorder and usually occurs with transitions from mania to depression. The exhausted manic, who may have gone days without sleeping finally falls asleep, only to wake up profoundly depressed. A milder version of this probably underlies the common experience of "getting up on the wrong side of the bed."

In addition to examining videotapes of these transitions, we can study them physiologically. We can wire up a person and measure brain waves, heart rate, electrodermal skin conductance, and other traits. This has been done with persons who suffer from panic attacks, bipolar disorder, and MPD. As you might expect, the switch is very interesting physiologically. Often it is characterized by a burst of physiological disorganization; for example, the heart rate suddenly varies widely before stabilizing at a different rate than before. During this period of disorganization it appears as if the physiological controls that usually stabilize functions such as heart rate are briefly suspended. For example, MPD patients often show an eight to ten beats-per-minute difference in heart rate between alter personality states. When the patient switches from alter A with, for example, a heart rate of sixty-five beats per minute, to alter B with a heart rate of seventy-five beats per minute, it is not a gradual increase. Rather, during the switch interval, which typically lasts about one to two minutes, the heart rate may be chaotic, suddenly jumping to seventy-five beats per minute as alter B stabilizes. The patient's brain waves likewise exhibit diffuse chaotic activity. Often there are high levels of what we call muscle artifact caused by dramatic facial changes, which obscure the underlying brain electrical rhythms. When the switch is complete, however, we often see significant changes in the type and patterning of electrical brain activity.

One final point emerges from research on switching. Transition pathways (as defined by behavior and physiology) between two discrete behavioral states are often not reciprocal. That is, the nature of the switch from A to B is not the same as from B to A. Falling asleep and waking up may include the same set of states, such as wakefulness, drowsiness, and sleep, but they are different processes. One easily observable difference involves motor release phenomena. As we fall asleep, our bodies often twitch and jerk as we pass from a waking state through drowsiness to sleep. These twitches are exceedingly rare, however, as we go from sleep through drowsiness to awakening.

In MPD patients, this directional pathway process sometimes leads to a "you can't get there from here" caveat when a therapist attempts to interact with a series of different alter personalities. Certain alters are just not available from other alter personality states, and therapists must learn to traverse each MPD patient's unique behavioral state architecture.

GENERAL PROPERTIES OF STATES

In considering some general properties of discrete behavioral states, we find a number of variables to be important in defining them.

One is emotion, or affect. We can all recognize within ourselves certain behavioral states—angry states, sad states, happy states—that have a strong emotional component as a defining principle. If you think about how you think and behave when you're very, very angry and how you think and behave when you're very, very happy, you'll realize that there are some very big differences in who "you" are under those two conditions. Those differences are emotional and perceptual. They are also apparent in your regulatory physiology. When you are very, very angry your heart is banging away, your muscles are tense, and catecholamines (such as adrenaline and noradrenaline) are pouring into your system. This is a very different physiological state from when you are happy.

Another emotion that can prompt a switch is fear. If you think back to the opening example of driving down the highway when someone cuts in front of you, you are flung into a state with elements of fear and fight or flight physiology: An adrenaline electric shock snaps through your body as you have the emergency response. That is a switch: You are switching into an emergency response state, and your physiology is rapidly altered; whatever you were thinking about previously is gone from your awareness. You are now utterly focused on the here and now. That is an example of a switch and a special state that some of us have too frequently on the road these days.

Activity and energy levels also must be noted as functions of behavioral states. There are certain states in which you have a very low level of energy and activity, and other states in which your level of activity and energy is very high. We often cycle through these states during the work day. We can sense where we are in our mental state space by noticing our levels of energy and arousal. Attention level is also a function of state. In certain states, you can maintain a high level of sustained attention, while in other states it's very difficult to concentrate.

CHANGING STATES

We are finding in the laboratory that changing mental states has a dramatic effect on what people recall about themselves. It strongly influences the kinds of information that people will tell you about who they are and what they believe in. I am not speaking only of MPD patients, who have serious problems with memory and often cannot recall some of their behaviors; indeed we see a similar phenomenon in normal college students. In the laboratory, we can demonstrate that in different mental states, subjects will give us very different histories about themselves in response to the same probing questions. And they will give us very different associations to the same list of cue words.

Even more interesting is what happens if you have subjects in one state and they give you associations to a list of stimulus words. Then you switch states on them, perhaps by giving them a mind-altering drug, and say, "By the way, here are some words that we had last time. I want you to tell me which are the words that I gave you and which are the words that you gave me." What is quite dramatic is that in a different mental state, the subjects often don't recognize their own words. In fact, they do much better at recognizing the source of words that you gave them than they do at recognizing their own associations. This shows that our ability to remember what we have done, who we are, and what we think has some very strong state-dependent aspects.

WHEN TIME STANDS STILL

Time perception is another marker of mental state. In certain mental states, one finds state-specific effects such as time dilation, where time seems to slow down. Events seem to happen in slow motion. This is characteristic of states of extreme emergency where things slow down and perceptions become very vivid. If you read personal accounts of such experiences, over and over again you find people describing very traumatic events in which they experience time as slowing down and actions occurring in slow motion. Psychedelic drug states are also frequently characterized by time dilation. Perception of time can expand or contract according to state of consciousness. After all, we all know that time flies when you're having fun.

SENSE OF SELF AND THE MOOD WE'RE IN

Your sense of self is very much a function of the particular mental state that you are in. If you're feeling good, you are also much more likely to be thinking and remembering positive things about yourself. If you're feeling depressed, you are much more likely to be recalling negative things, because your ability to remember good things about yourself is impaired. What we spontaneously bring up and remember about our own attributes, abilities, and behaviors is strongly state-dependent.

While this holds true for all of us, it manifests very dramatically in psychiatric conditions such as bipolar disorder. The extremely depressed person feels hopeless, useless, and worthless, considering him- or herself the lowest form of life, even deserving of death. Fifteen or twenty minutes later, that same person has switched into a manic state and is the most grandiose, self-promoting character you have ever seen.

I can remember the first time I saw this happen as a medical student. Making my rounds in the morning, I saw a young woman curled up in bed in a fetal position, covers over her head. Incredibly depressed, she was totally unable to function, even to wash herself or brush her teeth. She was obsessed with her failures. When I came back twenty minutes later, I found her leading everybody, including the nursing staff, in jumping jacks, shouting "SOUND OFF, ONE, TWO, THREE, FOUR!" She had an enormous amount of energy and vitality and was in total command.

PERSONAL TOOLS TO ALTER MENTAL STATES

ACTIVITY

We have a set of tools that can be used to alter states of consciousness. One of the most useful is activity. Not only does activity level vary with whatever mental state we're in, but we can use activity level to change our mental state. People work out not only to change their bodies, but also to change the way they feel. There is more to exercise than cardiovascular conditioning and weight control. Exercise can be a mental-state altering activity. When people are prevented from doing their morning run or afternoon workout, they miss it in part because they miss the way it makes them feel. For them, there are special mental states that are associated with physical activity. These states can be very helpful for relieving tension and stress and healing the body.

POSTURE

Posture also turns out to be a very effective tool for changing states of consciousness. We see this dramatically in infants, where picking up or holding infants, and thereby changing their postures, is helpful when they are distressed. This is a tool that parents use all the time to manipulate their young children's emotional states. Certain postures, such as standing on one's head, can be state-altering in adults. Disciplines such as yoga work, in part, by using specific postures, often coupled with breathing techniques, to help induce special states of consciousness. We can even change our mental state with more subtle shifts in posture. For example, just taking a deep breath, pushing your shoulders back and lifting your chin can change your mood from dejected to more positive and confident.

CONTROLLED BREATHING

Controlled breathing turns out to be an especially powerful way of altering mental state, because breathing is a gateway between the conscious and the unconscious. You are probably largely unaware of your breathing, but you can bring it into your awareness and you can control it. People who practice meditation techniques or martial arts that stress breath control as part of the concentration of Chi, or energy, learn that breathing is a very powerful state-altering tool. By changing your breathing—its rate, rhythm, and depth—you can produce profound alterations in consciousness. (You can also produce distressing mental states with breathing; for instance, many anxiety-prone persons experience panic attacks when they hyperventilate.)

THINKING CAN MAKE IT SO

There are many cognitive ways to change states. We can all think ourselves into a funk if we try hard enough. We can also think ourselves out of a funk, but often we need some outside help to do this. This is one of the ways in which psychotherapy and cognitive therapy techniques help people. Psychotherapy is particularly effective at helping people who are sliding down the slippery slopes of certain "state" pathways. By exploring what the person is thinking and feeling and gently challenging cognitive distortions, therapists can help people alter their associative pathways and prevent them from slipping into a depressed or anxious state in response to experiences that had previously triggered these responses.

MEDICATION AND VIRTUAL REALITY

Of course, we all know that different kinds of drugs can be powerful devices for altering mental states. I will not elaborate on psychoactive drugs here except to observe that we routinely conceptualize these experiences in terms of discrete behavioral states; for example "getting high." Another powerful state-altering tool involves the manipulation of an individual's perceptions and sensations without the use of drugs. In the old days, this was frequently accomplished through sensory deprivation, which can produce a psychotic-like state if it is carried too far. Nowadays, subtle new tools such as computer virtual reality effects are poised to carry these powerful state-altering capacities to new levels, with potentially dangerous consequences. It is the computer-game-playing, videogaming youth in our culture who are the most likely to both encounter and exploit this potential.

INTERPERSONAL EFFECTS

A variety of interpersonal processes can affect mental states. For want of a better word, I shall call these "empathy." There are many interpersonal processes associated with different mental states. Mental states are highly communicable. We read them in others all the time as part of our primary evaluation of people. Mental states such as anxiety or depressive states can be transmitted from one person to another, as can charisma, which is, to some extent, a shared state process in that the audience becomes entrained en masse by the politician or the performer.

Researchers such as Tiffany Field study the entrainment of physiology between mother and child. Even when they are not in physical contact, a mother and her infant or toddler often have synchronized heart rates.[11] Sharing states may be a crucial part of the bonding or attachment process between mother and child.

CREATIVITY AND STATES OF CONSCIOUSNESS

Not only do artists hope to affect the mental state of others, they often make use of altered states of consciousness to enhance their own creative process. A couple of years ago, I had the chance to talk to a group of writers and painters about mental states, with an emphasis on issues of creativity. When I began talking about switching and the issues associated with transitions from one state to another, I got an incredible response from these artists. Many became emotional as they talked about the difficulties they had in transitioning into their particular creative states. They began to talk about the set of routines, tricks, and rituals they would perform to try to kick themselves over the void between their everyday states of mind into their special creative states. They talked about how frightening that process was, because, for many of them, it was almost like jumping into an abyss. Some had obsessive routines involving arranging the pencils on their desks. Others would have to do something dramatic to get themselves going. But all of them resonated with the idea that there was, in fact, a special set of creative mental states. The writers and painters insisted that these creative states were very different from their ordinary states and required that a special effort be made to achieve them. Otherwise, they felt they would simply be going through the motions of their art, even though a person looking at their work might not be able to see that, for them, it wasn't the real stuff.

When I surveyed another group of writers, I found that about a third of them reported having some sort of an alter ego that emerged while they were in their writing states. They said it was as if they were watching themselves write, standing back and reading the words rather than writing them. They would describe sometimes being amazed by what they were reading.

PEAK EXPERIENCES: THE NIRVANA

I would like to finish with a brief discussion of peak experience states—the Nirvana. When we examine a variety of peak states, some common characteristics emerge. Transcendental and spiritual mental states typically involve a narrow temporal bandwidth. There is a sense of being in the *immediate* moment, the ever present here and now. People in these states are not thinking about anything in the past or the future. They are in the ever present NOW. Time perception is cleaved away from the experience and they exist in an eternal moment.

In peak experience states, action and awareness merge and become part of one and the same process. This often seems to be associated with the subsidence of internal voices, ruminations, obsessive thoughts, or other mental intrusions. A sense of stillness or profound peace accompanies this internal quiet along with a loss of preoccupation with self. Sense of self seems to be tightly bound to many emotional states, but during peak experience states, self melts away. One is not aware of or has very little awareness of self. Typically, when a person is in a transcendental state, there's very little reflection on the nature of the state itself. Indeed, as soon as you try to examine it, the experience is gone; as soon as you begin to reflect on it, it fades.

Peak experience states are rewarding because they enable us to just *be*. It is not as if they are a means to another end. They *are* the end. The individual does not feel the need to seek something beyond this experience. There is only the wish to be able to reexperience such a state when it has faded.

ON TO THE NEXT CENTURY

As we move into the next century, we are going to see an increasing awareness of the role of discrete behavioral states in our daily lives. We have focused on states at the behavioral level. But it is important to remember that states can be defined at all the levels at which we study consciousness. They can be defined down at a molecular level, and up at a behavioral level. But no matter which level we look at, the concept of states as discrete units of consciousness provides what we call an isomorphic construct, one that allows us to link various domains of knowledge about the mind, the brain, and the body. Indeed, if we could just put together all that we already know, we would suddenly know a great deal more. There is potentially enormous synergy in the knowledge that we already have about the brain, mind, and body, and organizing these domains of knowledge offers the tantalizing prospect of translating from one level to another. This in turn puts us in view of a time when we may use alternate states of consciousness to not only heal the mind and body, but to repel intimations of illness well before they take hold. The following chapters will continue to explore our consciousness states and how they can be used in positive ways.

JAYNE GACKENBACH, PH.D.

I first encountered Jayne Gackenbach at a talk she gave for the American Psychological Association's conference in Toronto. I thoroughly enjoyed her talent for presenting complex scientific material in an entertaining and easy-to-understand way. After reading her books and journal articles, I knew I wanted her to be a part of the Smithsonian series. And of course, she was a hit.

Dr. Gackenbach brings an important anthropological expertise to neuroscientific research. In addition to her affiliation with Canada's Athabasca University and Saybrook Institute, she is past president of the Association for the Study of Dreams, managing editor of the Lucidity Association, and has more than seventy professional publications and fourteen book chapters on dreams and higher states of consciousness.

Dr. Gackenbach is editor of *Conscious Mind, Sleeping Brain: Perspectives on Lucid Dreaming* and, most recently, *Psychology and the Internet: Intrapersonal, Interpersonal, and Transpersonal Implications*. Her first book, *Control Your Dreams*, was featured on the cover of *Psychology Today*, excerpted in *OMNI*, and selected for the Behavioral Science Book Club. She is currently working on a new book, *The Traditional Death of Crow Woman*. And she even has time for dreaming.

CHAPTER THREE

Sleep and Consciousness

JAYNE GACKENBACH, PH.D.

Freud helped us focus on consciousness with the idea that there is an unconscious mind and a conscious mind, and never the twain shall meet. They are separated because, according to Freud, we are driven by unconscious impulses to the point where we may ask ourselves, "Who the heck is driving this car called 'me'?"

I have been interested in this question for most of my life. I'm a first generation baby boomer, born in 1946. I've done all that baby boomers were supposed to do, including living in New Mexico in the '60s. After fulfilling the prerequisite baby boom agenda of the '70s, I shaved my legs after finishing my master's thesis on a feminist topic and went on to get my doctorate. In looking for a topic for my dissertation, the question of consciousness came up as I watched the death of an elderly friend. My professional quest became tied up with my personal quest: What's dreaming, and what's not dreaming? And since I began working with the Central Alberta Cree, I realized that these questions raise another one: What's real, and what's not real?

Thus my research, my writing, and a lot of my thinking have been involved with dreams and sleep, and in particular the experience of consciousness during sleep, or lucid dreaming. During lucid dreaming you are sound asleep, which we popularly think of as being unconscious. You're whacked out and lying there in bed. If that isn't unconscious, I don't know what is. Yet at the same time, some people say they know they're dreaming. This seems to be a paradox. How can you know you're unconscious when you're unconscious? If you're unconscious, you can't be conscious. You get a sort of waffly feeling just thinking about it, so ingrained in our society is the idea that consciousness and unconsciousness are mutually exclusive. If you have had the experience of knowing you are dreaming while you are dreaming, then you know what it is like. Typically it's fun and you enjoy it. If you've never had this experience you may scratch your head and feel confused. For twenty years I've pursued these questions. I'm still wondering who's driving this car, while I'm awake and while I'm asleep.

I am going to try to walk the thin line between addressing the person who has done some reading in this area and the person who is interested in but not really informed about contemporary psychological thinking. I shall try to bridge that gap by beginning with a general discussion about the biology of sleep and dreams, and then moving on to consciousness in sleep and the various forms that consciousness in sleep can take as it develops.

BRAIN-BODY ACTIVITY DURING SLEEP AND DREAMS

There are three major measures of sleep that are used in the sleep laboratory: brain waves, eye movements, and muscle activity. Waking consciousness is generally compared to the two most familiar categories of sleep: rapid eye movement or REM sleep, and non–rapid eye movement or NREM sleep. In a polygraph record, one of the major markers of differences in sleep states is eye movement: It is very intense in REM sleep relative to NREM sleep. Eye movement is even more frequent and jerky during REM sleep than it is during waking.

Muscle activity during sleep is also interesting, especially when you compare the muscle activity that occurs during NREM sleep with that which occurs during REM sleep. Waking muscle activity is high relative to NREM muscle activity, which is moderate. In other words, while we are awake our muscles are ready for use, while during NREM sleep, we don't use our muscles nearly as much. On the other hand, there is virtually no muscle activity in REM sleep. For all practical purposes, during REM sleep, we are paralyzed from the neck down!

When you go to bed at night, you snuggle into your favorite sleeping position. You may be a side sleeper or a back sleeper or a stomach sleeper, but once you get yourself settled, a fairly standard sequence of events occurs: You start in light sleep, progress to deepest sleep, emerge to light sleep, and then begin the pattern again. You cycle between light sleep and deep sleep throughout the night, about every hour and a half. This ninety-minute cycling is a circadian rhythm and we actually experience it throughout the day and night. This rhythm is particularly noteworthy in sleep because of the movement in and out of REM. Although REM is associated with dreaming, this association is not absolute: there is also mental activity that we might call dreaming that occurs in NREM sleep. However, for the most part, dreams tend to cluster in REM episodes.

Furthermore, the dreams of REM sleep are phenomenologically distinct from those of NREM sleep; that is, they feel different to the dreamer. There's been an argument in dream research literature about whether or not REM sleep is the biological marker for dreams. That's how it was touted when REM sleep was discovered in the early 1950s. Then, with subsequent research, sleep and dream scientists became disillusioned with that simplistic mind-brain equation and concluded that dreams go on all night long to one degree or another, and that they merely cluster in REM.

As is often the case in science, we have come almost full circle and now realize that there are real phenomenological markers of mental activity, or mentation, during REM sleep that are distinct from those that occur during NREM sleep. One marker is bizarreness; that is, the strange otherworldly sorts of things so characteristic of our dreams. In an article by Harry Hunt in the journal *Dreaming*, the scientist showed that attempts to equate the bizarreness of REM sleep mentation to the bizarreness of NREM sleep mentation have not worked. In other words, REM dreams are distinct from NREM dreams in that the former are weirder! REM dreams by the early morning hours last from thirty to forty minutes and have elaborate story lines and complex shifts and transitions. Your mother's got a purple face. A raccoon is walking upright and talking to you. You are experiencing this sort of thing during these early morning hours in REM sleep. That's the kind of stuff that real dreams are made of!

REM episodes get longer as you continue sleeping, indicating that most of your dreaming happens late in the sleeping cycle. During this time, you are paralyzed from the neck down, your eye movements are jerky and rapid, your heart rate fluctuates, your breath rate changes. Sometimes when you wake up from an especially intense REM dream you're panting, your heart's pounding, you're sweating, and you mutter, "Thank goodness that was only a dream!" If that happens, you have come out of REM sleep. If you suffer from ulcers, your stomach secretes twenty times the amount of stomach acid during REM sleep that it does during NREM sleep. If your child has asthma and he wakes up with an asthma attack, he's most likely waking from REM sleep. If you have angina, your heart problems will most likely occur during REM sleep. In other words, REM sleep doesn't seem to be good for your physical health. It stresses the body. It pushes all these different systems more than while you're awake (unless you're jogging ten miles, obviously). In addition, while all these systems are in overdrive, the brain is increasing its activity. What is going on?

FUNCTIONS OF REM AND NREM

During REM sleep, new information you have gathered during waking is processed and stored into memory. By new information, I mean everything from a casual glance at a stranger in a shopping mall, to learning how to drive, to sorting out your feelings about your child leaving home for college. Our personal experience of processing and storing information is dreaming. A dream world is created and it feels real. Even if you know it's a dream at the time it still feels real. In a dream if you jump up and fall down, you feel the thud. Although when you wake up you realize that it was a dream and tend to minimize and dismiss it, the feelings of its reality are there while the dream is going on.

The question becomes, why do we need to hallucinate every night so vividly that we think it's real? These hallucinations inspire strong emotions as well as feature bizarre events, and the body responds to the felt reality of dreaming. It is fortunate that we are paralyzed from the neck down because if we weren't, there is good evidence that we would get up and act out the dream. A famous illustration is the case of a Toronto man who got up from bed in the middle of the night, got into his car, drove across town, and killed his mother-in-law. A colleague of mine testified at the court case. Later, he brought the man to his sleep laboratory in Boston. My colleague discovered that, during this man's REM sleep, his muscle activity did not flatten out. He had enough muscle activity to get up, drive a car and, in this case, murder someone.

In brief, the function of REM sleep is information processing, and the function of NREM sleep is body maintenance. In NREM sleep, growth hormone release peaks. Another piece of evidence that supports the restorative function of NREM sleep is that high pre-sleep metabolic rates are associated with higher levels of delta or deepest sleep. So if you're working on getting your metabolism up you are going to need more delta sleep. Also, higher brain functions appear to be somewhat reduced during delta sleep. Slightly less brain oxygen is consumed and, as noted, psychological events related to delta sleep are sparse.

So why do we experience REM sleep? As noted, there is pronounced activity on a biological level. In addition, one's inner self and unconscious motives and drives are manifest in REM dreaming. REM sleep plays a role in the reorganization and restoration of brain processes that mediate the flow, structure, and storage of information, some of which are problem-solving, memory consolidation, information processing, and creativity.

Furthermore, as we go through life, there are changes in the amount of REM sleep we experience. Infants experience huge amounts: Fifty percent of a newborn's sleep cycle is spent in REM-type sleep, compared to twenty-five percent of an adult's. It is clear from these data that REM sleep serves some sort of information processing function. It turns out that while babies have almost all of their brain neurons at birth, the communicating aspect of the neurons, or synapses, which connect neuronal cells, have just begun to grow about a month before birth. Without the ability to communicate with one another, the neurons are virtually useless. Of course, there are enough synaptic connections at birth for some basic survival behaviors. For instance, a newborn will recognize his mother's voice and has perfect visual acuity for about eight inches, the distance to his mother's face as he is nursing. But for a newborn to see clearly beyond this distance would be confusing to the baby and disruptive to the bonding process with the mother, which must occur to ensure the newborn's survival. Nevertheless, at birth, there are many neuronal connections still to be made. After all, getting that thumb in the mouth without poking one's eye is a fairly major task! Learning to coordinate visual input (thumb) with motor output (moving it to mouth) takes synaptic connections. This growth of the synapses probably occurs during REM sleep. Because newborns have so much to piece together in terms of simply getting all their potential motor activities working properly (among many other tasks), it is no wonder that they need huge amounts of synaptic growth time, or REM sleep. Along the same lines, a premature infant will show as high as seventy-five percent REM sleep, as there are even fewer connections between neurons.

Other evidence pointing to REM's information-processing function involves the degree of activation of the right hemisphere of the brain. Although the difference between the functions of the right and left hemispheres has been over-simplified in the popular press, the left, more logical and linear hemisphere tends to dominate brain activity during the day. At night, however, the right hemisphere increases its neuronal activity, at least to the level of the left hemisphere. Consequently, creative and visual information, which is best processed in the right hemisphere, becomes more apparent and dominant during REM. This more holistic information is considered more emotive than left hemisphere processing. In fact, some scientists believe that moderating emotions is a major function of REM sleep.

On another psychological level, REM may serve some compensatory process function, as hypothesized by the founder of the psychoanalytic movement, Sigmund Freud. Personally important experiences may be repressed during the day, and thus you'll see a reciprocal emphasis in dreams at night. More often than not, however, research has shown that there is a connection between presleep experiences and dream experiences during REM and NREM sleep. What you've been thinking about before you go to bed at night, you'll see in your dreams that night.

This is especially evident in children. When my son was about eight years old, we were impressed with the advertisements for a movie called *Gremlins*. Naively we went to the theater, but during the gremlins' first transformation from cute, furry creatures into sharp-toothed lethal monsters, we left for the lobby. Not surprisingly, that night at about two a.m., I felt a small body crawl into bed with me. The gremlins from the film had awoken my son with a nightmare!

But to simply reduce dreams to rough reproductions of waking events is also to reduce their importance. Most dreams occur during the REM sleep cycle, when we process new information into our memory banks. Therefore, dreams are always autobiographical and unique to each individual. Many professionals who work with dreams clinically and scientifically argue that dreams represent the cutting edge of the self and that to attend to dreams is to deepen self-awareness.

WHY DO WE FORGET OUR DREAMS?

If these experiences of the night are so biologically and psychologically important, why do we typically forget our dreams upon awakening? The norm in the dominant European culture of North America is dream forgetting. The average adult sleeps about eight hours a night, and of that, about two hours is REM or dreaming sleep. That means we usually have at least four dreams every night without counting the NREM sleep mentation. Very few individuals remember even one dream a night, let alone four! People remember an average of four dreams a month, which would be about one a week. Typically we forget our dreams. Dream scientists have come up with three major hypotheses on why we do this: repression, salience, and interference.

The concept that we forget our dreams because we are repressing unpleasant emotions and experiences is classically Freudian. This is the idea that the part of our inner selves that we are not ready to deal with may emerge in dreams; thus, we forget them. Some Freudian analysts might argue that if you remember a dream, you're ready to deal with that material. Although there is some scientific evidence for the repression hypothesis, it is probably not the major reason we forget our dreams.

The salience hypothesis states that some dreams are so powerful, you cannot forget them. You wake up in the morning and your life has been changed, or you hope like mad that your life has not been changed. When my children were about nine and four I had a dream that they were crossing the street at a crosswalk with a friend of theirs. All three got hit by a car and were killed. I recall waking up and being absolutely terrified. I jumped out of bed and went to check on them. They were both sound asleep and in good health. Nonetheless, the fear would not leave me, so I did something that I rarely do: I knelt by my bed with tears running down my face and prayed to God that this dream might never come true. It still sends a shiver down my spine to even think about it! That is a dream I cannot forget, and I still get anxious any time I know my children will be in a crosswalk.

Despite experiences of this sort, according to scientific research the major reason we forget our dreams is something quite simple: interference. It's the same reason why, if I said, "Tell me about your breakfast this morning," you probably wouldn't remember much about it, but you might start to extrapolate by saying, "I normally have yogurt and fruit, so I must have had yogurt and fruit." You might remember some details, but I doubt that you would include details such as the number of glasses on the counter or other ordinary details about the kitchen. If you got a new tablecloth, you might mention it. But if it's something that happens every day—such as eating breakfast—it's probably not high on your need-to-recall list. Things interfere with your memory of breakfast, such as the family's rush to get to work and school because mom overslept. When we wake up from a dream, most of us immediately think, "Got to get up. Got to get ready for work. Got to get the kids dressed. Got to get breakfast." It's forward thinking and it interferes with the recall of what was just happening to us in our dreams. Occasionally we simply lie there and drift when we awaken, but still the simplest things can interfere, such as moving our legs or opening our eyes. Or we will wake up and think, "I was dreaming. I don't have a clue what it was. But I was dreaming." When my son was three years old he didn't like being awake while I slept so he would come into my bedroom, lift my eyelid, and cheerfully announce to me, "Wake-up time, Mommy!" I went through a rather long period of dream forgetting due to his well intentioned interference.

There are some other factors that may contribute to dream recall. When I moved to Canada I started working with the Central Alberta Cree and quickly found out that their dream recall was quite high, both in terms of research and personal observation. For instance, I recall a Cree friend looking at me with the most puzzled expression when I asked him if dreams were important in his home life. I kept repeating the question and in turn was puzzled when he did not answer right away, as I knew English was his first language. Finally, he looked at me with the most perplexed look and said, "That's like asking me if I brush my teeth." It is such a common experience to share and value dreams among the Alberta Cree that to ask if they do seems the silliest of questions.

Because of this work it has occurred to me that perhaps part of the large dream-forgetting characteristic of North Americans of

European descent is our cultural taboo against attending to this sort of material. We're not supposed to pay attention to our inner lives. We're not supposed to take them seriously. In fact, one theory is that the dreams we have during REM sleep are garbage, and that they are merely the way the brain makes sense of the brain stem's presumably random firing of neurons. According to this perspective, recalling dreams is recalling garbage and couldn't possibly be healthy. This theory has been generally debunked. I am not saying that every single thing you dream every night is important, but I do think there's a moderate position.

METAPHORIC MAGIC IN DREAMS

One of the cornerstones of dream work is understanding the concept of metaphor. If you are a poet or an artist you are already probably quite familiar with metaphor. Otherwise, you might be surprised to find out that we experience metaphor in virtually every aspect of our lives, ranging from advertising logos to pet names we give to those we love. Metaphors are verbal expressions based on similarity, words from one domain that express similar attributes when applied to another domain. Thus I say about my 1989 Plymouth Sundance, "I've got a gas guzzler." The car does not literally drink gasoline the way I guzzle diet cola, yet you understand that I get poor mileage.

Dreams speak to us in a language of metaphor. That is to say that dreams in one sense are a language you see, that you experience, and that moves you emotionally. But when it comes to trying to understand the meaning of dreams, you begin to realize that there is something more going on. The main language dreams use is the language of visual metaphor. While awake, we may use words that evoke images but we don't directly live the images. In dreams, we live the visual image of the metaphor.

Let me illustrate. Recently I was on my way to deliver a speech, following which I planned to visit my mother in Pennsylvania. I had a dream that I was walking down a road when I saw a bright yellow plastic lounge chair sitting there. I remember looking at it and thinking that I would have to get it off the road because a car might run over it. When I woke up I was completely puzzled and wondered, "Why on earth did I dream of a relaxing kind of chair sitting on a road?" I spoke to one of my colleagues about the dream and she quickly said, "Perhaps you need to relax when you're on the road." I thought, of course, the business trips where I try to steal a few days of vacation have often been so busy and stressful that I end up not relaxing. The dream caught in a visual metaphor the idea that I needed to relax while I was on the road.

To go a bit further with this analysis, my response to the dream was that there was potential danger involved in relaxing in the chair on the road. This spoke to my anxiety about my forthcoming talk: If I was too relaxed about it I might not do well. The metaphor also spoke to my anxiety about spending time with my mother: In the past this sometimes proved to be tense. Even my response in the dream—concern about getting the chair off the road before it was destroyed by a passing motorist—added further meaning to the visual metaphor. I needed to protect my downtime.

WHY ARE WE BLIND TO OUR OWN DREAM METAPHORS?

As a colleague pointed out as he read this in draft form, "Why is it that I can understand the metaphors someone uses to express his thoughts, but I find it difficult to understand the metaphors in my own dreams? In neither case have I consciously chosen the metaphors that were used." A stronger statement of his position would be, "I can better understand the metaphors in someone else's dreams than I can my own. My clarity fades the closer I am emotionally to the dreamer." I can understand the metaphor a student or friend may bring me from her dream much more quickly than I can one from my children, and I can be blind-sided by my own metaphors. This is the nature of self-awareness.

One finding of research into the dreams of those who have worked on developing their self-awareness is that their dreams become increasingly transparent in their use of metaphors. These people will often point out how straightforward and simple their dreams now seem. This idea was developed by psychologist Ernest Rossi in his classic book *Dreams and the Growth of Personality*, in which he argues that ultimate self-awareness in dreams manifests itself in the experience of dream lucidity; in other words, knowing you are dreaming while you are dreaming. Rossi details a sequence of stages that his patient, Davina, went through in her dreams during the psychotherapy that moved her to dream lucidly:

> The developing lucidity of Davina's dreams up to this point suggested three stages in the process of evolving consciousness and personality transformation. First there was a process of many divisions in her state-of-being, manifested by different images of herself in the same dream, that led to the hypothesis that a process of psychological change was in progress. Second, a process of self-reflection then mediated her shifts from certain states-of-being to new dimensions of awareness. Third, she then began a process of actively participating in using this new awareness to (a) remove blocks hampering her self-development, and (b) resolve the old hurts to her child-self.... Davina's constructive use of the process of lucid dreaming is in striking contrast to the rejection of lucidity by other dreamers who are not oriented to self-development. When an individual is lacking in a certain level of self-awareness, developmental blocks are experienced and the dreamer rejects the process of lucid dreaming.

LUCID DREAMING: MAXIMUM SELF-REFLECTION?

So lucid dreaming is when you know you're dreaming while you're dreaming. You're sound asleep and dreaming, believing that the dream is reality, when for a variety of reasons you recognize that it is a dream and that you are in fact asleep. Typically people react initially with a sense of wonder and fun. However, this initial excitement also often awakens the dreamer. Additionally, your consciousness is limited while you're unconscious.

There are various ways to conceptualize lucid dreaming. One is in terms of the self-reflectiveness that attaining such a state of consciousness might imply. The late Canadian psychologist Alan Moffitt and his colleagues at Carleton University developed a scale measuring self-reflectiveness in dreamers based on Rossi's therapeutic work.

The classic position has been that in most dreams we are not particularly self-reflective or critical of our dream surroundings, events, and characters. In keeping with this position, the lowest level of Moffitt's self-reflectiveness scale begins with "The dreamer is not in the dream." Researchers have found that this is one of the first dreaming experiences that children have. It takes quite a while until they move toward the next stage of thinking, when they can begin to construct their selves enough to have a self in a dream. One day when I was telling my then seven-year-old son about a dream I'd had, he looked at me with an irritated expression. I asked him what was wrong and he said, "How come you get to be in your dreams, and I don't get to be in mine?" I remember thinking that that was a fairly sophisticated observation. Without explaining that he has cognitive limitations, I assured him that eventually he would get to be in his dreams and, of course, this came to pass. Although occasionally young children appear in their dreams as active characters, more often than not they are observing, they have a sense of it happening out there somewhere. The ability to integrate a sense of self in one's dreams is a developmental benchmark.

The midway point on the self-reflectiveness scale is when the dreamer becomes completely involved in the dream. This is where many of us remain, so completely absorbed in the dream that if it is a nightmare we are relieved when we finally awaken. Eventually in a dream, we experience some kind of reflective activity, such as thinking about an idea. So in the dream we might mutter to our dream selves, "This isn't quite right." This happens when we utilize the highest form of logical thought, called formal operations. The reality is that we think at this higher level only about half the time—even when we're awake!

At one of the higher levels on this scale, the dreamer has multiple levels of awareness and is simultaneously participating in and observing the dream. This would be a dream where you're watching yourself doing something, and you're in it and out of it at the same time but it still feels real. Another example would be a false awakening dream, where you dream that you wake up, and then you really wake up and realize that you only dreamt you woke up. Did you ever do that two or three times in a row? You know you're dreaming, you wake up, and then you dream you wake... and then, and then, and then... After all, waking up can get scary! I recall doing it once four times in a row, and I was getting pretty scared, thinking, "What's real and what's not?"

Another example of the slipperiness of reality that these dream experiences can subject us to is the dream that was so real, you relate its events to a friend as if they really happened. Your friend looks at you as if you're crazy, and only then do you say in embarrassment, "I dreamt it!"

These things get very slippery. What's dreaming and what's not dreaming? What's real and what's not real? It can get quite confusing. A colleague of mine uses in his presentations a photographic slide of a huge toilet with a little person standing there looking at it. It illustrates the dream where you are telling yourself, "It's okay, you're awake, you can pee!", when another part of you replies, "No. You're asleep. Don't go!" Did you ever lose that argument?

At the highest level of Moffitt's scale, the dreamer consciously reflects on the fact that he or she is dreaming. This is the lucid dream. It is the experience of, "Hey, wait a minute, this is a dream," or "That's why I can fly like Superman!" I recall one of my students telling me that he often could tell he was dreaming. I asked, "How did you figure that out?" He replied, "Well, I know I'm dreaming if I'm in an airport and my car is there and it's blue, because my car's not blue. I know my car is purple. Ergo, it must be a dream." I recall thinking that, if that were me in the dream and there was a purple car instead of a blue one, I'd think, "Oh well, something must have changed and I now have a purple car." I'd just drift along accepting whatever came my way. In contrast, this student has a very critical attitude in waking, which influences his dreaming style; thus, he is often able to identify that he is dreaming. However, his degree of reflectiveness, or critical attitude, is actually quite rare.

Although most dream researchers consider having a lucid dream the highest level of self-reflectiveness, I believe that it's merely the basement of the potential of consciousness in sleep and, in fact, the potential of consciousness in the twenty-four hour cycle.

LUCID DREAMING PROOF

The initial verification of the possibility of knowing you are dreaming while you are dreaming is primarily due to the work of my colleague Stephen LaBerge. By now his work has been replicated in several sleep laboratories and, I think, enables us to say with reasonable certainty that you can be awake in some sense while you're asleep.

Here's how we know this. When you're in REM sleep you're paralyzed from the neck down. The task was to come up with a way to signal to the polysonographer who is monitoring your sleep electronically, "Hey, I know I'm dreaming." You cannot kick your leg because of REM paralysis. But it turns out that you do have control of your eye movements. For instance, while in a dream if you think, "I'm going to move my eyes way to the right and then way to the left" and then your dream self does it, that's what really happens to your physical eyes.

LaBerge devised a technique to enable a sleeping person to signal dream researchers when she or he was dreaming. The signal was a prearranged set of eye movements, such as a left–right eye movement marking the onset of lucidity, that reached the sleep lab technician through electrodes attached to the corners of the subject's eyes. Then the technician would awaken the subject and ask, "What was going on before I woke you?" (Interestingly, dream researcher Keith Hearne in England developed a signaling technique at about the same time that LaBerge did, with neither scientist knowing of the other's work.)

INDIVIDUAL DIFFERENCES IN LUCID DREAMING

Most of the research I have done over the last twenty years has dealt with individual differences in lucid dreaming. Why do some people seem to have these experiences with relative ease while others do not?

To begin with, I have been concerned with the spontaneous incidence of these experiences of consciousness in sleep. I was interested in knowing when this occurred normally—that is, when a dreamer was not programmed to try to have the experience. When my students and I asked college students if they ever had the experience of knowing they were dreaming, fifty-eight percent said they had had such a dream at least once in their lifetime, while twenty-one percent had it once or more per month. There is some indication that due to the media attention given to dreams in general and lucid dreams in particular in recent years that this spontaneous incidence may have increased. That is, once people hear that it is possible to dream lucidly, they often go home and do it!

In our study, we found the strongest individual differences were in terms of the superior spatial skills of lucid dreamers. People who spontaneously experience lucid dreams seem to know how to maneuver well in physical and mental space. You may wonder, "What do you mean that having the ability to dream lucidly is associated with getting around in space?" I mean this quite literally. For instance, we measured people who frequently reported having lucid dreams and those who didn't, and looked at the integrity of their vestibular systems. The vestibular system is a system of body balance involving the inner ear, and one of the primary mechanisms we use to orient ourselves in the space around us and affects, for instance, how much we tilt when turning a corner on a bicycle, whether we can easily balance on one foot, or whether we can tell which way is north.

Before the experiment we weeded out people who got motion sickness or had an obvious vestibular problem in order to ensure our subjects had reasonably healthy vestibular systems. We used standard clinical tests of the integrity of the system and found that for those that were not having lucid dreams very often there were marginal problems with their vestibular system. We also found the same thing when we tested them on an apparatus called a stableometer. This apparatus gives the subject the sensation of balancing on a platform which rests on a ball. Frequent lucid dreamers could balance on the platform the best.

Another aspect of spatial abilities is called field independence. Have you ever known someone who, no matter where they are, never gets lost? Even if there are no buildings or mountains they seem to know how to find their way around with some sort of internal compass. These people are field independent. Such people can be relatively independent of the physical environment and still accurately orient and maneuver themselves in space. Again, we found that people who were spontaneous lucid dreamers also tended to be field independent.

We also found that lucid dreamers are able to manipulate complex spatial objects in their minds. For instance, we asked them to rotate a three-dimensional object in imaginary space and match it to a representation of another three-dimensional object on a test page. The frequent lucid dreamers were able to do this much more accurately than those for whom consciousness in sleep rarely if ever occurred. To try this you might look at a familiar object in your kitchen, say a blender. Then open up the blender in your mind and imagine it rotating ninety degrees to the left. If this is a relatively easy thing for you to imagine, then you may have these sorts of spatial skills. The idea of moving objects in mental space is related to the ability to move in physical space. Specifically, when you're in a dream, you're in what feels like a real world with spatial parameters. Although the laws of physics aren't quite the same in the dream world as they are in the waking one, you still have to maneuver in this mental space as though it were a physical space.

I was also interested in personality variables which might be associated with people having lucid dreams. Although there were some personality differences between lucid- and non-lucid dreamers, there was nothing that was remarkable. For instance, there was some evidence that lucid dreamers were more androgynous; that is, they were comfortable expressing both the masculine and feminine parts of themselves. Lucid dreamers are also more likely to take mental risks, such as being willing to be hypnotized. They are also more self-oriented than non-lucid dreamers, at least in terms of awareness of internal aspects of the self.

MEDITATORS AND LUCID DREAMING

In some populations, you get remarkable increases in the incidence of lucid dreaming. I was given access to meditators who lived and practiced meditation at a nearby university. Five groups of meditators using the transcendental meditation technique reported having lucid dreams once or more per week, significantly more often than did non-meditators enrolled at another nearby university. It is important to note that these groups were not meditating in order to have lucid dreams; rather, lucid dreams seemed to be one of several positive outcomes that emerged from the practice of meditation.

It turns out that meditation increases performance on various spatial measures (especially field independence), as well as the frequency of lucid dreaming. Moreover there are some schools of meditation that maintain that consciousness in sleep is a marker of the development of higher states of consciousness.

WHAT HAPPENS IN A LUCID DREAM?

In comparing the content of lucid and non-lucid dreams, we found very few differences. The differences we did find, however, are worth mentioning. First, people tend to characterize their lucid dreams as much more remarkable than their non-lucid dreams. This is true at least for people who have had them somewhat infrequently. The more lucid dreams you have, the more ordinary they appear. They don't necessarily get boring, you just get used to this state of mind in sleep. Therefore, I think our self-evaluation findings may be affected by novelty; once the newness of lucid dreaming wears off, we no longer perceive lucid dreams as extraordinary and studies have indicated that the content of lucid and non-lucid dreams are quite similar.

Somehow being aware that you are dreaming seems to open certain dream potentials: When you're dreaming and you know you're dreaming you can, to a point, control the dream. While it is possible to have some felt sense of control over non-lucid dreams, there is not the immediacy of lucid control.

Another difference is that references to sounds are more frequent in lucid dreams, as are kinesthetic (body touch) references, which leads us to believe that the vestibular system is somehow more implicated.

Also, there tend to be fewer characters in lucid dreams, which is interesting from a psychodynamic perspective. If you view every character in a dream as an aspect of yourself, then having fewer of them would imply more integration of the aspects of self, a positive interpretation. On the other hand, a negative interpretative perspective might hold that lucid dreams are more narcissistic in nature.

Paul Tholey, a sports psychologist from Germany, points out that lucid dreaming has the potential to further one's growth process. He illustrates this by telling about a lucid dream he had about his deceased father. In the dream, he tried to talk to his father to no avail. Finally he confronted his father and was able to hear some legitimate criticisms from him without undue defensiveness. Finally the father and dreamer characters merged into one, which Tholey interpreted as a resolution of some of his issues with this parent.

HOW TO HAVE A LUCID DREAM

You may be asking, "How can I have this thing?" Research has found that there are some things you can do before sleep and/or during sleep or naps to encourage lucid dreaming. As you are falling asleep, you may want to simply suggest to yourself that you will know you will be dreaming.

To further facilitate the likelihood of dreaming lucidly you might ask while you're awake, "Am I dreaming?" Then, while you're still awake, do a reality check. For instance, if you read your watch in a dream and then read it again a moment later, the time is often dramatically different. But if you look at your watch twice while you're awake, only seconds pass.

I do not recommend that you question yourself like this while you're awake if you have problems identifying what's real. Certainly we can go on and on about nothing being real and get lost in the whole philosophy of it, but let's put that aside. If you are reasonably confident that you know what's real and what's not, then you might ask yourself that question every time a light blinks. So when you stop at a traffic signal and the light changes from red to green, ask yourself, "Am I dreaming?" When you turn on a light in a room, say to yourself, "Am I dreaming?"

One thing that's received a lot of attention over the last few years is a biofeedback sleep mask designed by Stephen LaBerge, which monitors your eye movements to identify when you're in REM sleep. When you are in REM sleep for a pre-specified length of time, a light blinks on the inner surface of the mask. When you see this blinking light in your dreams you have trained yourself while awake to then ask, "Am I dreaming?" With sufficient motivation on the part of the mask wearer, LaBerge has successfully used the mask to help induce lucid dreams.

There are two other pre-sleep activities that may help you start dreaming lucidly: meditation, and the cultivation of high dream recall. I mentioned the effects of meditation earlier and have also found that cultivating the skill of remembering dreams increases the likelihood that you will know you are dreaming while you are dreaming. This may simply be the result of increased inner attention developed by recalling dreams.

When it spontaneously occurs to you that you are dreaming, it is likely to happen in one of three ways: when you are having a nightmare, when your dream features incongruities, or when you simply know you are dreaming from the beginning of the dream. In the case of nightmares, the bogeyman may be chasing you and you suddenly realize it's only a dream and are relieved. By incongruities I mean those oddities in dreams that do not occur while you are awake. For instance, I once had a dream of an old man with a tin can growing out of his head. It occurred to me in the dream that this may be a dream. All too often we blindly accept these strange events in our sleep, but sometimes we question them and learn we are dreaming. Finally, subjects who spontaneously report lucidity tell me that they just knew they were dreaming from the onset of the dream. I believe this may be an indicator of the development of higher states of consciousness.

LUCID DREAMING IS ONLY THE BEGINNING

Why would you want to have a lucid dream? Perhaps you would like to develop greater self-awareness, get rid of nightmares, solve work problems, or even improve your tennis stroke. If you're a tennis player and you want to angle your wrist in a new way to get that shot exactly right, you can practice in your imagination and that can be helpful. But the dream is the strongest realm of images to which we have access. To practice there feels real. Some sports psychologists have worked with athletes, training them to practice their sport in lucid dreams. In any case, it's fun, it's enjoyable, and it has some psychological as well as pragmatic potentials, but lucidity is only the beginning.

In my research program and my books, I have conceptualized lucid dreaming as the bargain basement of consciousness in sleep. Witnessing dreams and sleep are indications of higher forms of the development of consciousness. Psychologist Charles Alexander has conceptualized these higher states of consciousness as postrepresentational.

Let me explain. The way we think is representational; that is, when I think, it is always about "something." There is a representation of something. Thus when I think about my children, I have feelings that represent them, I have ideas or cognitions about them, I have a mental image of them, and I have a felt sense of how it is to touch them. But in all these forms my children are still represented. Even when I think about myself there is still representation: me the teacher, me the mother, me the middle-aged woman, me the dream expert, and so forth. There is always something that is represented in my consciousness.

In post-representational levels of consciousness our thoughts, feelings, and sense of body are without content. There is no object of our attention. At this level, consciousness has also been called pure or transcendental consciousness. The idea that consciousness can have its own integrity, can know or refer to itself without an object, without a thing to be conscious of, has been around for thousands of years in some philosophical systems from east Asia. However, for those of us in the West it can feel like a peanut butter concept: You know what it is, but explaining it is like trying to talk with peanut butter in your mouth.

Some traditions assert that the clearest marker of the development of these states of being is consciousness in sleep. These states have been called spiritual or mystical states. One of the first steps toward consciousness in sleep is having a lucid dream. Still, in a lucid dream, although you know you're dreaming, while you're dreaming you're still caught up in the dream activities. It's exciting and fun but you're anything but detached. When you move into the higher forms of consciousness in sleep, you are more likely to feel detached.

I examined these sleep consciousness forms in research with an elite group of meditators who practice an advanced form of transcendental meditation. This group was on a program of practice (planned activities including meditation) for all but two hours a day. They were extremely sophisticated observers of these states of consciousness. Lucid dreaming was described to them as a dream in which they are actively thinking of the fact that they're dreaming. One of these meditators wrote of his lucid dreams, "I'll become aware of the dream as separate then aware that I am dreaming. Then I begin to manipulate the story and the characters to create whatever situation I desire. [At] times in unpleasant situations, I'll think as the dreamer, 'I don't have to put up with this.' And I change the dream, or at least I back out of the involvement."

"WITNESSING" A DREAM

A higher form of consciousness in dreams was described by someone in this group as "witnessing" a dream: "A dream in which you experience a quiet, peaceful inner awareness or wakefulness, completely separate from the dream." Another person wrote, "Sometimes, whatever the content of the dream is, I feel an inner tranquillity of awareness that is removed from the dream. Sometimes, I may even be caught up in the dream, but the inner awareness and peace remains. It is de-embedded." Therefore, in witnessing dreams, there is a feeling of separateness.

One of the classic characteristics of the development of consciousness is a continued de-embeddedness, or detachment. We think of this as wisdom; somehow things don't shake us up so much when we get older and (we hope) wiser. As we move through life we become de-embedded or detached, to use the more common term. Being detached does not mean that we don't care. Rather, it means we've been through many different experiences and have learned how to let things wash over us.

WITNESSING IN DEEP SLEEP

Witnessing in deep sleep or relatively dreamless sleep can be described as a dreamless sleep in which one experiences a quiet, peaceful inner state of awareness and wakefulness. One participant explained it this way: "It's a feeling of infinite expansion and bliss and nothing else. Then I become aware that I exist, but there is no individual personality. Gradually I become aware that I'm an individual, but there are no details of who . . . where . . . what . . . when . . . eventually these details fill in and I might awaken."

This state of consciousness has also been called the void, because there is no content or object of awareness. Here's a description of witnessing deep sleep from a mathematics professor who has been meditating for twenty years on a regular basis: "One experiences oneself to be a part of a tremendous composite of relationships. These are not social or conceptual, or intellectual relationships, only a web of relationships. I'm aware of the relationship between entities without the entities being there. There's a sense of motion, yet there's [nothing] to gauge motion by . . . it's just expansiveness. There are no objects to measure it. The expansiveness is one of light, like the light of awareness. Visual, but not visual; more like a light in an ocean. An intimate experience of light."

In my book *Control Your Dreams*, I argue that as you grow more self-reflective in dreaming, you generally move toward lucid dreaming and on to witnessing dreaming, and witnessing deep sleep. However, you don't have to be lucid in order to experience witnessing in sleep. Some people get so attached to lucidity that they find they need to let go of it before they can develop the detached perspective of the witness. You can become as attached to knowing you're dreaming while you're dreaming as you can to anything else. After all, when you have a lucid dream, there is still an object of awareness in it: the dream itself.

There are several lines of evidence both biological and psychological that support this developmental model, or at the very least, suggest that there is a relationship between these states of consciousness in sleep. I have summarized this research in a book I coedited,

Dream Images: A Call to Mental Arms. I shall briefly highlight some of it here.

It has been found that increases in REM density have been associated with both the lucid state in non-meditators and for meditators who claim witnessing half the night or more. Alpha brain waves are experienced in early and pre-lucid episodes and they're associated with witnessing dreams and sleep. Fred Travis, whose work appeared in the journal *Dreaming*, has pulled some of this EEG brain work together, and Lynn Mason, studying subjects in a sophisticated sleep laboratory, has reinforced his model. Travis says that in meditation you have moments of transcendence or unity, which isn't to say that you might not also have it when you're running or crocheting or nursing your baby. What these and most of life's activities may have in common is a focused sense of total connection, total communion with the universe. Travis and others have measured those experiences in meditation and it turns out that they're identical to your EEG every time you change states of consciousness. That is, moving from sleeping to waking to dreaming sleep. The implication is that perhaps there is a state of consciousness which underlies waking, dreaming, and sleeping which I have identified herein as pure or transcendental consciousness.

In this chapter I have highlighted the research on sleep and dreams with an emphasis on the experience of consciousness in sleep. The potential far-reaching implications of consciousness in sleep are just beginning to be investigated if not appreciated. We are at the entry of a new era in our understanding of such states and their implications for full human functioning.

Deepak Chopra, M.D.

When Deepak Chopra heard that Karl Pribram, of whom he has long been a fan, was a part of my Smithsonian series on the Brain and Consciousness, he immediately accepted my invitation to participate. Dr. Chopra is known worldwide for his extraordinary ability to combine complex scientific findings and ancient wisdom in a fascinating manner to educate and inspire all who encounter him. The author of twenty-three bestselling books, including *Perfect Health* and *Ageless Body, Timeless Mind,* he has also produced a number of television and video programs in conjunction with PBS, including the immensely popular *Body, Mind, and Soul: The Mystery and the Magic.*

Formerly chief of staff at Boston Regional Medical Center, Dr. Chopra also taught at the Tufts University and Boston University Schools of Medicine and built a successful endocrinology practice in Boston. He served on the National Institutes of Health Ad Hoc Panel on Alternative Medicine and presently heads the innovative Chopra Center for Well Being in La Jolla, California.

CHAPTER FOUR

Quantum Physics and Consciousness

Deepak Chopra, M.D.

I would like to introduce you to the paradigm that has been the consciousness paradigm in Vedic tradition—the ancient science of healing from India—for thousands of years. And I also want to introduce you to some concepts about healing based on this paradigm.

Our paradigm in science, until recently, has been based on a materialistic interpretation—the Newtonian world view—that is a result of a sensory interpretation of the universe. In other words, the premise is that the senses, or the scientific instruments which are prostheses of the senses, give us an accurate picture of the world. I think it would be fair to say many scientists now recognize that it is not really true that the senses give us an accurate picture of the world, or even that scientific instruments give us an accurate picture of the world. In fact, the so-called objective world is a response of the observer—literally a result of the interpretations we make in our consciousness and of the kinds of instruments that we use to make those observations.

A number of years ago, an experiment with kittens was conducted by scientists at Harvard Medical School. From the day of their birth, some of the kittens were raised in an area painted with horizontal stripes: all the visual stimuli in their environment were horizontal. Another group was raised in an area with vertical stripes, and that was all that they could see. And when these kittens grew up to be wise old cats, the group that was exposed to the horizontal stripes could see only a horizontal world, bumping into furniture legs, for example, as though they were not there. The kittens that grew up in a vertical world had exactly the opposite problem. Of course, this had nothing to do with the belief system of these cats. When their brains were examined, one group of cats did not have interneuronal connections to see a horizontal world, nor did the other group have interneuronal connections to see a vertical world. The initial sensory experience of these kittens, and how they interpreted that experience in their consciousness during the critical days after birth when their sight developed, actually shaped the anatomy of their nervous systems. Ultimately, these kittens perceived only that which they had been conditioned to perceive and interpret in the first place.

Some psychologists have an interesting term for this—they call it "premature cognitive commitment." Premature, because we make it at a very early stage of our lives. Cognitive, because it influences the anatomy of the nervous system with which we cognize, or know, the world. And commitment, because it commits us to a fixed reality. Some scientists will tell you that, right now, the nervous system you are using will take in less than one billionth of the stimuli that are present. And the stimuli that your nervous system does take in are those that reinforce your notion, your idea, your interpretation of what you think exists out there. If you have already made a commitment to reality, then that which exists outside the framework of that commitment will be edited out by your nervous system, which you are using to make observations. And depending on the kind of receptors you have, depending on the kinds of observations you want to make and the questions you are asking yourself when you make those observations, depending on all that, you perceive a certain limited segment of reality. After all, the human nervous system can perceive only wavelengths of light between 400 and 750 nanometers. And if we happen to agree on our sensory observations, and the interpretations of our sensory observations, we collectively have a framework for interpretations that we agree upon.

We call this methodology "science." And we usually presume that science is a methodology for exploring the truth when, in fact, science—as it has been structured and has functioned until recently—has really not been a methodology for exploring the truth at all. Rather, it has been a methodology for exploring our current conceptual framework of what we think the truth is. The territory that we have explored has been a function of the map that we have in consciousness. And as that map, that conceptual framework, changes, then of course the territory that we begin to explore begins to change as well.

The fact that perception is a learned phenomenon, that perception depends on the kinds of instruments we use to make observations, should be made clear by examining the mechanics of perception in any living species. The eye cells of a honeybee do not respond to the usual wavelengths of light that you and I respond to. But because they are sensitive to ultraviolet, a honeybee looks at a flower, even though it doesn't see the flower that you and I see, and senses the honey from a distance. A snake would experience that same thing as infrared radiation. A bat would know it as the echo of ultrasound, which means nothing to you or me. A chameleon's eyeballs swivel on different axes, so we cannot even remotely imagine what something would look like to a chameleon.

So then, what is the real shape of the world? What is its real texture? What is its real fragrance? What is it really like? I believe these to be appropriate questions because what the world is really like depends on who is making the observations. It also depends on what kind of questions the observer is asking when making those observations. Sir John Eccles, a well-known neuroscientist, once said, "I want you to know that there are no colors in the real world, that there are no fragrances in the real world, that there's no beauty and there's no ugliness. Out there beyond the limits of our perceptual apparatus is the erratically ambiguous and ceaselessly flowing quantum soup. And we're almost like magicians in that in the very act of perception, we take that quantum soup and we convert it into the experience of material reality in our ordinary everyday waking state of consciousness."

As a result of trusting our senses to give us an accurate picture of the world, we have built up a scientific edifice that is based on a materialistic interpretation of reality. Our senses are supposed to give us an accurate picture of the world, but we know that they don't. After all, our senses tell us that the Earth is flat. No one believes that anymore. Our senses tell us that the ground we're standing on is stationary. We know it's spinning at dizzying speeds, and hurtling through space at thousands of miles per hour. Our senses tell us that a thing has color, texture, shape, and size. And we tend to believe that these attributes define the intrinsic nature of the object of our perception, when in fact, they define the intrinsic nature of the observer and the instruments that the observer is using to make those observations. So based on the old paradigm, we have structured a system of biology that has until now been based completely on a mechanistic worldview of the human body.

Science, in its attempts to cure illness, looks at mechanisms of disease and tries to elucidate those mechanisms in the hope of understanding how to interfere with them, and thereby eliminate the disease. For example, if we can understand how bacteria multiply and then interfere by administering an appropriate antibiotic, we shouldn't have infections anymore. If we know how cancer cells replicate at the level of DNA, then we can interfere by using the appropriate anti-cancer agents, called interleukins, and we shouldn't have cancer anymore. Whether at the level of genetics, molecular biology, or biochemistry, all of science attempts to understand the mechanisms of disease and then seeks to interfere with those mechanisms in the hope of eliminating them. However, I believe there is a basic fallacy here.

Yes, it is important to understand the mechanisms of disease and learn how to interfere with them. This approach has been extremely successful in the treatment of acute illness and has saved many lives. Nevertheless, it is important to recognize that the mechanisms of disease are not the same as the origins of disease. Origins of disease have to do with the daily expressions of life in the human mind and the human body. These daily expressions include the basic acts of eating, breathing, digesting, metabolizing, eliminating, and, most important, the movement of consciousness—which is thought, and feeling, and emotion, and desire, and memory. These fluctuations in consciousness influence each of these expressions of life in both our bodies and our minds.

If we continue to confuse the mechanisms of disease with the origins of disease, even though we may be extremely successful in the short run, we will not influence significantly the power of disease to cause illness and death in a given population in the long run. Rather, we will only be successful in replacing old epidemics with new ones. So today, for example, instead of epidemics of polio, smallpox, malaria, and tuberculosis, we have epidemics of HIV disease, cancer, degenerative disorders, cardiovascular disease, alcoholism, drug addiction, obesity, and diabetes.

Moreover, if we are to understand the mechanisms and origins of health, then we have to go beyond the origins of disease. Health is not the mere absence of disease, but a state of well-being that is physical and emotional, and, according to the Ayurvedic world view, spiritual. We must ask the crucial question that science has not posed but has relegated to the realm of philosophers: "What is life?"—not merely in its expressions, but also in its essence. I recently asked a California physician friend of mine if he could define life for me. He replied, "Yes, of course, it's a sexually transmitted incurable disease."

If we continue to focus merely on mechanisms of disease and interfere with them, we may even help sow the seeds of illness in the future. It has been estimated through a number of studies that about eighty thousand people die per year in the United States as a direct result of antibiotic-resistant infections acquired in hospitals. Simple infections like streptococcus and staphylococcus, which used to be so easy to treat, are now becoming resistant to all forms of therapy as a result of the indiscriminate use of antibiotics. It is known that the number one cause of drug addiction in the world is not street drugs, but medications that are prescribed by physicians. Despite the fact that there are more people doing research on cancer than have cancer, the age-adjusted mortality from cancer has increased slightly over the last three decades. I attended a National Institutes of Health meeting a while ago and one participant remarked that more people are living off cancer than are dying from it!

There is something wrong with a model that looks primarily for a magic bullet. It is estimated that about eighty percent of the population of the United States swallows a medically prescribed chemical every twenty-four hours. If you can't believe you ate the whole thing, have a couple of Alka Seltzers. You can't go to sleep at night, take a sleeping pill. You're feeling anxious, there's a tranquilizer.

You have an infection, there's an antibiotic. You have cancer, there's chemotherapy, radiation, and surgery. You're having chest pains, you can pop a nitroglycerin pill. Better still, have a bypass operation. All these approaches are based on an incomplete model of the human body that excludes consciousness altogether. And it is consciousness that is, in fact, the phenomenon, and matter that is the epiphenomenon, or by-product, in human physiology, and probably in the physiology of this organic universe in which we live.

So let us examine a model that is at the same time extremely ancient and extremely modern. It is a model that says that the human body is not an anatomical structure that is fixed in space and time. The human body is more like a river alive with energy, information, and intelligence. It has a cybernetic feedback loop and can influence its own evolution and its own expression. It has the ability to learn from mistakes and the ability to make choices. The human body is literally a river of energy and information—the "real you." But the real you cannot step into the same flesh and bones twice, just as you cannot step into the same river twice, because in every moment of your existence you are renewing your body more easily, more effortlessly, and more spontaneously than you can even change your clothes. Technically speaking, the physical body that you use to leave a room is not the one that you walked in with earlier. Through a number of physiological processes, you renew your body in every second of your existence. For example, in the simple act of breathing, each breath we inhale contains ten to the power of twenty-two atoms from the universe. It is an astronomical amount of raw material that comes from everywhere and ends up as our heart cells, brain cells, and kidney cells. With each breath that we exhale, we are breathing out ten to the power of twenty-two atoms which have their own origin in every cell of our bodies. So we are literally breathing out bits and pieces of our heart and kidney and brain tissue, and speaking technically again, we are all intimately sharing our organs with each other all of the time. The great American poet Walt Whitman once said, "Every atom belonging to you as well belongs to me." This turns out to be not a metaphor of poetry, but a fact of physiology.

Researchers have done mathematical computations based on radioactive isotope studies which suggest that, right at this moment, in our physical bodies we may have a million atoms that were once in the body of Jesus, the Virgin Mary, or Buddha; of Leonardo da Vinci or Michelangelo; of Mahatma Gandhi or Mother Teresa; of Saddam Hussein or anyone else who comes to mind. In the last three weeks, a quadrillion atoms have circulated through our bodies that have circulated through the bodies of every other living species on this planet. We could think of a tree in Africa, a squirrel in Siberia, a peasant in China, and we have raw material inside of our bodies that was circulating in that tree or squirrel or peasant three weeks ago. In less than one year, we replace ninety-eight percent of our physical bodies. So, literally, we make a new liver every six weeks at the atomic level. A new skin once a month. A new stomach lining every five days. A new skeleton—it seems so hard, and solid, and permanent, but it is a dynamic structure—and speaking technically again, we replace it every three months. Even the raw material of our DNA that holds the memories of millions of years of evolutionary time, comes and goes every six weeks, almost like migratory birds. So if you think you are your material body, then according to this paradigm, you have a bit of a dilemma. Which body are you talking about? The physical body is recycled elements— recycled earth, water, and air—matter in all of its solid, liquid, gaseous, and quantum mechanical forms. And it comes and goes in the twinkling of an eye.

Any time I explain the quantum mechanical model to my friends and colleagues, they ask me that if it is really true that the human skeleton replaces itself every three months, then why is the arthritis still there? If it is really true that the blood vessels replace themselves every six to eight weeks, why are they still blocked? The answer I give is that through our own conditioning, we generate the same impulses of energy and information that lead not only to the same behavioral outcomes, but also lead to the same biochemical processes, and that these biochemical processes are under the influence of our consciousness, our memory, and our conditioned responses.

Our physical bodies, according to the Vedic paradigm, are just the places that our memories and our dreams call home for the time being. Perhaps we are confusing the horse with the rider, and the molecules on which we ride do not make up the essential persons who are using the molecules to express themselves. There is a wonderful moment in *The Tempest* by Shakespeare when Prospero says, "We are such stuff as dreams are made on." And perhaps, that is not a metaphor anymore. As I was writing *Ageless Body, Timeless Mind*, I received a call from a cardiologist in Chicago who wanted to refer a patient to me, a young woman who'd had a heart transplant for a condition called cardiomyopathy, a chronic disease of the heart muscle. After she was returned to her hospital room, she started to have intense cravings for Chicken McNuggets™ and beer. At the same time, she began having dreams about a young man. This young man would tell her that his name was Tommy So-and-So and that "I really love you because you have my heart."

After the young woman was released from the hospital, she went to the library, searched the obituary columns, and discovered Tommy So-and-So. He was nineteen years of age, and had consumed a lot of Chicken McNuggets and beer just before he had a fatal motorcycle accident. If I had heard this story ten years ago, I would probably have given both the patient and the cardiologist a hundred milligrams of Thorazine and called in a psychiatrist. But since then, I have looked at histories of transplant patients and reviewed studies of the physiological structure of the mechanisms of memory, and I have come to realize that it is not as outlandish a story as it appears to be.

These kinds of experiences are leading us into the world of science today, and particularly into the world of biology, where I believe we are witnessing the climactic overthrow of the superstition of materialism. Whether it is a fax machine, or a radio, or a television, or a computer—all of these technologies are based on a very simple premise: the essential nature of the material world is not material. The essential stuff of the universe is non-stuff. An atom, the basic unit of matter, is not a solid entity, but a hierarchy of states of information and energy in a huge void. And today, if you went to a quantum physicist and asked her what is the true nature of the human body, she most likely would tell you the same thing. The human body is made up of atoms. The atoms in turn are made up of subatomic particles that are moving at lightning speeds around huge empty spaces. And the subatomic particles are not material things. They are fluctuations of energy and information in a huge void. Seen through the eyes of a physicist, the human body is proportionately as void as intergalactic space. If you could see the human body as it really is—not through the artifact of sensory experience, which we know is unreliable, but as it really is—then you would see that 99.999% of the human body is empty space. And the .001% that appears to be material is also empty space; it just gives the appearance of solidity. In other words, the human body is really made out of nothing.

As you go beyond the facade of molecules, you enter the subatomic cloud. Go beyond the cloud and you end up with a handful of nothing. So the question is: What is this nothingness from whence everything seems to come—including this physiology, this body? Is this nothingness just a void, or could it be the womb of creation? Is it even vaguely possible that nature goes to exactly the same place to create a galaxy of stars, or a rain forest, or a human body, as it goes to create a thought? Because what is a thought, after all, if not a fluctuation of energy and information? We get so used to experiencing thoughts in purely linguistically structured and verbally elite terms, because presumably we all hear them in English, and sometimes with an Indian accent, and we assume that thinking must be a purely human phenomenon. In fact, if we conceive of thoughts as information and energy, then that might be the basic activity of the universe itself: that human thought is just a localized concentration of energy and information in a universe that is alive with energy and information. These thoughts, likewise, are quantum events in the same field of pure potentiality that one calls the unified field these days, and that to think that thought is, at the same time, to manufacture a molecule. Thoughts may be quantum events that transform themselves into space/time events. The great Sufi poet Rumi, who lived in the Middle East about a thousand years ago, once said, "We come spinning out of nothingness, scattering stars like dust.... Look at these worlds, spinning out of nothingness. This is within your potential."

The pioneering research by Dr. Candace Pert and her colleagues in the 1970s provided evidence of a biochemical basis for awareness and consciousness, and showed how our internal chemicals—the neuropeptides and their receptors—act as messengers communicating information over a network linking all of our systems and organs. What we envision is what Dr. Pert called a "mobile brain": a brain that exists not just in the head, but throughout the body.

So when scientists began to look at the cells of the immune system such as T-cells, B-cells, microphages, and leukocytes—cells that are protecting us from infection, cancer, degenerative disorders, and the ravages of aging—they found receptors that were identical to those found in nerve cells. In other words, our immune cells are, in a way, eavesdropping on our internal dialogue. The conversation is going on all of the time. In fact, it is going on right now as you are evaluating what I am saying, agreeing or disagreeing. It goes on in sleep. It goes on in dreams.

If you ask a neurobiologist today if there is an essential difference between the immune system and the nervous system, he will tell you there isn't any. The immune system is a circulating nervous system. It may not be thinking in linguistically structured thought, but behaves identically. It has memory. It makes choices. It has learning ability. And if by mind we mean information and energy, the immune system is as sophisticated as the nervous system in the expression of its information, its energy, its memory, its learning ability, and its adaptability.

So when today you say, "I have a gut feeling about such-and-such," you may not be speaking metaphorically at all because your gut makes the same chemicals that your brain makes when it is having those thoughts. In fact, I would suggest that your gut feelings are probably more accurate because gut cells have not yet learned how to doubt their own thinking.

Evidence like this is leading at least some of us to hypothesize that the body is the objective experience of consciousness, just as the mind is the subjective experience of consciousness. You cannot take a thought or emotion and localize it and observe it through a microscope or in a test tube. No neurologist has actually observed the mind when dissecting the brain. No neurosurgeon has found this thing called the mind when operating on the brain. The evidence that the mind exists at all is circumstantial. And yet—because we have subjectively experienced thoughts, feelings, emotions, desires, instincts, and drives, because we have fallen in love with someone and have passion about certain things—I think that everyone feels, quite reasonably, that he or she does have a mind. The evidence for this may be circumstantial, but we have had direct knowledge of it through our own subjective experiences. It is possible that the human body is just the epiphenomenon of the mind in that it is the objective experience of consciousness. There is a Vedic expression dating back thousands of years that says, "Curving back within myself, I create both the experience of the mind and the body. Curving back within myself, I experience my mind subjectively, I experience myself objectively, but in fact, I am beyond both." And Rumi also said it very elegantly: "Out beyond ideas of right doing and wrong doing, there is a field. I will meet you there."

I believe it is becoming clear that the mind and body are inseparably one in every bit of their expression. What may not be so clear is that mind and body may be inseparably one, not only in the physiology of a human being or an animal, but in the physiology of our planet and possibly the physiology of our universe: that information, energy, and matter are inseparably one in every aspect of the entire universe. After all, Einstein clearly showed that energy and matter were essentially the same thing. One only needs to add one more ingredient: information. Mind and body as one is a real phenomenon of nature and expresses itself through self-referral cybernetic feedback loops. It influences its own expression. It has the ability to remember, and it has the ability to learn. For this reason, one may not want to call it merely information, but intelligence. Intelligence is information that is alive. And we may be part of a living, organic, metabolizing, thinking universe.

That mind and matter may be inseparably one in every aspect of the cosmos is a theory that is the basis of an aphorism in Vedic texts: "As is the microcosm, so is the macrocosm. As is the atom, so is the universe. As is the human body, so is the cosmic body. As is the human mind, so is the cosmic mind." Of course, "cosmic mind" sounds spiritual, but one need not call it that. One can call it a "non-local field of information with self-referral cybernetic feedback loops."

The pioneering work of Dr. Robert Ader, Dr. Herb Spector, and many others who established the field of psychoneuroimmunology shows what this inseparability of mind and matter is, and how it can make the difference between life and death. One of the early experiments involved mice who were given a chemical called poly-I:C, a substance known to stimulate the immune system and strengthen an animal's defense against disease. For a few weeks, every time the mice were given the poly-I:C, they also were exposed to the smell of camphor. Later, the mice were exposed only to the camphor, and their immune cell count increased, even without the chemical. In another experiment, rats were given cyclophosphamide, a chemical known to suppress and eventually destroy the immune system, along with a saccharine solution. When the chemical was withdrawn and the rats tasted just the saccharine solution, their immune cell count continued to drop until they died. What was the crucial difference between life and death in these two groups of mice? It was nothing other than the interpretation of the memory of the smell of camphor and the taste of the saccharine solution, memory that had become part of the cellular structure of the immune system. Memory is not simply in the brain; it is in all of the cells of the body.

You might ask, "Has this any relevance to us?" And the answer is, yes, it seems that it does. It is estimated that the average human thinks about sixty thousand thoughts a day. That is not surprising. What is a little disconcerting is that about ninety percent of the thoughts we have today are the same ones we had yesterday. We have become bundles of conditioned reflexes and nerves that are constantly being triggered by people and circumstances into predictable outcomes. We have become the victims of the stale repetition of outworn memories. And the irony, of course, is that my tormentor today is myself left over from yesterday.

There is an ancient Vedic aphorism that says, "If you want to create a new body, then you must step out of the river of your own memory and see the world as if for the first time." And another says,

"If you want to create a new body, then you must learn how to use memories and not allow memories to use you." Lord Shiva in ancient times said, "I use memories. I do not allow memories to use me." In these simple statements are the mechanics of freeing oneself from conditioned response. All behavior in animals is conditioned behavior. What we do not recognize is that much of the repertoire of human response to situations, circumstances, people, and things is also conditioned response. As a result, we are generating the same impulses of energy and information that lead to the same outcomes again and again, whether they are behavioral responses or even biochemical responses.

This may not be as far out or as abstract as it appears to be. A number of years ago, a study was published at Ohio State University where scientists examined the metabolism of cholesterol in rabbits. They fed groups of rabbits diets that were extremely high in cholesterol, and to their amazement, the scientists found that one group of rabbits did not have high cholesterol levels or hardening of the arteries despite being fed the same diet as the other groups. After careful investigation, the scientists discovered one difference between these healthier rabbits and the others: The technician who was feeding the healthier rabbits would take them out of their cages to pet and cuddle them. Then he would feed them the same toxic diet. As a result of this experience—you can call it love, or you can call it the flow of information, depending on your bias—these rabbits presumably had a different set of neuropeptides and metabolic substances transferring the cholesterol into a different metabolic pathway. And this made the crucial difference between life and death from heart disease, the number one killer in our culture.

So here you see a very clear example of consciousness influencing the processes through which the body assimilates food, in this case into a metabolic pathway that generates high cholesterol or one that does not. Scientists now look at this very carefully, and there is an increasing amount of evidence that the sight, taste, and smell of food are influenced by what is going on in your awareness — whether you like the food or not, whether you perceive it as nourishing or not, the amount of time you take to eat it, and what other emotions are part of your consciousness. Are you feeling hostility, anger, anxiety? All of these will influence the way that food is metabolized in your physiology. This is further evidence that consciousness is primary, and that matter is secondary.

Some years ago, scientists from the University of Miami School of Medicine published a report in the Journal of Pediatrics about their study of premature infants. They divided the infants, born ten weeks early, into two groups and fed them the same formula. For one group, holes were drilled in the incubators through which an investigator would reach in and stroke the baby three times a day for approximately five minutes. Of course, they did not call it stroking—they called it "kinesthetic tactile stimulation"—which is the Orwellian medical term for stroking. And God forbid, call it love. Nevertheless, babies who received this kinesthetic tactile stimulation for five minutes, three times a day, gained an average of forty-nine percent more weight than those who were not stroked, leading the investigators to conclude in an accompanying editorial that kinesthetic tactile stimulation was a cost-effective strategy because you could save three thousand dollars per baby. We can be sure that Blue Cross will soon have a billing code for this procedure!

More recently, cardiologists and epidemiologists have begun to look more closely at risk factors associated with deaths from cardiovascular disease. Despite the fact that we know what the risk factors for heart attacks are—smoking, hypertension, high cholesterol, and family history—it seems that if you really look at the data these days, you will find something else in the case histories of the majority of people who die of heart attacks before the age of fifty-five. The studies have found that the number one predictor of fatal heart attacks is job dissatisfaction. The second most common predictor is a lack of self-happiness, and more precisely, a sense of meaninglessness or purposelessness in life.

Another result of these studies, also replicated in France, was the discovery that more people die of heart attacks at a particular time. At nine o'clock on Monday morning, more people die than at any other time. This is a stunning and extraordinary accomplishment for which only the human species can take credit. Presumably, no other animal knows the difference between Monday and Tuesday. And what is the difference? It is an idea, simply an idea. You cannot observe ideas through any scientific instrument that I know of. You cannot localize them in a test tube. There is no measuring device that tells you the strength or weakness of an idea. Ideas are utterly ephemeral things in this abstract space that we call consciousness. But ideas can be harbingers of disease, destruction, devastation, and war. They also can be the force of healing. Our bodies are fields of ideas, and ideas are self-generated. They come about as a result of meaning and interpretation, which happens somewhere in consciousness—whatever that consciousness is.

I would like to define consciousness by calling it awareness that has at least three components: attention, intention, and memory. And one might also say that attention, intention, and memory are energy and information. Therefore, consciousness and the quantum field of information and energy in nature may be identical things. They may be just different ways of stating the same thing: that the essential ground of nature is nonmaterial. It is made up of energy and information fields, and these energy and information fields express themselves in human physiology and also through the human nervous system as thought and memory, intention and attention—all those things that we experience subjectively in every moment of our existence.

This seems to be the new paradigm, and it is consistent with the paradigm that has existed in Vedic tradition. It says that consciousness conceives, it governs, it constructs, and it becomes matter. Our physiology is part of an organic universe that has a similar physiology where microcosm and macrocosm mirror each other in every aspect.

We can go further, at least from the perspective of Vedic tradition, because as soon as you say, "I have a thought" or "I make this observation" or "I have this interpretation," you imply that somebody is there to think the thought. In other words, a thinker is distinct from the thought. To even use the expression "I have a thought" implies that there is someone who is having thoughts, and that someone is presumably distinct from the thought itself. The molecules of the body have a very short shelf life; they come and go in approximately one year. Thoughts, feelings, emotions, and desires have a longer shelf life; they constantly outlive the molecules through which they express themselves. But Vedic science says there is a field of awareness that goes beyond the thought and the place where the thought is manufactured: It is the thinker of the thought. The Sanskrit term to describe this is *atman*, and the closest translation is the word "soul." Of course, if you were to go to a scientist, at least based on the old paradigm, and say that there is such an entity as the soul, the scientist likely would say, "I'd like to believe that, but please show me where it is. Where is the evidence?" Just as a few years ago, if you asked about the mind, this same scientist would say, "What is the evidence for the existence of the mind? After all, it is only circumstantial."

In the last century, some scientists would even weigh a person before death and then again immediately afterward to see if this animating force we call the mind actually had left. And since there was no difference in weight, scientists at least came to one reasonably good conclusion: Whatever it is that constitutes the real you, the thinker of the thought, we can say with a certain amount of scientific certainty that it probably doesn't weigh anything!

In our own century, the brilliant scientist and neurosurgeon Wilder Penfield was intrigued by the notion of interpreter, thinker, thought generator, choice maker. Dr. Penfield is well known to those who have researched the field of neuroscience. Yet, there is a part of him that is not well-known — not an unusual circumstance when one's personal beliefs or aspirations do not fit the fashion of the day. Niels Bohr had a spiritual side. Albert Einstein had a spiritual side. And so did Wilder Penfield.

Frequently, when he would operate on his patients under local anesthesia, he would use an electric probe to stimulate different parts of the sensory cortex of the brain, and as he was doing so, the patient would begin reliving experiences from many years before. For example, one woman said, "I'm six years old. I'm at my birthday party in a green meadow. My mother is wearing a blue dress. We're having chocolate cake. I can taste the cake. And I can smell the daisies."

In other words, by stimulating a certain part of the sensory cortex, Penfield was able to elicit the full-blown experience on the level of the senses. He had stimulated that place in the brain where these experiences were recorded, so that the patient could actually smell the daisies, taste the cake, and see the meadow. Yet, when Penfield asked her, "Are you at the picnic?" the patient responded, "No, I'm in the operating room." He wondered then, where was this interpreter who knew the difference? On the level of the senses, the interpreter was attending her birthday party, and yet there was a silent witness behind the scenes, you might say, who determined that the party in the meadow was a hallucination.

On another occasion, Penfield stimulated the motor cortex in a patient and the patient's arm began moving upward. He asked, "Are you moving your arm?" and the patient answered, "No, my arm is moving up." Then Penfield did something clever. He instructed his patient, "Instead of allowing your arm to move up like this, when I stimulate your motor cortex, make it move somewhere else." And the patient did so. Penfield was intrigued. Who was this person who made this choice? And where was this person who could override this movement as he stimulated the motor cortex?

After a number of experiments, Penfield observed, "I cannot find the choice maker. I cannot find the interpreter. All I can measure are the effects of the choices, the interpretations, and the decisions once they're already made. Then I can localize them in the brain. But I can't localize this person, this choice maker that is making those choices."

Today of course, through instruments like positron emission topography, and through evoked potentials, it is possible to measure the effects of a flicker of an intention a microsecond after you have it. But who is forming those intentions? And where is the person? We cannot localize it, either in the human body or in the brain. We can only measure its effects. So right at this moment, if I choose to drink a glass of water, or take off my shoes, or make a phone call, or eat ice cream, there is actually an infinity of choices available to me this second. And if I choose any one of them, you wouldn't find it either in this body or in this brain; you wouldn't be able to localize the one who is making those choices. You would only be able to localize the effects of those choices once Me—the choice maker, the interpreter—has already made them. In other words, you will not be able to find the essential Me in this body.

The question then is: Why can't you find Me in my body? And the answer may be relatively simple. The reason you can't find Me in my body is that I'm not really here. If you go into any bookstore and look in the metaphysical section, you will find a number of books on so-called out-of-body experiences. Yet, the real mystery is how do we get an in-body experience, because technically speaking we're not even here.

Imagine you are listening to Beethoven on the radio and you tear the radio apart, hoping to find Beethoven inside. You won't find him there because he really isn't there. The radio is an instrument that traps the music and localizes it into space and time. We can localize any experience to a certain place in space and actually see it or observe it in moments of time. Every experience is a space/time event. And so is this human body of ours a series of space/time events. It has moments in time. It has a beginning, a middle, and an ending. The human body starts as a speck of information on the DNA, and after being fed becomes a three-dimensional structure in space and time. All experiences are space/time events — every single experience. Anything that you observe materially is a continuum of space/time events. But the field whence space/time events comes is neither space nor time; it is the potentiality of space and time.

If you ask, "Well, since I'm not in the body, then where am I?" the answer is: That is the wrong question. As soon as you ask "where," you imply a location in space for something that does not occupy space; you imply moments in time for something that is timeless and eternal. Of course, if you read a description of spirit — whether in the Jewish, Eastern, or Christian tradition — you will find that the spirit is nonlocal. It is abstract. It is dimensionless. It has no existence in time and it occupies no space. Dimensionless, spaceless, and timeless, yet called a real force, at least in spiritual traditions. Abstract, yes. Mysterious, yes. Intellectually incomprehensible, yes. But possibly real. After all, gravity and time are abstract forces, but they are real forces, too. We acknowledge the existence of gravity and time, and maybe it is time to acknowledge the existence of spirit.

Einstein said that a field is not a model for actual space/time events. A field is the continuum of probability amplitudes — or possible measurements — for space/time events as functions of time. And what Einstein called the "field of potentiality" that gives rise to space/time events, is what ancient Vedic culture and many other spiritual traditions call spirit. It is just a different way of defining the same thing.

According to Vedic culture, the closest we can get to the thinker of the thought — the one that manufactures the thought, the interpreter of the thought—is in the spaces between our thoughts. So between every thought you have is the potentiality of a thought. A thought also is a space/time event in a sense because a thought occupies space in this place we call consciousness. And a thought has moments in time. A thought has a beginning, a middle, and an ending. Emotion is a thought that also is a sensation at the same time. And emotions have a slightly longer shelf life, but they are also space/time events. So let's say we have a thought here...a thought here...a thought here...a thought here. Between every thought is a little space.

Right now, there must be spaces between my thoughts, because I am orchestrating the syntax, the grammar, and the sequence of these words. Otherwise, there would only be a jumble of words, a word salad that would not make any sense whatsoever. Perhaps this is not making sense anyway, but the fact is that the thinker of the thought is sequentially choreographing the process. And if you examine the space between thoughts, you see that one of the attributes of the space is silence. It has to be silent because if it is not, then it is no longer the thinker, it is the thought.

Another attribute of the space is that it is a field of infinite possibilities, because in every space and between every thought is the possibility of an infinity of choices. As the evolution of our own consciousness goes to higher levels of awareness, you and I become infinite choice makers in every moment of our existence. And because the infinite choice maker is in the silent spaces between the thoughts, we come to the question, at least in Vedic philosophy: Is it possible that the thinker who is orchestrating my thoughts is the same thinker who is orchestrating your thoughts? After all, the one here is silent and is a field of infinite possibilities; and the one there that is making the interpretations and evaluations right now is also silent and is a field of infinite possibilities. Is it possible that the thinker who is manufacturing the thoughts that I am enunciating now is the same thinker who is manufacturing the thoughts that you are experiencing now through your nervous system?

The teachings of many spiritual traditions say there is only one mind, and that this one mind is expressing itself in different forms, different guises, and different localized concentrations of energy. But is it the same thinker? Vedic science says yes and no at the same time. It is the same thinker because it is silent and it is a field of infinite possibilities. Yet, it is a different thinker because even though it has infinite choices available to it in every moment of its existence, it is not making the same choices. If I look at a snowstorm, I might suddenly make the choice or have the idea, "Maybe I should be in Hawaii, or maybe I should go skiing." Another person could look at the same snowstorm and get the idea, "Maybe I should shovel the driveway." With that same stimulus, the space/time event is quite different. We each have unique experiences. In every situation and in every circumstance involving persons and things, we have unique experiences.

The Vedic term for this phenomenon is "karma," defined incorrectly by most dictionaries as meaning fate. The correct translation is action or experience. So, every time you perform an action or have an experience—no matter what it is—it qualifies as a karmic episode. And every time you perform an action, that action creates memory, and memory becomes the potentiality for desire. Every thought that you have is either a memory or a desire. Action generates memory. Experience generates memory. Memory becomes the potentiality for desire. And desire generates action or experience once again.

The only reason that you and I are different (if we are different at all) is that we have metabolized different experiences in the past. We have walked through different gardens, we have knelt at different graves, we have laughed with different people, and we have hummed different songs. We have metabolized every wisp of experience that has come our way, and then we have converted that experience into an expression of material reality in both the forms of our bodies and the experiences of our world.

If I were to rephrase the modern science paradigm, I would say that on the level of the senses, there is a material world made of recycled elements. If you go beyond the material world, you will find fields of information and energy. Go beyond these fields of information and energy, and you will be able to measure space/time events as functions of time which created those fields of information and energy. Go beyond that, and you will come to the unified field that is one of pure potentiality for space/time events that precipitates into material events. These same things have been described in Vedic and other ancient traditions and concepts as the body, the mind, the soul, and ultimately the spirit.

What science calls the unified field—the potentiality of the forces of nature that transform themselves into material events—is nothing other than consciousness itself. The ultimate implicate order unfolds into the explicate order of space/time events; and there is one seamless wholeness underneath all of this where we are part of a web—a cosmic web—that is inseparably interconnected with every one of its components.

We could hope that science will attempt to study the field through objective means. However, there may be another approach: the subjective methodology of spiritual traditions that is based on the ability to access the space between thoughts. If we could slip into the space, we might discover that this is our window, our corridor, the transformational vortex through which the human psyche communicates with the cosmic psyche. And for that, we really do not have any sophisticated technology. Rather, it is simply the ability to go beyond the internal dialogue and access the spirit. Franz Kafka said it beautifully: "You need not do anything. Remain sitting at your table and wait. You need not even wait. Just listen. You need not even listen. Just learn to become quiet and still and solitary. And the world will freely offer itself to you to be unmasked. It has no choice. It will roll in ecstasy at your feet."[5]

At that point, the realization comes spontaneously: The observer, the process of observation, and the object of observation are essentially the same thing. The seer and the scene are one. There is no phrase in science to describe this experience of unity consciousness. Perhaps it can only be called love—not as a sentiment nor as an emotion, but as the experiential knowledge of unity. It is the experiential knowledge that you and I are not only made up of the same stuff, but we may be the same being in different guises.

JOHN SPENCER, PH.D.

I met Dr. John Spencer in the early 1990s when we were both speakers at a national health care conference. His involvement in developing the Office of Alternative Medicine at the National Institutes of Health put him at the forefront of information and research on mind-body issues, making him the logical selection when I was planning the Brain and Consciousness series. Dr. Spencer has always been willing to update me on breakthroughs in the area of mind-body medicine and was also very helpful in advising me on medical issues for a follow-up Smithsonian series on Energy and Consciousness. His generosity with his time and knowledge is a tribute to his dedication to informing the public about the latest research and best choices in mind-body medicine. Dr. Spencer is an innovative and caring professional. His comprehensive 1999 book, *Complimentary/Alternative Medicine*, written with Dr. Joseph Jacobs, former director of the Office of Alternative Medicine, NIH, sets the stage for the direction of health care in the next century.

CHAPTER FIVE

Mind-Body Medicine

JOHN SPENCER, PH.D. AND
KAREN SHANOR, PH.D

*"Asthmatics sneeze at plastic flowers. People with a termi-
nal illness stay alive until after a significant event, apparently willing themselves to live until a graduation
ceremony, a birthday milestone, or a religious holiday. A
bout of rage precipitates a sudden, fatal heart attack. Spe-
cially trained people can voluntarily control such "invol-
untary" body functions as the electrical activity of the
brain, heart rate, pain, bleeding, and even the body's
response to infection."*

—KENNETH PELLETIER, PH.D., M.D.[1]

Several months after starting work at the Office of Alternative Medicine, National Institutes of Health, I was asked to deliver a talk at a
retreat sponsored in part by the Menninger Foundation. It was
springtime in Kansas, with many budding flowers and trees. I had
suffered from allergies for almost five years and was taking Seldane
twice a day. But I had forgotten my medication at home. When I
arose to speak, I experienced a severe sinus headache that stayed
with me for the next hour and a half. This was, by the way, not an
uncommon occurrence when I did not take my medication, especially during the spring.

At some time during the talk I mentioned my predicament and
at the talk's completion, to my surprise, a middle-aged man came

forward and introduced himself as a body-energy healer. He suggested that he might be of help. We went to the back of the room where he asked me to sit down, close my eyes, and relax. I am not sure what he did at this point although I was aware of what seemed to be hand movements around and over but not touching my head. For what seemed to be about five minutes nothing happened. Then I perceived a red line, which appeared around and followed the curvature of my left eyelid. This was followed by a mild sensation of heat within my cranium, a perceptible flash of light that appeared as a ray going directly into my nose, and then complete drying of mucous in my nose along with the release of any pain. The whole procedure lasted less than fifteen minutes. Later, the man explained that he had sculpted healthier schemas in electrical energy fields around my head, changing the abnormal firings of electrons to a more balanced and harmonious state. The biggest and most pleasant surprise was that one treatment was sufficient for me to be completely free of any more sinus problems. Since that time I have required no further medication.

This anecdotal and personal report would never be accepted by most scientists as an account of healing, and perhaps would not be accepted by some non-scientists either. It is, as defined by classical methodology, a biased, unverifiable, subjective report. Reasonable questions that skeptics might ask would include: How accurate was the diagnosis of sinus condition in the first place? Could my experience be replicated on five, ten, or a hundred other patients with similar symptoms? Are some people less likely to respond to this or other types of mind-body treatments than others? And of course, the opposite question: Are some people more likely to respond to this kind of treatment? And why? Might not my sinus condition simply be going into remission? Perhaps. But it did disappear quite suddenly.

Later I asked Elmer Green, one of the pioneers in biofeedback and formerly of the renowned Menninger Clinic, to explain the profile of treatment failures in mind-body procedures. His response was that mind-body treatments were most likely to fail with those "people who deny the existence of a higher power, whether consciously or unconsciously." This was, I thought, a most profound statement about the role of belief in healing.

SCIENCE'S STUDY OF CONSCIOUSNESS

While science has an important and necessary role to play in determining which therapies are valid and reliable, the study of the mind and consciousness is exceedingly complex. For example, the range of what we call consciousness is broad, extending from deathlike coma to the fully awake state, with components that can be influenced through the use of direct or subtle relaxation, visual imagery, and even hypnosis. Describing the makeup of what we call the mind and consciousness is equally difficult because it can be abstract, comprising thoughts, ideas, fantasies, and objects. Sometimes this makeup includes a more personal and unclear side where hallucinations and images occur that can become distorted by either external forces (the environment) or internal forces, (drugs, or a disease process such as schizophrenia). It is at this dimension of consciousness where the real mystery or lack of understanding of the mind and body's interaction can be found; it is also here that immense potential for the treatment of patients might exist.

Mind and body were sent their separate ways, ideologically, during the time of Descartes in the early to mid-seventeenth century. Science developed and usually concentrated only on the physical world, what could be seen, or somehow understood and measured by the five senses. Mind waves or molecules such as neuropeptides are not visible to the naked eye. So it was understandable four centuries ago, when scientific investigation was in its incipient stage, that scientists would limit their methods and investigations. Today, however, with extraordinary advances in technology and quantum physics, scientific research has become far more sophisticated. While we still cannot see energy systems with the human eye, we can detect and measure many with our technological eyes. We not only detect electromagnetic forces, but use them to be able to "see" and measure different bodily functions, and to heal as well. Scientific methods and technologies have improved significantly and continue to do so.

Science is now creating ways of examining how mind and body "talk" to each other. The discovery of neurotransmitters—messengers to and from the brain and every cell in the body—and the use of precise information systems give science the tools with which to "eavesdrop" on these mind-body conversations. As in most other situations where two entities are continually and intimately "conversing," the mind and the body influence each other in many ways, for better or for worse. To continue this analogy just a little further, the brain-mind does more of the thinking in this marriage, and the rest of the body does more of the hard work of functioning each day. However, we also know that every cell in the body does some kind of thinking and deciding, as well as communicating to the rest of the body; much of the communication, but by no means all, goes through the nervous system. And the brain-mind control center tries to do two very complex things at the same time: keep everything functioning at an optimal level and under control, and facilitate continual physical and mental growth.

Only in response to some outside threat does the mind-body system veer away from these two priorities. Then resources are directed toward saving the mind and body from whatever is threatening, such as an illness or injury. Every organism has the instinctive drive to do whatever it can to survive. The mind-body team does, too. It not only has the mandate to survive, and usually the resources to survive an attack, it also has the intelligence—often subconsciously—of how to get away from a threat to the system; and, if attacked, how to recover. Recovering from the damaging effects of an attack is referred to in medical terms as healing. In most cases healing is done within the system. You nick your finger and healing forces come through the bloodstream and other channels to heal the cut. Other times the system may benefit from outside help, which can come in many forms.

"Who has the disease is more important than the disease he has."
— HIPPOCRATES

Because we are each unique with our own histories, cultures, and belief systems—as well as our individual genetic blueprints—each person heals herself or himself, and is able to express this healing power in special ways. To best understand the mind-body connection and its impact in the arena we call medicine, it is essential to understand how consciousness (mind as abstract entity) influences the brain (a physical part of the mind) to produce physiological and chemical reactions in the body, which lead to and may promote the sensation of well-being or what we call healing.

THE ROLE OF THE BRAIN IN HEALING

Much clinical study has been devoted to demonstrating that the brain is able to control functions such as breathing, heart rate, and blood pressure, and even more specific areas such as cellular firing from various organs. And over the last few decades there has been an increasing recognition that the brain in fact is subject to the will of the individual. This is especially apparent with emotional attitudes, which can result from a variety of sources including self-thoughts and personal interactions with other persons and the environment. Just as brain chemicals can change thoughts, so too can thoughts change the chemistry and functioning of the brain. Sir John Eccles, a Nobel laureate in neurophysiology, calls "extraordinary" the way our mental thoughts affect our physical being at the most basic level.

Psychosomatic medicine, previously not taken very seriously by conventional medicine, is now considered a more integral part of health care. Consciousness, emotions, attitudes, spiritual beliefs, thoughts, and expectancy sets are all actively involved in healing, in both positive and negative ways. Most importantly, the individual can bring all under control.

THE PLACEBO EFFECT

"Placebos Prove So Powerful Even Experts are Surprised!" This recent headline in the *New York Times* science section confirmed the power of the human mind. Most of us are used to hearing placebos mentioned in connection with a study of a new drug, in which a sugar pill or other inert substance having no known medicinal power is used as a control. Some patients are given the drug, for example, and others are given a sugar pill and told it is the new and powerful drug. If the drug is shown to be significantly more effective than the placebo in curing the malady, the drug is considered effective. Of course, the patient doesn't know whether he or she was receiving the placebo or the real thing.

In early studies, the physician or other researcher did know. Then double-blind studies were devised where neither the subjects nor those who gave out the pills knew which was the drug and which was the placebo. That change in methodology came about when it was realized that the expectations of the researcher or physician could significantly affect the outcome of the study.

In the last twenty years, more and more research has focused on the power of the placebo effect. "Placebo" means "I shall please" in Latin, and when we strongly believe that a pill, surgery, or other procedure will affect us in a certain way, most of us experience a bodily change consistent with that belief. This is referred to as the placebo response. In the case of medications, studies suggest that up to sixty-five percent of the drugs prescribed by physicians may depend on placebo action for their effectiveness.[2]

In two recent studies, one focusing on heart patients and the other on men with prostate problems, the power of the placebo was evident. In the first study, when placebos were given to patients with various types of cardiovascular disease, improvement in symptom remission such as pain with angina pectoris was seen in as many as thirty to eighty percent of patients, and twenty-five to thirty-five percent showed improvement in certain areas after heart attacks.[3] In the second study, men were treated with placebos to bring their enlarged prostate glands back to normal size. Urologists found a thirty to forty percent cure rate six months after the treatment.[4]

Sometimes expectations can outweigh the power of the drug itself. Two decades ago, a study was done at the University of California at Los Angeles where one group of subjects was given a strong dose of amphetamines (stimulants) and told they were receiving tranquilizers. Based on their expectations, these subjects became extremely relaxed. Not only that, a group given tranquilizers and told they were receiving amphetamines became very energetic and restless, as if they actually had received a substantial dose of stimulants.

Placebos are about fifty-five to sixty percent as effective in controlling pain as aspirin or codeine. And in a recent review of studies of modern antidepressants, University of Connecticut psychiatrist Irving Kirsch found that the placebos worked as well as the drugs.[5] The placebo response has even been shown to be as effective as some surgical procedures; one astounding study was described in the *New York Times* science article:

> Doctors in Texas are conducting a study of arthroscopic knee surgery that uses general anesthesia in which patients with sore, worn knees are assigned to one of three operations—scraping out the knee joint, washing out the joint, or doing nothing. In the

"nothing" operation, doctors anesthetize the patient, make three little cuts in the knee as if to insert the usual instruments and then pretend to operate. Two years after surgery, patients who underwent the sham surgery reported the same amount of relief from pain and swelling as those who had had the real operation.[6]

THE POWER OF EXPECTATION

How do placebos work? Expectancy theory as studied by psychologists explains that what the mind expects to happen often does. Just as Pavlov's dogs learned to associate the sound of a bell with being fed meat and later salivated at the sound of the bell even when no meat was forthcoming, we develop certain expectations of people and situations based on former experiences. Walking into a doctor's office, seeing professionals in white coats, or the smell of disinfectant may produce for some people an expectation of relief from symptoms, and make others feel worse (this is called a nocebo).

Response expectations are strong because throughout an average day we encounter much ambiguity. We may see a person from a distance with a certain color hair and height and fill in the facial details, thinking them to be someone we know. If we regularly have coffee with caffeine to wake us in the morning, we likely will be just as stimulated by a cup of decaff if we don't know the change has been made. Our brain often fills in the blanks and details of situations that are similar to those with which we are familiar. We are able to read so quickly because we relie on this filling-in process. All we have to do is see part of a word or phrase and our mind fills in the rest based on our previous experiences, and on knowing the general form of certain words. Thus we don't have to look for every single letter or even every single word in a phrase or paragraph. (Many readers may have missed the two purposeful typos in this paragraph.)

Expectancy theory became one respected explanation of the placebo effect when neuroscientists realized that the brain, immune system, and endocrine systems are closely linked. Chronic stress can create a cascade of biological events involving a number of chemicals in the body, such as serotonin, interleukins, cortisol, cytokines, and many others. Many studies show that stress lowers our resistance to disease. And the reverse can happen as well: Our thinking can reduce stress, our expectations can strengthen the immune system.

The brain generates two types of activation patterns from networks of neurons firing together. One type comes from information from the outside world, such as sights, smells, tastes, sounds, and kinesthetic data. The second type is based on feelings and memories stored in the brain and in cells throughout our bodies. These two patterns interact to affect our perceptions of present events. In fact, research shows that previous experience has enormous influence on what we expect to happen next. We can see this illustrated in the Japanese study in which subjects exposed to fake poison ivy developed real rashes. The subjects' systems were responding to past experiences and information that a leaf which looks a certain way would create an allergic reaction, a rash. The leaf in the study looked like poison ivy, but was not the real thing and had no physiological way to cause a toxic reaction. The rashes the subjects developed were based on their belief that the poison ivy leaves were real and their expectations that exposure to them would produce a rash.[7]

Also coming from our previous experiences and aligned with our expectations is what is known as "remembered wellness." Cardiologist Herbert Benson asserts that following a therapeutic intervention such as relaxation, a memory of past events begins to trigger a physical response which could be a past thought of strength, peace, and/or confidence, all of which are found in a part of consciousness associated with prior good health.[8] The goal is to resurrect these thoughts and feelings and move them into an even more active part of consciousness. Accessing the memory of remembered wellness can be accomplished through any procedure that quiets both the mind and body. Biofeedback, relaxation, and meditation have been used to demonstrate that a variety of health conditions are influenced and changed by first quieting the mind. Benson and R. Schneider showed that subjects who practiced the systematic "relaxation response" were able to significantly lower their high blood pressure.[9] Sometimes remembering a beautiful scene or wonderful vacation can help a person recreate happy, healthy feelings, thereby changing body chemistry and actually increasing immune capacity.

Prior learning as well as previous experiences continually shape our thinking and how we respond to present day situations and stimuli. The goal is to respond in positive and healthful ways instead of negative ones. In some situations people remember illness and trauma. For example, a woman in her forties realized in therapy that every year at the same time in November, she experienced severe pain in her throat and lungs. After remembering that that was the time of year her father had died of lung cancer when she was a teenager, she was able to connect the pain with her memories instead of thinking she was actually suffering from a disease. When she decided to spend this time every year remembering her father consciously and in more positive ways, she no longer had to feel physical pain, or somatize his memory, and her loss of him.

Even the colors of various drugs can influence their effectiveness. In our culture red, yellow, and orange pills tend to be associated with a stimulating effect, while blue and green pills are associated with a tranquilizing effect. Drug companies draw heavily upon psychological research in the design of every pill, taking into account previous experiences of potential consumers as well as the most effective color, shape, and size for a specific type of medication.

GOOD HEALTH AS AN ACTIVE ENDEAVOR

Since variables such as past memories, beliefs, expectations, attitudes, cultural settings, and hope can and do influence healing outcomes in either positive or negative ways, every therapeutic intervention has a mind-body component. And in addition to reacting to events based on our past experiences, perceptions, and expectations, we can take active roles in maintaining our health. Although we may be exposed to or even have certain viruses or bacteria in our system, we don't have to become ill.

In his seminal book, *Who Gets Sick: Thinking and Health*, Dr. Blair Justice writes of two Harvard Medical School pediatricians' investigation of the question of who gets sick. Over the course of a year, Drs. Roger Meyer and Robert Haggerty extensively examined the one hundred members of sixteen families at regular intervals:

[They] made throat cultures on all family members every three weeks and did various laboratory and clinical tests for signs of streptococcal illness. More than fifty-two percent of the streptococcal acquisitions by family members were not associated with illness. In other words, tests established that for most of the infections that family members acquired, illness did not result.

All families had approximately the same potential contact with streptococci, as judged by their number of school-age children, degree of neighborhood crowding, and other kinds of contacts, including the fathers' working environments. Throughout the study year, families commented on the connection between acute family crises and the onset of illness. The researchers determined that both streptococcal illnesses and other respiratory diseases were about four times more frequent after episodes the families defined as stressful....Families with high levels of chronic stress had significantly more streptococcal illness as well as more acquisition of microorganisms....[10]

The study also concluded what many other studies have shown: In addition to stress, fatigue and poor nutrition also lower our resistance to illness. Justice goes on to show that feeling blue or in some way being unable to adequately handle situations leaves us more vulnerable to viruses as well as bacteria: "For example, herpes viruses seem to remain in the body until the immune system is 'unbalanced' by negative moods or poor coping. Some diseases that have unclear or unknown etiology, such as systemic lupus erythematosus (SLE), may depend on a virus that becomes active only when a susceptible person is having trouble coping or feels chronically distressed." [11]

So in addition to a healthy exercise routine, good nutrition, and getting eight or more hours of sleep a night, what can we do or think to help prevent illness? University of Chicago psychologists Suzanne Kobasa and Salvatore Maddi offer one solution. They found in their research with two hundred business executives that those who stay healthy under stress possess the three Cs—they have a sense of control, see problems as challenging rather than debilitating, and have a sense of commitment to life: "They are deeply involved in their work and families and this commitment gives them a sense of meaning, direction, and excitement. They have acquired 'hardy' personalities, which helps to protect them against illness." [12] This sense of control does not indicate a tendency to control other people or one's environment, but as some psychologists have suggested, "a belief that one has at one's disposal a response that can influence the adversiveness [sic] of an event...." Often this means the way we look at things. [13]

The Kobasa-Maddi research team also studied over 150 lawyers in private practice, looking at strain symptoms such as nervousness, headaches, and insomnia. Once again attitudes and beliefs played powerful roles: "The lawyers who believed in the importance and value of what they were doing and had a sense of purpose experienced the fewest symptoms." [14]

Thousands of stringent studies done over the last forty years show similar results. Good health is an active rather than passive endeavor. Good nutrition, exercise, healthy lifestyles, and our attitudes and beliefs are powerful allies in preventing disease.

BIOCHEMISTRY AND THE MIND-BODY

Candace Pert suggests that the brain is more than just a system of anatomical pathways and the sole ruler of the body. In addition to the well-described and well-known brain connections, there is an interacting and dynamic molecular system of a type of amino acids known as neuropeptides which function as messengers between cells and various organs and other mechanisms in the body such as the immune, endocrine, and gastrointestinal systems. These neuropeptides, or molecules of emotion, carry information to and from the brain to systems throughout the body, forming a dynamic information network linking mind and body.

We also know that the immune system is active and can be trained and taught varying degrees of responsiveness. Just as in Pavlov's classic study, it has been shown that rats can be conditioned by using a stimulus such as a drug that will suppress immune function, and pairing it with a sweet solution such as saccharin. Later when only the saccharin solution is given (and would not produce any response without prior pairing with the drug) the immune system "thinks" that the saccharin is the drug and continues to suppress immune function.

Researchers then turned from rats to humans to study what pioneer researcher Robert Ader named "psychoneuroimmunology" (PNI), the interconnections among the mind and the immune system. In 1991 the conservative *New England Journal of Medicine* published a landmark report showing a direct link between mental state and disease.[15] Many other studies have showed a similar correlation.

And intense and stressful situations have consistently been found to impair immune system functioning, whether it is the effect of exams on college students, space flights on astronauts, the loss of a loved one, or an emotional argument between friends or lovers.

In their chapter in Daniel Goleman and Joel Gurin's, *Mind-Body Medicine*, Janice Kiecolt-Glaser and Ronald Glaser write that researchers have shown that

> …immune system cells can respond to chemicals once thought to affect only the nervous system and that nerve cells respond to chemical messengers secreted by the immune system, which provides a plausible means by which the two systems might communicate with each other. Changes in levels of stress hormones can also modulate immune function…and nerve cells connect the brain to the spleen and other organs directly involved in producing immune system cells.[16]

Humans can also learn to self-regulate their own immune systems by visually imagining ways to change the content of white blood cells. All of this suggests continual back and forth communication between the brain and the rest of the body, particularly the immune system. The most likely candidates to carry out such intricate and effective communication are the many "messenger molecules" that appear to be both listening and talking. Body and mind are no longer separate in our scientific models, but are working together in health and in healing.

BODY WORK AND BALANCE

Many people form strong impressions about others on the basis of snap judgments and first impressions. If you happen to be an especially keen observer, you will be able to tell a great deal about that stranger. You will know how confident she is by her posture. You will perceive sources of stress and possible childhood trauma. You might even have a good idea whether or not she is an honest person. You could make a good guess about her nutritional practices and lifestyle. And if you walk across that crowded room for an introduction, you will know much as you shake her hand and hear her voice. Body language offers strong and essential information.

In addition to revealing information, physical characteristics such as gestures and facial expressions may conceal more important emotions such as fear, hurt, and depression. In turn, the body can become distorted by responding to emotions in unhealthy ways. For example, many of us tend to hold our breath when we are frightened. When angry, we might tense up our bodies or rigidly put our arms by our sides or fold them front of us, as if holding back our instinct to fight. We might slouch or curve our shoulders inward because we are not feeling confident. Posture broadcasts a great deal about strong emotions and experiences, and the rigidity and distortions in muscles and our skeletal framework can eventually keep us from feeling or expressing emotions in a natural and healthy way. A number of exercises, deep massage, or other systematic pressure on the entangled muscles and nervous system can lead to better balance and health.

Physical treatments such as these and mentally positive messages to overcome unhealthy emotions can create a form of feedback to the brain, teaching healthier responses to situations and feelings. For example, instead of holding our breath when we feel stressed, we can learn to take a slow, deep breath, which is healthier for the whole system. Or mentally, instead of giving ourselves negative messages about the busy day, we can tell ourselves that, while we have a great deal to accomplish, we might as well enjoy our activities instead of complaining or focusing only on what is not going as well as we'd like.

The argument that healing origins exist and can aid in the treatment of illness at a cellular or biochemical level is difficult for many people to grasp and understand. However, most people can understand this by remembering how their feelings and attitudes change when they exercise, receive a massage, or practice a body work procedure such as tai chi. Such activities make us feel relaxed and energized. It is at this somatic level, through touching or gentle manipulation, that latent responses to memories and feelings may be probed for. These emotions that are blocked may break down and clog an invisible energy flow inside the body called by names such as prana, chi, or libido. The feelings are first cleared by touching, manipulation, releasing emotions, talking, and directing the mind to help clear the pathways and increase energy. John Upledger, for example, asserts that blocked paths of energy can be cleared by craniosacral therapy, which readjusts various muscles—especially those around the head and neck—to free up the energy pathways.

POTENTIAL SOURCES OF MIND-BODY ENERGY

If it is true that a dynamic interaction occurs between mind and body, where might the energy come from to produce the activation of healing in the body? Within the body, it is likely there is neuro-electric activity that is measured by the electroencephalogram (EEG) or electromyogram (EMG). This internal energy is thought to activate cell firing of thought patterns which signal problems to the physical body and may even change patterns of physical functioning. If a person is anxious or fearful, for example, this energy would be very different than if that same person were calm. And if this energy is blocked the body would not function as well, nor would the mind have energy it needs to think, learn, and react effectively to external events.

It is thought that a second internal energy source known as chi flows through the body. While Western science has not yet developed instrumentation to observe chi directly, many people claim they can feel it. Eastern medicine believes that this energy moves throughout the body in pathways called meridians, which are all connected in a massive and very well delineated network. It is along these meridians that acupuncture points are distributed. The concept of chi is very similar to the idea of the quantum field in modern physics in that chi is thought of as an imperceptible and pervasive substance which can condense into solid material objects or carry out the essence of material objects and their relationships in wave form.

What is now being described and considered important in understanding sources of energy is that which is found *outside* internal organs (but perhaps associated with or in some line or perimeter) using magnetometers—sensitive instruments that pick up and record physical excitation and energy several feet away from, but considered part of the individual. This might indicate that a potentially controllable energy medium exists in another dimension, with its own set of parameters, and more importantly, unique to each person! Bioenergy or therapeutic touch healers who claim to be able to sense this field of energy have themselves been studied and found to be conductors of some energy force measured by direct activation of electrical resistance through the use of meters attached to their fingers. Could it be possible that energy outside the body but associated with specific "target" organs is under some degree of control? And furthermore, that that energy is related to the health or dysfunction of that organ or other part of the body?

The implication for healing begins to expand, and we might ask: Where might the source be? In addition to the integration of the body and mind, we are beginning to scientifically tap into an energy system, which may be spiritual in nature. The Bible and other scriptures describe a spiritual realm that coexists with the physical world during life, and at death leaves the body. This force, flexible and operating but not visible in our dimension, may well be a source of external energy, internal energy, or both.

The many accounts of healing in the Bible allude to a tremendous force of energy, present and used. Christians relate this energy force to the indwelling of the holy spirit. Its energy activation for healing is most completely maximized by the use of prayer. Similar energy is described by other beliefs although explanations of the sources may vary. The ancient Greeks referred to a life force called *pneuma*. The Chinese concept of chi has an energy component, and preliminary scientific research on the effectiveness of chi gong masters, those who purport to direct chi for healing purposes, shows promising results. The Japanese word for a similar concept to chi is *ki*, and yogis call it *prana*.

If this all sounds a bit far-fetched, it is important to remember that over the last decade, a number of scientists worldwide have been studying the healing powers of energetic fields, especially electromagnetic fields (EMF). While it is known that massive amounts of EMFs, such as those emitted from electrical power lines, can be dangerous to living organisms, it appears that minute amounts and varied wavelengths and frequencies can be therapeutic in a number of areas, including bone and soft tissue repair. Scientists at such universities as Johns Hopkins and Georgetown are researching these healing possibilities. Collaborative efforts are being carried out between the U.S. and a number of Russian scientists who have long been developing technology in this area, such as biophysicist Eugene Khizhnyak and physician Larissa Khizhnyak, authorities on the use of millimeter wave technology for healing purposes. This is a fascinating and promising area as we learn more about healing energy, especially energy forces outside of and surrounding the body, which seem to be under some intelligent control.

SELECT THERAPEUTIC MODALITIES

Some of the better known mind-body therapies include biofeedback, cognitive therapies, hypnosis, meditation, relaxation, yoga, prayer, and therapeutic touch. While the term "mind-body" implies utilization of the brain, all therapies use and involve the brain in some way. Even acupuncture, which involves the insertion of needles in specific body meridians, and massage, which employs soft or deep tissue work, and/or skeletal or muscle manipulation (as is practiced in chiropractic) are interrelated with a person's attitudes and expectations. Just because a medical treatment is found to be clinically significant, it may or may not be useful for everybody. Just as Hippocrates pointed out that who has the disease is as important as the disease he has, healing is predicated on who is being treated—and his or her belief in the treatment and the healer.

BIOFEEDBACK: MIND CONTROL OVER
BODILY FUNCTIONS

In the mid-1970s the health director of a populous East Coast state almost resigned his coveted post, a job he loved. His migraine headaches had become disabling. A physician, he had tried every headache medication, experiencing little success and a backlash of devastating side effects. At the peak of his career, he felt his professional future was at stake, as well as his ability to be a good husband and father. He was desperate; so desperate, in fact, that he tried a then revolutionary concept called biofeedback to cure his migraines. And it worked.

Today, biofeedback is recognized, understood, and successfully used by the medical establishment for a number of medical problems, including migraine headaches. The method uses instruments to provide information, or feedback, to patients about what is happening in their bodies in a number of areas, including heart rate, breathing rate, temperature, sweat response, and brain waves. Then patients are taught methods to regulate these functions, receiving constant information about their bodily status to know if they are reaching their intended goals. In the case of migraine headaches, for example, patients may be trained (often with thermal feedback, using finger temperature) to warm their hands by increasing the blood flow. Then they learn to increase the blood flow in their heads, a means of headache prevention or treatment.

We are always receiving feedback from our bodies and reacting to it in natural ways. If we start huffing and puffing too much while we're walking, we know to slow down. If we hold a child in one arm too long, that arm gets tired and we either switch arms or set the baby down. If we feel hunger pangs, we eat.

However, we usually do not learn to be aware of those bodily functions that were long thought to be out of our control, such as heart rate, pulse rate, muscle tension, breathing rate, body temperature, sweat response, digestive functioning, and even our brain activity. Special instruments used in biofeedback give us information about these bodily functions. Then we can learn to be aware of these signals on our own and to regulate them in healthy ways. The state health director learned through biofeedback techniques how to reduce muscle tension throughout his body (especially in his head and neck) and to regulate the flow of blood in his head, which prevented further migraine headaches.

As with a number of procedures that don't rely on drugs or surgery, the concept of biofeedback caused a furor in the medical community when introduced in 1961 by a respected researcher at Yale. Psychiatrist James Gordon, in his book *Manifesto for a New Medicine*, stated

> [When] Neal Miller first suggested that the autonomic nervous
> system could be as susceptible to training as the voluntary nervous

system, that we might learn to control our heart rate and our bowel contractions just as we learn to walk or type or play tennis, his audiences were aghast.... [T]his was a kind of scientific heresy. Everybody knew that the autonomic nervous system was precisely that—automatic, beyond our control. The fabled feats of Indian yogis—their claimed ability to slow the rate of their hearts and their breathing and to profoundly alter their body temperatures— were regarded as a masochist's perversion, a charlatan's tricks, or neurological accidents.

Miller persisted... and soon proved that if he simply offered a perceptible recording of autonomic behavior—sounding a high-pitched tone, for example, till elevated blood pressure decreased or cold hands warmed—people would be able to use this information to correct their internal functioning.[17]

Biofeedback worked, and in the last forty years physicians, psychologists, and biological information technicians and engineers have developed intricate sensors and methods to enable millions of people to be aware of and control even the most subtle of their bodily functions. Today, biofeedback is used clinically for many disorders besides headaches, including high blood pressure, circulation problems, cardiac arrhythmias, asthma, chronic pain, Raynaud's disease, anxiety, teeth clenching and grinding, incontinence, irritable bowel syndrome, menstrual discomfort, and even diabetes.

That diabetes could be prevented or at least ameliorated was astonishing to many in the medical community, because it seemed if any malfunction in the body could be considered purely physical it would be diabetes, as it centers around the biochemicals glucose (blood sugar) and insulin (a hormone secreted by the pancreas). Normally glucose—a major source of energy for body cells—enters the cells from the bloodstream with the help of insulin. In diabetes mellitus (the full medical name), the sugar delivery system breaks down either because the pancreas makes too little insulin (Type I diabetes) or because the cells in the body have for some reason become resistant to insulin (Type II diabetes). When glucose cannot penetrate the cells correctly it builds up in the bloodstream, spilling out into the urine. Diabetes has long been thought to cause such severe problems as nerve and eye damage and accelerated cardiovascular disease.

"Mind over metabolism" is how Duke University's Richard Surwitt describes his and other research which shows that stress plays an important role in the onset and aggravation of both types of diabetes. Surwitt says that controlling that stress may "play a key role in keeping sugar levels in check."[18] Angele McGrady's 1998 review of the literature substantiates that medical variables like glucose tolerance and blood sugar levels are moderated and changed through both relaxation and biofeedback; and blood circulation, which is impaired in diabetes, can be improved by using thermal biofeedback.[19]

Researchers are also using biofeedback treatments for conditions associated with irregular brain wave patterns such as epilepsy and attention deficit hyperactivity disorder (ADHD) in children. When attached to an EEG, we can see which brain waves we are producing and in what quantity. Children, for example, can be taught how to change and focus their brain waves to enhance concentration. For example, EEG training in children with attention deficit disorder (ADD) reveals that they can be taught to normalize, or increase certain electrical frequencies that are thought to be involved in sustaining attention. In numerous studies these children typically are also able to increase their IQ scores and show improvement in not only attentiveness and academic performance but show a decrease in hyperactivity. Some children are able to reduce and in certain cases eliminate the need for medication. Adults with ADD also respond to this treatment.

Biofeedback seems to have the potential to cure and prevent many health problems. Interestingly, when patients are told prior to the procedure that biofeedback is a waste of time and money, they have more difficulty adapting to and successfully controlling various physiological processes. This might be considered a good example of an expectation or "set" that may act as a negative variable, and again reveals how important our minds are in assisting with healing.

Biofeedback increases the range of information the brain is continually collecting and acting upon and by doing this, consciousness itself is expanded. While psychotherapy may nurture the soul, biofeedback is its physiological complement.

Whether a person uses instrument feedback data to learn to better self-regulate bodily functions, or other methods such as visualization or relaxation, continued and numerous research results confirm that there are many ways we can take control of our health and our lives. And as one might predict, this capacity to take control over intricate physiological workings generalizes to a person's having more confidence in their ability to affect many areas of their lives. Helplessness turns to confidence. Over-dependency gives way to more personal power.

COGNITIVE THERAPY

Psychologist Albert Ellis and psychiatrist Aaron Beck are credited with the development of a form of psychotherapy called cognitive therapy, which is based on the belief that the messages we give ourselves—our "self-talk"—create the direction of our lives and affect what happens to us each day (or at the very least, affect how we perceive and deal with what happens to us). For decades Beck, at the University of Pennsylvania, has used his cognitive approach as a treatment for depression, and studies have shown that cognitive therapy can be as effective as antidepressant medication. Beck asserts that many people are depressed because they give themselves overly negative messages. While negativity has long been associated with depression, cognitive therapists believe that negative thoughts can often *cause* the depression.

In cognitive therapy, patients learn to recognize their negative and self-deprecating thoughts, and to see how such thoughts have often become automatic and deeply ingrained in their perception of the world and all that happens to them. Patients then learn to replace negative messages and patterns of thinking with more realistic and optimistic thoughts. For example, a depressed person may engage in a distorted thinking pattern such as focusing only on the negative aspects of a situation and disregarding the positive, or generalizing a small bit of misfortune to everything in her life. Such a person might generalize getting caught in a traffic jam to "everything bad always happens to me." Dr. Ellis teaches his patients to stop catastrophizing, or making mountains out of every little inconvenient molehill. For example, he might help the student who flunks a test to change his internal message from "I can't do anything right. I'm stupid and a loser," to "It's not fun to do poorly on a test, and I don't like it. But I'll find a way to do better."

Here's another example. It rains on Saturday. The negative thinking person might say to himself, "Oh, it always rains on my day off. Even the weather is against me." A better and more realistic way of thinking might be, "Well, I'm sorry it's raining on my day off, but we do need the rain, and it offers me a good chance to get caught up on my correspondence."

Rain or no rain, an important coping mechanism is to find the silver lining whenever possible, or the opportunity even a crisis may afford us. If we are constantly feeling victimized or angry that we're not getting our way, we don't have the mental attitude to benefit from and overcome our misfortunes. We instead feel depressed and defeated—low in energy and desire to move ahead. Pessimism breeds passivity and what psychologists refer to as learned helplessness.

In his book *Learned Optimism,* Martin Seligman shows how looking on the bright side of things generates more hope and sense of control in the individual, attributes shown in numerous studies to be associated with personal fulfillment and physical well-being. In addition, upbeat people feel more energetic, and often focus the energy on more health promoting activities, such as exercise, good nutrition, and relationships. A positive cycle then develops in many phases of a person's life; even expectations play a healthier role.

Much research, including Seligman's study of learned helplessness and Candace Pert's focus on neuropeptides, suggests that hostility, anxiety, and other negative emotions deplete the immune system, leaving an individual vulnerable to disease. In one interesting study in 1985, psychologists Michael Scheier and Charles Carver asked college students to answer true or false to questions such as the following:

1. In uncertain times, I usually expect the best.
2. If something can go wrong for me, it will.
3. I always look on the bright side of things.
4. I'm always optimistic about my future.
5. I hardly ever expect things to go my way.
6. Things never work out the way I want them to.
7. I'm a believer in the idea that "every cloud has a silver lining."
8. I rarely count on good things happening to me.[20]

"At the end of the semester, students who had scored high in optimism reported fewer physical symptoms like headaches and upset stomachs than students who had scored lower on the scale. In another study of college students, pessimists reported almost twice as many infectious diseases, and visited a physician twice as often as optimists."[21] And a review of much of the research done this decade concluded that optimistic people adapt in more healthy ways—psychologically and physically—to stress.

When cognitive therapy is used along with biofeedback or relaxation, it is called cognitive-behavioral therapy, or CBT. CBT is really a form of talk therapy in which the therapist works with the patient to think through steps initially that may be dysfunctional, such as negative attitudes toward health conditions, and then helps the patient develop and practice healthier steps. Some of the biochemical processes involving brain chemicals or neuropeptides mentioned earlier in this chapter may be undergoing some reconstitution throughout this process.

The term of treatment varies but even one exposure may be helpful. For example, fifty-two patients phobic about dentistry were enrolled in a cognitive intervention which involved restructuring their negative perceptions. After one hour of treatment they had substantially decreased their negative perceptions about dentistry, and showed a large decrease in anxiety.[22]

Since it has been shown that optimism is such a healthy attribute, parents often ask what they can do to encourage it in their children. Psychologists generally agree that what we hear from our parents and teachers about life and how the world works has a major effect on whether we become optimists or pessimists. Researchers have shown that the following strategies can help toward raising an optimistic child:

1. Be consistent;
2. Be positive;
3. Be responsive;
4. To the extent that you can, program the child's world to be consistent, positive, and responsive;
5. Give the child responsibility and encourage independence;
6. Set realistic goals;

CBT has been proven helpful in alleviating symptoms of other related mental health problems, such as depression, anxiety, and anxiety disorders.

HYPNOSIS AND MIND-BODY ISSUES

Hypnosis can be used in a number of ways to address medical problems. Pain control is one of the most common. Whether for surgery, childbirth, dentistry, or the management of chronic illnesses, hypnotherapy by a trained practitioner or self-hypnosis can be very effective. Just about anybody can be coached or taught to go into a hypnotic trance, which is basically a relaxed state of focused attention.

A fascinating study done in 1995 on what actually happens physiologically when hypnosis is used to control pain showed that conduction

7. Involve the child in a variety of age-appropriate activities;
8. Teach the child not to generalize from specific failures;
9. Teach the child to have a general sense of confidence from his or her successes;
10. Encourage problem-solving;
11. Help the child to see failure as a challenge to do better next time;
12. Encourage humor as a way of coping;
13. Be a role model of realistic optimism;
14. If the child expresses pessimistic views, challenge them;
15. As best you can, screen the child's peers and teachers for pessimistic tendencies.

(Source: "Healthy Attitudes, Optimism, Hope and Control," by Christopher Peterson, Ph.D. & Lisa Bossio) of the electrical and chemical action of nerves and muscles slowed under the hypnotic state. And so did the brain electrical activity.[23]

Hypnosis has been successful in controlling pain experienced by cancer patients, helping to alleviate some of the side effects of cancer treatment such as nausea, anticipatory nausea, and vomiting, and has been used along with conventional methods as actual treatment itself. In one study, Carl Simonton, a radiation oncologist, and Stephanine Matthews-Simonton, a psychotherapist, applied hypnosis along with traditional medical treatment for cancer patients. They first trained patients to relax and then visualize their immune system's white blood cells (which they imagined as powerful sharks) attacking and destroying cancer cells (weak prey), or, using a similar theme, allowed these patients to develop their own images. The Simontons clinically tested this procedure with 159 medically incurable cancer patients given one year to live. Sixty-three were alive two years after their diagnosis. Of these, twenty-two percent showed no evidence of cancer and nineteen percent demonstrated tumor regression, suggesting that hypnosis and visualization may in some way increase immune function for certain people.[24]

In addition, several recent studies involving healthy subjects have shown that hypnosis can alter certain immune system responses. Karen Olness and her colleagues carried out groundbreaking research with children at Minneapolis Children's Medical Center. The children (aged six through twelve) who learned a simple form of self-hypnosis using imagery to relax deeply, and who were given additional hypnotic suggestions to increase salivary immunoglobulin—the immune substance in saliva—showed a striking increase in their levels of IgA, one of the saliva immunoglobulins. The combination of self-hypnosis and hypnotherapy were effective in strengthening the children's immune systems. In a later study with adolescents, the same researchers found that self-hypnosis training resulted in significant changes in the activity of white blood cells.[25] Once again, the immune system was helped by hypnosis. And finally, when hypnosis is used shortly after a person has been badly burned, it is possible to decrease the severity of the body's reaction to the burn.

Brain wave research shows that hypnosis does have measurable effects on the brain. At the same time, other methods of deep concentration, such as the relaxation response or some types of meditation can at times initiate some brain wave changes related to hypnosis.

MEDITATION AND RELAXATION

Meditation and relaxation are similar in some respects. They both require the body to become quiet, with eyes either open or closed. A person may focus on something such as a thought, sound, or breathing, or endeavor to empty the mind of all thought and sensation. Three decades ago Herbert Benson, a Harvard cardiologist working with psychologist Robert Keith Wallace from the University of California at Los Angeles, reported that experienced meditators could in fact produce dramatic changes in their physiologies while meditating. Specifically, they were able to decrease their pulse and respiratory rates, decrease oxygen consumption, decrease blood lactate levels, and change EEG patterns. The combination of these physiological changes with decreases in anxiety and hostility in the subjects studied was first described as "the relaxation response." Other exercises with a body focus such as yoga, tai chi, or more thought-directed activities such as focused meditation, hypnosis, and visual imagery also produce similar physiological effects.

This relaxation response is more complex than originally conceived and may consciously or unconsciously incorporate an individual's personal and spiritual beliefs. For example, researchers found that, for some, saying the rosary can produce physiological effects similar to those produced by the relaxation response, as can other repetitive, inspirational thoughts or prayers which are meaningful to a particular person. In addition to alleviating headaches, high blood pressure, anxiety, and stress, recent studies have shown relaxation and meditation to be useful in controlling epileptic seizures, moods, and pain—including chronic low back pain and surgical pain.

MEDITATION

Twenty years ago when we suggested that our patients meditate to facilitate better mental and physical health, we were often met with skepticism. Now people are flocking to meditation courses. Benson's

WHAT IS MEDITATION?

We hear three main questions from our meditation students: (1) What is meditation? (2) How do I do it?, and, from those who say they have tried meditating, (3)Why can't I get my mind calm and away from outside distractions?

Meditation is a special state of deep relaxation coupled with mental alertness. It is an inward, self-focused, reflective type of response that underlies and is a part of the relaxation response in many ways. While various traditions have different meditative techniques, the main objective is a quiet inner concentration, away from the many day-to-day distractions of life. Some meditators endeavor to sit quietly and empty the mind of thoughts, to be in the here and now, and to reach a level of awareness and consciousness where they are focusing completely within. Others focus on a particular thought or phrase. Or a meditator may focus on breathing, counting, or repetitive chanting as a method of decreasing intrusive, busy thoughts, sometimes referred to as mind chatter. All of these approaches are known to reduce stress and anxiety. To those persons who become anxious and frustrated because they can't seem to get rid of pesky, intrusive thoughts, we suggest patience and practice...and more patience and practice!

and Wallace's landmark work as well as thousands of scientific stud- ies have shown meditation's vast physical and mental benefits and have placed it in the wonderful position of being, as the Scottish phrase goes, "good for what ails you" without any negative side effects. Besides aiding in wellness, meditation has been shown to give people more energy and make them better thinkers, enhance mem- ory and concentration, and heighten creativity.

YOGA

Yoga, another form of relaxation and meditation, literally means to yolk together. It aims for the perfect union of body, mind, and spirit through a system of postures, breath control, sounds, and medita- tion. Within Hindu philosophy, there are at least eight main sys- tematic yogic disciplines. Hatha-yoga, the form of yoga most familiar to Westerners, focuses on physical mastery and includes breathing exercises, meditation techniques, and physical postures designed to stretch and balance the body, mind, and spirit. Hatha- yoga is known to relieve problems such as anxiety, headaches, depression, and fatigue, and has been incorporated into a treatment program for victims of post-traumatic stress disorder at the Baltimore Veterans Affairs Medical Center. These patients suffer from symp- toms such as nightmares, flashbacks, chronic pain, and hyper- arousal. Yoga is also extremely useful for rape victims because many are afraid of being touched and yoga provides a safe and comfort- able method for them to get in touch with their bodies again while significantly reducing stress and anxiety.

According to some researchers who have studied the health effects of yoga, a key mechanism is the controlled nostril breathing, which can involve breathing through one nostril at a time, as well as changing nos- trils and rhythms of breathing. Psychologist David Shannahoff-Khalsa of the Salk Institute has been able to demonstrate that yoga breathing techniques can significantly decrease the symptoms of those suffering from obsessive-compulsive disorder, an extreme tendency to obsess over certain thoughts or indulge in compulsive behavior such as washing the hands every five minutes throughout the day. [26]

Yoga is known to offer many health benefits, including improved cardiovascular functioning, regulation of hormones, better sleep, less stress during the day, and improvement of concentration and memory. In one study of patients suffering from osteoarthritis of the hands, those who participated in eight weeks of yoga were able to significantly reduce their pain during activity, and increased their range of finger motion when compared to a control group.

BODY WORK

What happens to the water flow when your garden hose is twisted? Better still—a car will chug to a halt if it doesn't have the proper fuel, or the mechanisms aren't in tune with each other and working properly. How well would our cars work if we treated them as miserably as many of us treat our own bodies?! Moreover, how effective would the ride be with the tires unbalanced and out of alignment? There are a number of effective body work approaches that balance, heal, and release unhealthy blocks in the system. These range from bioenergetics, developed by Alexander Lowen, in which various positions and activities release blocked energy and toxic emotions from the system, to Shiatsu, the traditional Japanese deep massage which aligns the body and has been shown to have significant healing effects, to, of course, chiropractic.

In 1874 Andrew Taylor Still, a physician upset with the surgical and medical practices of the time, became the first osteopath. In his research, he saw that "rapidly flexing and extending the spine could reestablish blood flow." [27] He then developed a system by which a practitioner could alter a body's skeletal structure to improve its functioning and overall health. Osteopathy enhances the body's ability to keep itself healthy and to combat sickness if, like a well-maintained car, it is taken care of.

The Alexander and Feldenkrais techniques are two other popular body work approaches. The former offers a set of positions to help get rid of constricting postures and movements, so the body is more flexible and energetic, and the mind more focused. Some lessons take place on the massage table, and others teach "correct" ways to sit, stand, and lift—generally, how to use the body to move correctly. The Feldenkrais method, which teaches movements that reeducate the brain and in turn enable it to communicate in new ways with the rest of the body, has been shown to dramatically help stroke victims and people with cerebral palsy to recover their physical abilities.

Using a different but equally effective approach, Rolfing is a popular, deep massage developed by Ida Rolf to restructure the mind and body by working on the attachments of muscles and bones and the nervous system. This is done by breaking up points of resistance in the muscles, usually through a series of ten basic sessions in which all areas of the body are treated. Later sessions can focus on specific problems.

The different body work approaches all assume that divergent parts of the body are connected and interact in some way. For example, it is thought that problems in the lumbar region or bursitis in the shoulder joint may be related to pressures or twists on the ankles and knees, that carpal tunnel syndrome may be in some way associated with muscular tensions in the pelvis, and chronic back pain may at times be linked to restricted breathing.

As physical blocks in the body are loosened and removed, it is not uncommon for emotions built up and stored during trauma to be released as well. When we are children, our bodies are flexible and growing. Yet each time we may have reached out—physically, perhaps with a hand to grasp a tantalizing object on the coffee table, or emotionally, perhaps with a self-conscious invitation to a dance—and were slapped or pushed away in some manner, our body recorded the event. After a number of such thwarted attempts to reach out, we learned not to be so adventuresome or trusting. Eventually the nervous and muscular systems become blocked in certain areas. And as time goes on, stress may create tight and tangled muscles in the neck and back.

Better circulation and more efficient use of the muscles and nervous system can also result in letting go of some of the blocks, trauma, and vivid intercellular memories of stressful incidents in our lives. As the energy, biochemicals, blood, and nutrients are able to get to and nourish every cell in our bodies, we feel better and our bodies are better able to ward off sickness.

BREATH CONTROL

In the midst of a jumbled, stressful day, pausing for a few long, deep breaths can do wonders. In a fascinating book, *Concepts of Life-Breath*, authorities compare Eastern and Western views of a person's breathing, energy, and union of the physical, mental, and spiritual components, examining the importance of every breath we take and the manner in which we take them.[28] And why not? Our lives begin with our first breath and end with our last. We know the importance of oxygen, which nourishes and facilitates the functioning of every cell in the body. Lack of oxygen for even a few minutes is known to kill brain cells and do substantial organic damage.

Shallow breathing starves us of energy. Meditation disciplines encourage deep breathing from the diaphragm, which is known to nourish essential body organs and heighten energy levels, increase metabolic rate, and revitalize stagnant areas of the body.

PRAYER

"Mystery Cancer," a 1998 *Newsday* article by Delthia Ricks, poses the possibility of the power of prayer in healing cancer. Jean Arth, a recent retiree who moved to Shelter Island with her husband, Joseph, worked as a sexton and organist at Our Lady of the Isle Catholic church. She was diagnosed with an unknown primary tumor (UPT) in January 1994. This type of tumor can remain elusive or may vanish after seeding tumors elsewhere; in Arth's case, new tumors appeared in the spine and later the abdomen. Tracking down a UPT often takes many hours of shrewd detective work, according to doctors. Arth had aggressive therapy and has been cancer-free for more than a year. Arth says she believes the reason she is cancer-free is because friends and parishioners were "storming the heavens for me. I really firmly believe that I've been blessed."[29] Is this a story of the power of aggressive cancer therapy, Arth's faith, her mind, her prayers, the prayers of her friends, or some combination of them all which has kept her cancer free? No one knows the answer but the question is provocative at the very least.

At around the same time, *Forbes* published an article by John Christy titled "Prayer as Medicine." Christy provided evidence that "people who pray and attend religious services are healthier than their skeptical peers" based on the proposition that health is affected by state of mind, which can be influenced by religious beliefs.[30] One example can be found in the higher survival rates following heart surgery and consistently lower diastolic blood pressures of patients with strong religious faith.[31]

The proliferation of such articles over the last few years demonstrates people's increasing interest in how mind, belief, and attitude may all come together to aid in healing. Prayer may be a much more central factor in all of this than was previously suspected.

Spirituality refers to a belief in a higher power which, according to some, may dwell inside us in a region such as the mind or the soul.

It is difficult to separate spiritual or religious belief in a higher power—a very personal experience—into variables that lend themselves to research methodologies. Those who are spiritual do not always describe themselves as religious. A person may consider him- or herself spiritual yet not espouse a specific religious tradition, while someone else could be strongly affiliated with a religious group and not be spiritual. One of the problems involved in introducing formal religion as a variable in psychosocial research involves the way the religion is defined and used. There is disagreement among researchers about the precise definition of religion and whether religion is a unitary phenomenon or involves a set of separate attitudes. Simplistic and limited notions of religion include religious affiliation and frequency of church attendance. Also, membership in a religious denomination is often confused with religious participation and the two are often mistaken for belief and adherence. Another issue is how to equate religious belief that may only be situational or temporary, such as belief that manifests itself only when someone is diagnosed with cancer or incurs injuries in a car accident.

PRAYER AND MEDICAL CONDITIONS

A groundbreaking study by cardiologist Randolph Byrd evaluating the role of prayer in healing has encouraged numerous subsequent investigations. During a ten-month period, a computer assigned 393 patients admitted to a coronary care unit at San Francisco Hospital to either a group that was prayed for by home prayer groups (192 patients) or a group that was not remembered in prayer. The study was designed according to rigid criteria, the kind usually used in clinical medical studies. It was a randomized, double-blind experiment in which neither the patients, nurses, nor doctors knew which group the patients were in. Various religious groups were recruited to pray for subjects in the prayed-for group. These prayer groups were given the first names of their patients as well as brief descriptions of the patients' diagnoses and conditions. Prayer group members were asked to pray each day but were given no instructions on how to pray. Each person prayed for many different patients and each patient in the prayed-for group had between five and seven people praying for him or her.

The patients in the prayed-for group differed from those in the unremembered group in several areas. They were five times less likely to require antibiotics; they were three times less likely to develop pulmonary edema; none of them required breathing tubes while twelve in the unremembered group required ventilatory support, and few patients in the prayed-for group died.[32]

Evidence of the power of prayer keeps mounting. A 1995 study at Dartmouth-Hitchcock Medical Center found that one of the best predictors of survival among 232 heart surgery patients was the degree to which the patients said they drew comfort and strength from religious faith. Those who said they did not have faith had more than three times the death rate of those who did.[33]

A number of studies have indicated that in the elderly population, frequent church attendees have lower blood pressure, lower rates of stroke, and survive longer than infrequent attendees. Likewise, numerous studies have found lower rates of depression among the religiously committed. In their research, D.B. Larson and M.G. Milano present a strong case for integrating religion and spirituality into therapeutic treatment, especially in the mental health arena. In a 1996 publication on the relationship between religion and mental health, they provide evidence of how religious and spiritual commitment are associated with a lower prevalence of depression, suicide, and overall rates of rehospitalization of patients with schizophrenia.[34] Religious involvement or participation is associated with an improvement in overall emotional functioning for those suffering from mental disorders, and the presence of religion in a person's life is linked with a decrease in the risk for tobacco, alcohol, and illicit drug use.

Many more studies need to be done to better understand what role religion and spirituality can play in the prevention, onset, status care, and resolution of illness to persuade health care communities to integrate religion and spirituality with conventional medicine. We are just beginning to educate health care providers about this. The accreditation Council for Graduate Medical Education has only recently implemented two requirements specifically related to religion, and in 1997 there were thirty medical schools teaching courses on religious and spiritual issues. Eighteen medical schools have each received $25,000 grants to sponsor courses that inform future physicians of the role of religion and spirituality in the lives of patients and provide students with tools to address these issues. This is an important beginning to bringing medicine back to treatment of the whole person: mind, body, and spirit.

THERAPEUTIC TOUCH

In the 1930s, Rene Spitz found that babies raised in spotless northern European foundling homes and fed sufficiently did not thrive. In fact, many died. In contrast, Spitz noted while on a visit to Mexico that orphans in an impoverished and dirty institution were doing far better physically and emotionally. In trying to understand why these infants did so much better, Spitz found that every day, neighborhood women came to feed, hold, rock, and sing to these babies. He concluded that human contact and love had not only sustained these little ones emotionally, but also provided essential nourishment for their physical development.[35]

Two decades later, University of Wisconsin psychologist Harry Harlow showed in his ground-breaking research with baby monkeys that the desire and need for touch was even greater than that for food![36] And Deepak Chopra tells of how researchers found that laboratory rabbits that were handled and cuddled by a technician were much healthier than those who were not.

The healing power of touch is recognized in numerous healing capacities: the power of human contact, hugs, the value of having a loving dog or cat, and a particular approach, therapeutic touch, used by a wide variety of health professionals including nurses in hospitals and the scores of volunteers who now come to hold or give daily therapeutic massages to premature babies. Therapeutic touch or TT, as it is often called, does not require direct physical contact. It generally begins with the practitioner attempting to evaluate certain energy flows by placing the hands several inches above a person's body and redirecting accumulations of tension. Scientific studies of therapeutic touch show that it decreases anxiety, pain, and depression, and promotes relaxation.

Caring touch is life giving, and while research data are very important, we don't have to wait for thousands of scientific studies to acknowledge something we already know—the power of love.

EXERCISE

In the early 1970s at Mercy Hospital in San Diego, psychiatrist Thaddeous Kostrabala could be seen leading a regiment of joggers— patients who had been hospitalized for severe depression. Dr. Kostrabala's innovative program of exercise for these patients created such marked improvement in their conditions that a number were able to get off medication and leave the hospital.

Today most mental health professionals acknowledge the connection between exercise and mood. The 1996 U.S. Surgeon General's Report on Physical Activity and Health noted that "persons who are inactive are twice as likely to have symptoms of depression than are more active persons." And those who exercise regularly are less likely to complain of depression or anxiety than those who exercise infrequently or not at all. A growing body of research is validating the importance of exercise for good mood and all-around good health.

And psychiatrist John Doherty, director of the Center for Innovation in Behavioral Health at New York Hospital–Cornell Medical Center, says, "exercise has a very positive effect on mental health from a number of perspectives. We know exercise helps regulate biorhythms, which improves sleep, and it enhances energy level and vigor. Exercise is also very important in maintaining physical health and controlling weight, which impacts on self-esteem."[37]

So from preventing depression to decreasing the pain of arthritis to keeping the whole body functioning at a more optimal level, exercise is an essential part of good moods and good health.

CHILDREN AND MIND-BODY APPROACHES

Children are especially good candidates for mind-body approaches because of their flexible minds and fertile imaginations. Some exciting results have already been documented on using biofeedback and learning approaches with children to alleviate problems such as bed-wetting, attention deficit disorder, and hyperactivity. Hypnosis and other relaxation techniques have proven effective in treating allergies and asthma. And when given the opportunity and proper training, children respond enthusiastically to exercise and even meditation and yoga as routes to better health and well being.

No matter what ages we are or what our previous experiences have been, we can all learn, grow, and exert more control over our lives. Norman Cousins, author of the best-selling *Anatomy of an Illness*, reminds us that

> We must learn never to underestimate the capacity of the human
> mind and body to regenerate—even when the prospects seem

most wretched. The life force may be the least understood force on Earth. William James said that human beings tend to live too far within self-imposed limits. It is possible that these limits will recede when we respect more fully the natural drive of the human mind and body toward perfection and regeneration. Protecting and cherishing that natural drive may well represent the finest exercise of human freedom. [38]

CHAPTER SIX

The Power of Hypnosis

KAREN SHANOR, PH.D.

"I can't believe that someone with your expertise and intelligence would talk about that quackery!" Pretty strong words from an otherwise enlightened physician who was appearing on my radio program on psychology in 1979. This nationally recognized authority on public health issues was referring to a program I had done about hypnosis a few days before. I was surprised, because at that time hypnosis was used regularly in therapy and had solid research supporting it. But maybe I shouldn't have been so taken aback, for the idea of hypnosis has provoked strong opinions and varying feelings for centuries.

In this chapter I will outline the history of hypnosis, describe what it is and what it isn't, and how it can be used. I will also explain how hypnotic trances are often an integral part of everyday life, and how we can use self-hypnosis to improve our lives.

A HISTORY OF HYPNOSIS

Franz Anton Mesmer (1734–1815), an Austrian physician, popularized hypnosis in Europe some two hundred years ago. He also believed that the correct use of magnetism could be useful to one's health and practiced both "animal magnetism" and hypnosis, which came to be called mesmerism. The science of those times was very much interested in the phenomenon of influence at a distance. So not so long after Newton had described the law of gravitation, Mesmer adopted the scientific metaphor of the day (just as we use information-processing metaphors) and became very successful in Vienna. However, for a number of reasons, some of them political, the medical community rejected hypnosis and it fell into considerable scientific debate until almost a century later when, in 1882, the famed French physician Jean-Martin Charcot (1825–1893), who attended to the most prominent families in Europe, endorsed hypnotism as a genuine science.

In the mid-1880s Sigmund Freud went to Paris to study with Charcot and later wrote that he was awed by Charcot's dramatic demonstrations of hypnotism: "I received the profoundest impression of the possibility that there could be powerful mental processes which nevertheless remained hidden from the consciousness of men."[1] Freud initially worked almost exclusively with hypnosis, trying to uncover the traumatic events at the root of people's psychological problems.

Then Freud stopped using hypnosis because, as he explained in his autobiography, he was trying to cure a woman of her attacks of pain by tracing them back to their traumatic origin, "when suddenly she woke out of the trance state, and threw her arms around my neck...I was modest enough not to attribute this event to my own irresistible personal attractiveness, and I was relieved from a painful discussion by the unexpected entrance of a man servant...."[2] So on that day, Freud discovered transference, the idea that patients often transfer to their therapists feelings and problems associated with people from their pasts, such as parents, siblings, teachers, friends, and lovers. He felt that in order to control or to work with the transference rather than simply to exploit it, he had to stop practicing hypnosis. So he developed the technique of free association as a method to tap into the deep unconscious.

Photographs of Freud's original study-consulting room in his home at 19 Berggasse in Vienna reveal his preferences in furniture placement during therapy sessions. When he practiced hypnosis, he used to sit beside the couch—the couch was originally placed there for that purpose. When he stopped practicing hypnosis, he moved his chair around behind the couch because he didn't like patients to look him directly in the eye. A picture of an archeological dig hangs right over the couch, reminding us of Freud's interest in archeology (an interest he shared with Carl Jung), which fit into his fascination with the unconscious.

When fear of the Nazis forced Freud out of Vienna, he first went to Paris, then settled for the remainder of his life in London. Interestingly, a picture of his study in London shows, in the place of honor, right above the couch, a picture of Jean Martin Charcot inducing hypnotic catalepsy. So at the end of his career, Freud returned to the beginning, to the origin of his interest in hypnosis, writing that the "pure gold of analysis might well have to be alloyed with the baser metal of suggestion."[3]

Most orthodox analysts today still feel that hypnosis ought not to be used because Freud declared it not usable. Still, many important movements in intellectual history have begun with hypnosis, abandoning it as soon as they got on their feet.

A PERSONAL ACCOUNT

I have found hypnosis to be very useful in therapy and, whenever possible, teach my patients self-hypnosis, a useful tool throughout life. Dr. Milton Erickson, a genius in the understanding and use of hypnosis (as well as a creative and compassionate psychotherapist), showed that the hypnotic trance occurs in many ways specific to the individual and the situation. This is probably one reason why hypnosis is often misunderstood. People usually feel more comfortable with a standard phenomenon to which we can give a precise label. But the mind doesn't work that way. While there are a number of standardized and specific approaches to hypnosis, the phenomenon itself is quite expansive, and even elusive, in that sometimes we don't even realize we're in a trance. Though hypnosis, like the human mind, is often hard to pin down and research adequately, that doesn't mean we should not try. Even the term "hypnosis" is understood differently by various experts and schools of thought. Presently within the academic community there is a debate over whether to define hypnosis as a trait or a state. I prefer Frank Putnam's designation of hypnosis as a consciousness state.

My first real encounter with hypnosis came in the early 1960s when I took Psychology I at Stanford University. As you probably know, a college's undergraduate class is a valuable source of subjects for research. The hypnosis study by psychologists Josephine and Ernest Hilgard—whose work I first mentioned in Chapter One— sounded most intriguing to me, and I volunteered. Prior to being hypnotized, I was interviewed for many hours by Josephine Hilgard. She took my family history and asked many questions about my personality, preferences, and style of thinking. As is often the case in such interviews, I learned a great deal about myself. There were many questions about aspects of my life I'd never considered. Dr. Hilgard was warm, accepting, and fun. In retrospect, I feel privileged to have spent such an insightful time with her.

As I recall, the next part of the research included about three sessions where I was primed to be induced into a trance by sitting in a bare room and focusing on a thumbtack in the wall until my eyelids got heavy. Then I was escorted into a laboratory where I was tested for a number of things. One might have been some sort of perceptual test. I seem to remember being strapped into a wooden armchair and tilted at about a thirty-degree angle. Of the rest, I have even vaguer memories.

I came out of the first two sessions doubting that I had really been hypnotized. My expectations, like those of much of the general public, were that I was supposed to have been unconscious, or at least in a deep, deep sleep. Yet I thought I had been aware of everything that had taken place at the time it was occurring, and, at least at that time, remembered afterward what had happened in each of the sessions. Even though I thought that I wasn't hypnotized during the two earlier sessions, I remember thinking, "Well, I'll go along with what they are asking me to do since I'm too relaxed not to. And anyway, I signed up to cooperate—why not just go along with it?" I felt that I could have resisted at any time if I had wanted to, but why bother?

During what I remember to be the third session, the experimenter asked me to go back in time in my mind to my senior English class in high school. Where did I sit? Who sat in front of me? What student was in back? (I now know that I was being asked to contextualize the past event, since much of memory is state- and context-dependent.) I was asked to picture and to feel the classroom in as much detail as possible, then write down my name and the date as if I were there. I did so. Then I was asked to do the same thing for another class two years earlier, and back and back in time. A part of me thought, "Isn't this interesting. I'm writing a date easily and confidently, but I'm not trying to calculate what the particular year is by subtracting from the present date in any way." I just seemed to know the right date for whatever grade I was being asked to recall. I remember being in fifth grade, then third, still writing my name and the date easily and spontaneously.

Then came first grade. I was shocked to see and feel myself holding the pencil very clumsily and printing my name in giant, crude letters. "Oh my gosh!" I thought, "I really must be hypnotized!" Even though I can't remember my exact exclamation, I vividly recall, and even can viscerally feel once again my excitement as some part of my mind realized what was happening!

A few years later, I learned that I had been a part of a landmark study that examined which types of personalities are most hypnotizable. The findings surprised those who had previously suspected that those persons most susceptible to hypnosis would score relatively low on an IQ test and be very, very suggestible—almost a hysteric in the clinical sense. But not so. The Hilgards found that almost everyone can be hypnotized to some degree under the right circumstances. Moreover, intelligent and independent individuals are some of the best candidates, especially those who can concentrate in a very focused way without being distracted by the stimuli around them. The person who can read a book in the midst of a New York subway ride, or while five little children are tramping through the house. Daydreamers and deep fantasizers also tend to be good hypnotic subjects, fitting into the category of "high absorbers." They are often able to easily switch from reality to fantasy, from analytic thinking to a more free-flowing type of thinking. [4]

The Hilgards' research led to their development of the often used standardized Stanford Hypnotic Susceptibility Scale for clinical settings. [5] Psychiatrist Herbert Spiegel has also developed a standardized written susceptibility test, as well as an eye-roll test in which a clinician evaluates how far a person can roll his or her eyes in an upward direction, as a quick way to determine hypnotic potential.

Years later in my graduate program in clinical psychology, I underwent hypnosis a number of times, experiencing many of the wonderful and varied possibilities of this powerful technique. As I was finishing my doctoral studies, I even allowed myself to be hypnotized before a couple of hundred other graduate students in the auditorium. It was time to decide what the next step in my life would be, and the session helped me to do this. Incidentally, throughout my graduate experience and training in hypnosis the same professor, whom I liked and trusted, did the hypnotizing. Good rapport is an important factor in maximizing the effectiveness of a hypnotic induction.

I've found self-hypnosis to be an invaluable tool, from finding a lost article to preparing myself mentally for the numerous lectures and media appearances I've done over the years. I regularly use self-hypnosis to focus my mind before writing sessions, or making important phone calls, or conducting especially challenging psychotherapy sessions.

My first attempt to recover a lost article by using hypnosis occurred in the late 1970s. I was desperate. I had misplaced my glasses, which I needed for driving. For two days I had been unable to locate them, and needed them to drive thirty miles to Washington's Dulles Airport to pick up an out-of-town friend. I had looked for them innumerable times without success. Yet I knew they had to be somewhere in the house. As I lay on my bedroom carpet doing my morning exercises, I paused a moment and hypnotized myself, suggesting that I would find the missing glasses within the next five minutes. Shortly thereafter, in a relaxed and casual manner, I got up off the floor and walked across the room to an alcove containing a stack of ten or more carefully folded sweaters. Without consciously thinking about my glasses (or much of anything, for that matter), I lifted the third sweater from the top of the pile and there, underneath, lying on top of the fourth sweater down, were my glasses! The hair on the back of my neck stood on end. Astonishing! What a great technique!

Well, why not? Some part of my mind knew where I had placed those glasses. In retrospect, I don't know if I should have taken pride in my brilliance in thinking of using self-hypnosis to find my glasses, or chided myself for getting them into such a stupid and unlikely location in the first place. There was no one else I could blame, since I lived alone at the time. These days, my family has a wry saying: "If Mom can't find it through hypnosis, then she wasn't the one who lost it!" A fun comment, but not necessarily the case.

Sometimes we resist the information hypnosis brings us from our subconscious. One of my patients did that. Jeff (not his real name) was a good hypnotic subject, and eventually mastered the self-hypnosis technique I taught him. Early one morning as he was leaving on a business trip to Peoria, Illinois, he realized he didn't have his plane ticket. After a frantic and thorough search of his house and possessions, Jeff sat down and hypnotized himself to think of where the ticket might be. The strong message he received from his subconscious was that the ticket could be found in the second pocket of his briefcase. Although he had searched there earlier, he felt pushed to look again. But he resisted. Instead, he canceled the trip to Peoria and went to his office. Later that night, he found the ticket...in the second pocket of his briefcase.

Our next psychotherapy session centered around why Jeff didn't want to make that trip to Peoria. It turns out that deep down he really didn't want to make the sale for his company, which was the reason he was being sent to Illinois. With more probing, Jeff realized that he felt that his present boss was not an ethical man, and he no longer wanted to work for him or the company. Jeff's conscious mind had for months suppressed the ethical concerns he had about his boss and his job. But his unconscious mind recognized the problems, and probably also realized that Jeff needed to make a career move to a company he truly believed in and felt comfortable making sales for. A month after that session, Jeff started working for another company. More than ten years later, he's still at that company and doing very well. Most important, he now looks forward to going to work each day.

Often the various facets of our minds are in conflict, even when we formally hypnotize ourselves. Later, I will talk about some of the informal ways we hypnotize ourselves each day. For now, I shall mention some common examples of self-hypnosis. Are you able to wake yourself up at a certain time without the use of an alarm clock? You are giving your unconscious mind a message which it is following. If you say, I'll wake up at 7:00 a.m. sharp, can you do it? All you have to do is believe that you can do it and practice and you can wake yourself up on the minute. We can also influence (self-hypnotize) ourselves in negative ways. If you feel you are going to have a miserable day—and you really believe it—chances are you will.

The cognitive approach to psychology is based on the power of the messages we give ourselves. Pioneers like psychiatrist Aaron Beck and psychologist Albert Ellis were some of the first to incorporate this approach into psychotherapy. Psychiatrist David Burns's popular book, *Feeling Good*, is a wonderful aid to using the cognitive approach. Dr. Burns has shown that even patients who had been hospitalized for severe depression were able to get out of the hospital, off their medication, and lead happy lives by changing the mental messages they were giving themselves. What a testimony to the power of positive thinking! So if you're always walking around expecting the worst to happen, don't be surprised if it does. Henry Ford, the inventor and industrialist, is credited with saying, "There are two kinds of people. Those who believe they can and those who believe they can't. And they're both right."

One of my favorite examples of auto-hypnosis was accomplished by the master of hypnosis, Milton Erickson. He writes in *Healing in Hypnosis* about the time when, as a twenty-year-old college sophomore in Wisconsin, he applied for a job at the local newspaper, *The Daily Cardinal*:

I wanted to write editorials. The editor, Porter Butz, humored me and told me I could drop them off in his mailbox each morning on my way to school. I had a lot of reading and studying to do to make up for my barren background in literature on the farm. I wanted to get a lot of an education. I got an idea of how to proceed by recalling how, when I was younger I would sometimes correct arithmetic problems in my dreams.

My plan was to study in the evening and then go to bed at 10:30 p.m., when I'd fall asleep immediately. But I'd set my alarm clock for 1:00 a.m. I planned that I would get up at 1:00 a.m. and type out the editorial, place the typewriter on top of the pages, and then go back to sleep. When I awakened the next morning, I was very surprised to see some typewritten material under my typewriter. I had no memory of getting up and writing. At every opportunity, I'd write editorials in that way.

I purposely did not try to read the editorials but I kept a carbon copy. I'd place the unread editorials in the editor's box and every day I would look in the paper to see if I could find one written by me, but I couldn't. At the end of the week I looked at my carbon copies. There were three editorials, and all three had been published. They were mostly about the college and its relation to the community. I had not recognized my own work when it was on the printed page. I needed the carbon copies to prove it to myself.[6]

When asked by Ernest Rossi, the co-author of *Healing in Hypnosis* and a brilliant hypnotherapist in his own right, why he decided not to look at his writings in the morning, Erickson answered:

I wondered if I could write editorials. If I did not recognize my words on the printed page, that would tell me there was a lot more in my head than I realized. Then I had my proof that I was brighter than I knew. When I wanted to know something, I wanted it undistorted by somebody else's imperfect knowledge. My roommate was curious about why I jumped up at 1:00 a.m. to type. He said I did not seem to hear him when he shook my shoulder. He wondered if I was walking and typing in my sleep. I said that must be the explanation.[7]

Erickson goes on to say that it wasn't until his third year in college when he took distinguished psychologist Clark Hull's seminar and began his own research in hypnosis that he better understood what had happened. Since then, he said, he has shown many of his students how to train themselves in this type of dissociative activity and hypnotic amnesia. After a while, Erickson added, the students would not need the alarm clock.

WHAT HYPNOSIS IS AND WHAT IT ISN'T

Professor Martin T. Orne offers this definition:

> Hypnosis refers to a state or condition in which the subject becomes highly responsive to suggestions. The hypnotized individual seems to follow instructions in an uncritical, automatic fashion and attends closely only to those aspects of the environment made relevant by the hypnotist. If the subject is profoundly responsive, he or she hears, sees, feels, smells, and tastes in accordance with the suggestions given, even though these may be in direct contradiction to the actual stimuli that impinge upon the subject. Furthermore, memory and awareness of self can be altered by suggestions. All of these effects may be extended posthypnotically into the individual's waking activity. It is as if suggestions given during hypnosis come to define the individual's perception of the real world....These effects are best understood as the consequence of the hypnotized individual's ability to focus his or her attention on suggested ideas and ignore other aspects of his or her external and internal environment.... However...it is not possible to hypnotize a person against his or her wishes.[8]

So hypnosis is a specific type of dissociation that involves focused attention and some degree of suggestibility. It is also often a normal part of everyday life. In fact, Dr. Melvin Gravitz, an authority on hypnosis, once reminded me that a number of us "walk around in a trance much of the time." And too many of us drive around in one.

Even though hypnosis is a normal variation on intentional processing, some people can become more absorbed than others, and some people are more suggestible than others. Most of the time our attention is relatively dispersed. Psychologist George Miller wrote a fascinating and famous paper called "The Magical Number Seven, Plus or Minus Two" that said every study of working memory and attention seems to come up with the same numbers—between five and nine things that we can think about and pay attention to at once. That is our working memory and attention span.

Stanford's David Spiegel suggests that what we do in hypnosis is cut the number of things down from seven plus or minus two to one or two things that we attend to with great intensity. Some of us have a higher capacity to focus than others, and may be referred to as high absorbers, who tend to be more highly hypnotizable. Those who have the capacity for hypnosis tend to tap into it spontaneously when focusing on something intently. This happens in peak performance. Spiegel tells of one of his former students who was very hypnotizable, and also a wide receiver for the Stanford football team: "When he was on, when he was playing well, he was aware of two things, the ball and the defender. And those twenty other big guys running after him, he paid no attention to. Nor was he aware of the sixty thousand people in the Stanford stadium. It's that kind of focused attention."

When the late Florence Griffith Joyner, the fastest woman on earth, won the Gold medal for the hundred-yard dash, they asked her what she was thinking about. She said, "I was just trying to relax." Now, here this body is tearing down the track, and she wants to relax! But good athletes and good performers know that. If you start telling your body what to do at that moment, you are going to mess things up. If you haven't learned what you have to do, you are not going to learn it while you're performing at your peak. Joyner had entered a kind of natural trance state.[9]

When a skill is learned and practiced enough, it goes from the attentional part of the brain to the automatic part. As with learning to drive a car with a standard transmission, you eventually do not have to think about shifting gears while you're driving. I remember telling my son (who was six years old at the time) that for his first piano recital he had to "overlearn" the piece. When he asked what it meant to overlearn something, I said, forgetting he was still largely in the concrete thinking stage of development, that I meant he should learn it so well, he could play it in his sleep. So a few nights later, he awoke me at around 2:00 a.m. to prove to me he had over-learned it, which he had. I was the nervous one at the recital, remembering, but never sharing with him, how I blanked out at one point while playing during my own first piano recital. Imagine my delight at not only witnessing his perfect performance, but hearing him say as we drove home, "That was fun. When's the next recital?" (I had, by the way, also hypnotized him for the recital.)

The absentminded professor is another good example of a high absorber. Albert Einstein was certainly known to get lost in his thoughts. I remember hearing a story that his wife sent him to the front hallway to put on his galoshes on his way to work. Forty-five minutes later, when she came into the hallway, she noticed he was still standing there, deep in thought, holding the galoshes.

While Einstein might have gotten a prize as an exceptionally high absorber, all of us compartmentalize—that is dissociate, or put out of our conscious awareness those things that we might ordinarily be aware of—to different degrees at different times. Probably while reading this you have not been aware of your body touching the couch or chair in which you're sitting, until I brought it to your attention. The more you focus on something in the center of your attention, the more likely you are to dissociate, or ignore things at the periphery. This can even be therapeutic at times—for example, in pain control—which will be discussed in more detail later on.

According to Spiegel, there is a related phenomenon called source amnesia, where you tend to forget where you obtained certain information. In an experiment, psychologists John Kilstrum and Fred Evans took highly hypnotizable people and told them in hypnosis that they would recall strange facts, such as the population of Kalamazoo is 73,000 people. And later in the course of a routine series of questions, they would ask, "Hey, do you happen to know the population of Kalamazoo?" And the subjects would come up with this number. Then the experimenters said, "Well, that's really remarkable. How did you know that?" And the subjects would scratch their heads and say things like, "Well, I was listening to a quiz show the other night...and you know, I heard that answer and it just struck me as strange," or "It just turned out to be the same size as my hometown." [10]

What the subjects did in this experiment was remember the content and forget the context—they decontexualized it. If you're very focused in hypnosis, it's like looking through a telephoto lens: You see something in great detail, but you don't see what's around it. The experiment's subjects lost the context in which they learned the information about the population of Kalamazoo, and attributed the acquisition of the information to themselves. And we all know that we're far less critical of our thinking than of anyone else's. [11]

Furthermore, if you think a hypnotic suggestion was given to you by yourself rather than by someone else, you're more likely to follow it. This doesn't mean that people who are hypnotized are robots or zombies. Spiegel says that his father, Dr. Herbert Spiegel, who has been using hypnosis as a psychiatrist since World War II, has had patients anxiously ask him whether he can take over their minds and make them do anything he wants. Dr. Spiegel looks at them with a twinkle in his eye and says, "You know, if I really had the power to take over somebody's mind and make them do anything I want, do you think I'd be sitting here with you?"[12]

HYPNOSIS AND THE BRAIN

Research on hypnosis and the brain is still in the incipient stage. Scientists are not unanimous in their theories as to which brain waves are most predominant during hypnosis.

It used to be thought that hypnotic activity affected mostly the right hemisphere of the brain, the more holistic side. We process music and sensation in the right hemisphere, and words and most math concepts in the left. The left is thought to be more linear than the right, and does one thing at a time. You might say that the left hemisphere is a type of linear processor, whereas the right hemisphere is more of a parallel processor. The narrow focus of the mind during hypnosis may mean that, in fact, hypnosis is more left-brained than right-brained. Research is under way to clarify this.

David Spiegel conducted brain research a few years ago that revealed that hypnosis can affect the parietal cortex up on the top of the head, and is very good at helping people modulate signals; that is turning them up or down like an amplifier in a stereo system.

CHILDREN AND HYPNOSIS

As we have seen, children tend to be very hypnotizable. I have hypnotized my son and then taught him self-hypnosis as soon as he was interested in learning, which was when he was about ten. He uses it in a number of ways: to get in the right frame of mind for his piano recitals, to learn material at school, to take tests, and in sports. Hypnosis can be used for anything that the mind can be used for. Since many of us, especially children around the age of eight, are often in trances, self-hypnosis is a way of choosing the trance we want. One psychotherapist I know hypnotized his children to help them relax and have a healthy night's sleep without nightmares or other disturbances. David Spiegel tells how he used to do something similar: "I often used to do a simple self-hypnosis exercise with the kids. I have them close their eyes and imagine they're floating. For example, my daughter might visualize floating down the river on the back of a swan, and all the things they are passing along the way. And then they get more and more peaceful and tired, and pretty soon they drift off to sleep. The children like suggestions like that. They find them soothing. One night I hadn't done this and my son, who was about eight, wandered out to the shed where I was working and said, "Dad, I need a professional." [13]

Spiegel agrees that teaching children, as well as adults, the technique of self-hypnosis could be a great aid. Each of us can benefit from learning a type of self-talk in which we can program ourselves and our bodies to do things that are helpful. And children can especially benefit from the self-regulation and study skills that self-hypnosis can offer.

Milton Erickson, the father of six children, taught them self-hypnosis when they were very young, and he used his hypnosis skills on them as well. When his son Robert was three, Erickson hypnotized him to refocus attention to alleviate the pain of a bad cut. Erickson agreed with his son that the injury hurt, but explained that it would just hurt for a little while. While washing the cut, he had Robert think of the color of the blood. Later on in the hospital, he suggested to Robert how great it would be if he got more stitches than his older brother had gotten for an earlier injury. No medication was used to deaden the pain while stitches were being taken, and the doctor was amazed to hear Robert ask for even more stitches than were necessary. [14]

In another instance, Erickson fixated some children's attention, leading them into a trance. He describes the incident this way:

I was in an airport in Denver, Colorado, at two o'clock in the morning waiting for my plane. I saw a tired mother coming into the waiting area with five children, all of whom were dragging their feet, whining, and whimpering.... These children were really raising a row with their mother, and she was saying so patiently, "Now, Johnnie, sit here please; Mary, sit there, please."

I watched that scene for a while. Then I went and got a big newspaper and returned. I stood in front of those kids and slowly tore a tiny strip the whole length of the newspaper and laid it down on the floor. I rapidly gained an attentive audience of six.

I tore another strip and I laid it crosswise. I tore another, and then I tore another, and I made quite a pattern on the floor. Then I went over and sat on the bench beside the oldest child, and I tore little, short strips and laid them in a pattern on the seat bedside the child.

"This is what I always do before I go to sleep," I told him. "When you look at those strips, you will also get sleepy."

I took hold of his hand, lifted it up, producing catalepsy, and then laid his arm very gently on his leg, dropping my hand down in front of his eyes. His eyes closed and I turned to the next child.

The mother was watching me with a great deal of interest and when I had finally finished with all five children, she looked up, saw her husband coming, and said to him, "Oh, John, Dr. Erickson has just hypnotized the kids for me." [15]

SOME THERAPEUTIC USES OF HYPNOSIS

Hypnosis has been used in innumerable ways. Erickson writes of a case where he hypnotized a young woman to increase the size of her breasts. She had been subjected to a number of hormone treatments to no avail. He suggested to her while she was in a deep trance that her breasts would become warm and tingly and start to grow. Although she didn't remember the suggestion, her breasts grew larger within two months, possibly because the hypnosis caused the blood supply to increase. Physicians sent other referrals to him, the results of which were equally successful.[16]

Dr. Helen Crawford and other researchers have shown hypnosis to be very effective in alleviating chronic pain, as well as the acute pain associated with childbirth, dental procedures, and skin transplants. It is used to alleviate muscle spasms, and even to get rid of warts. And, of course, hypnosis is used in psychological and psychiatric settings to help patients remember past events, control neuroses, deal with phobias, and change behavior in a variety of ways.

A recent use of hypnosis is in the area of burns, not only to decrease the terrible pain associated with them, but to minimize the seriousness of the burn itself. Some paramedics are now trained to take advantage of the approximately twenty-minute window of time it is thought to take a burn to completely manifest itself on the body. If paramedics can hypnotize the patient during this time to think the burn is less serious than it really is, they can minimize the depth and seriousness of the burn, resulting, for example, in a first-degree rather than a third-degree burn. (The body is told to respond as if it has been only slightly burned.)

MILTON ERICKSON'S UTILIZATION APPROACH TO HYPNOTHERAPY

There are a number of effective therapeutic approaches that hypnotherapists can use. Erickson's work offers an example of one I believe to be both effective and exquisitely respectful of the inner resources of the person being hypnotized (ethical, concerned professionals in the therapeutic community take what they do very seriously and value highly the people they work with). As they discuss the utilization approach to hypnotherapy in their book *Hypnotherapy: An Exploratory Case Book*, Milton Erickson and Ernest Rossi write, "We view hypnotherapy as a process whereby we help people utilize their own mental associations, memories, and life potentials to achieve their own particular goals." [17]

Erickson's utilization approach is described as a three-stage process: (1) Preparation: a period during which the hypnotherapist explores "the patient's experiences and facilitates constructive frames of reference" to guide the patient toward therapeutic change; (2) Therapeutic trance: in which the patient's own mental skills are taken into account and mobilized; and (3) "A careful recognition, evaluation, and ratification" of the change which has taken place in the patient as a result of the hypnotherapy. [18]

An important part of the preparation is, as I've mentioned earlier, to establish rapport with the patient. Then for the second stage, some sort of fixation of attention technique is used to initiate the therapeutic trance. Techniques used include counting, focusing visually on an object or picture, listening to tones, or some other focused activity. You will note that the common denominator here is a focusing exercise to eliminate intrusive and/or distracting stimuli, which is an essential requirement for trance. The authors write that in their view one of the "most useful psychological effects of fixating attention is that it tends to depotentiate patients' habitual mental sets and common everyday frames of reference" so that therapeutic learning and change can take place. [19]

Finally, it is important to remember that hypnosis is relatively simple, yet powerful. Professionals well trained in understanding the mind should use it judiciously and therapeutically only. Even the best-trained hypnotherapist may not be the best for a certain person. If you, for whatever reason, do not feel comfortable with your therapist, it's better to find one with whom you are comfortable working. Trust your intuition on this. In the next chapter Dr. Karl Pribram explores the scientific approaches taken to understand our mental powers.

KARL H. PRIBRAM, M.D.

Often referred to as the Einstein of the Brain, Dr. Karl Pribram prefers the title Magellan of the Brain, conferred on him by former student Paul MacLean, an eminent brain scientist in his own right. Just as Ferdinand Magellan (born in 1480 and the leader of the first expedition to circumnavigate the world) was relentless in his pursuit of geographical truth, Dr. Pribram continues in his ninth decade to be equally vigorous and unrelenting in his pursuit to understand the brain. He has always been way ahead of his time, as shown in science's recent confirmation of the holographic tendencies of the brain, which Pribram asserted long ago.

Stanford Professor Emeritus, head of the Center for Brain Research at Radford, and Distinguished Research Scholar at Georgetown University, Dr. Pribram was honored at Georgetown's first international, interdisciplinary conference on the Brain and Communication in April 1999. And in 1997 the Russian government honored him for outstanding contributions in the study of the brain. Dr. Pribram is not easy to keep up with as he travels all over the world, while continuing to carry out groundbreaking research on the brain. He inspires us all with his energy and his perpetual curiosity.

Having not seen Dr. Pribram since the 1960s at Stanford, I met him once again in 1990 when I found myself sitting next to him in a lecture on hypnosis given by Stanford Professor Emeritus Ernest Hilgard at an APA convention. When I saw Dr. Pribram the same day at a physics lecture, then at an artificial intelligence lecture, then at a lecture on chaos theory, I was inspired by his continual zest for learning, and his expertise in a myriad of disciplines, including mathematics and physics.

Trained as a brain surgeon at the University of Chicago, Dr. Pribram apprenticed under then famous Dr. Karl Lashley, and taught at Yale before his thirty-year tenure at Stanford University, during which time he collaborated with Harvard's B.F. Skinner, and wrote a groundbreaking book with Harvard's George Miller.

This brilliant visionary and explorer of the brain brings together in a few pages a world of knowledge about the mind, some of which is decades ahead of mainstream science. I am privileged that Dr. Pribram consented to contribute to this book his first chapter written for a general readership. This rich gift from Dr. Pribram is science of the brain and consciousness in a literary nutshell.

What if that tiny ant (mentioned on page 3) that only sees the bottom of the fingernail were to suddenly look up—to see the person and all around and above, including an expansive sky and an exquisite panorama of nature? In his way, Dr. Pribram is asking science to be curious and courageous enough to look up and take into account the larger picture, using breakthrough technological advances and interdisciplinary knowledge. He writes about understanding the brain/mind at the quantum level of radiation, converging energy levels, and oscillating waves of energy, as well as at the Newtonian material investigation of molecules and cells which encompasses most of current brain research.

Pribram emphasizes the importance of the whole and how everything is dynamic and interconnected. He illustrates the dynamics of language—mind as a verb, a process of "minding," rather than a thing. He shows how the continual interrelatedness of patterns of oscillating waves of energy, and the interference patterns of these waves which can create a hologram, operate throughout our brain encoding information from our five senses and more subtle energy systems within and outside of us, and how these quantum level processes interact with the material, linear parts of our larger nervous system, including the brain.

For decades, he has been revolutionary in his insistence that much in the brain occurs in a holistic and often holographic fashion, similar to the 3-D pictures the medical MRI takes of our body. The sophisticated technology and understanding of how wave forms (and magnetic forces in the case of an MRI) can resonate are confirming this holistic process in the brain.

Pribram believes that much of the quantum activity of the brain pertaining to consciousness occurs within the dendritic web. During a recent lecture at an international neuroscience conference in his honor Pribram declared: "If you remember anything from my talk it should be this: Dendrites, Dendrites, Dendrites!!!" Here is why.

As we know, the nervous system is made up of neurons. A neuron has a cell body with branches extending from that cell body. One of the larger branches is chemically different and can support a nerve impulse—a depolarization of its membrane that makes a sharp noise or visual spike on the electronic equipment used to measure it. This level of activity can be thought of as the circuitry of the brain (similar in a way to electricity flowing through a wire).

However, according to Pribram there is a very different process that occurs in the finer branches of the neuron, the area of the teledendrons and dendrites. (In more scientific terms: "At the distal end of an axon which it synapses (makes a junction) with another neuron, it splits into branches called teledendrons, which connect to the dendrites of another cell, its non-axon branches, through chemical synapses and electrical ephapses.") And the teledendrons and dendrites form a dense web of very fine fibers in which processing does not involve nerve impulses, but oscillating waves, energy, and other quantum processes. It's as if this web captures and resonates to/with certain frequencies. Pribram believes that what we become aware of, our conscious experience, may very well be based on what is happening in this processing web.

And finally, Pribram takes us to a different way of perceiving the mind/brain issue. Since information cuts across time, space, material, and non-material realms, instead of only considering the Cartesian distinction between matter and non-matter, we can think in terms of the "ideal" (the potential energy and possibilities around us) and the "real" that which we experience, create, and can continue to create from that energy.

CHAPTER SEVEN

The Reality of Conscious Experience

KARL H. PRIBRAM, M.D.
WITH SHELLI MEADE, SCIENCE WRITER

INTRODUCTION

As we enter the new millennium, we find ourselves in the midst of technological advances that offer exciting possibilities for the integration of ideas across many disciplines. The upsurge of interest in the scientific study of consciousness can be attributed to two such developments: access to images of the actively functioning human brain, and the information processing revolution.

However, after we have observed brain activity using the latest imaging techniques, we are left to wonder: What is the relationship between the brain process that has been identified during an experience and the experience itself?

And when we apply the innovations made in information processing to the study of our conscious experience, we are left to ponder the question: If consciousness is to be understood in terms of information processing, is what we experience a virtual reality or a true one?

Answering these two questions form the substance of this chapter. We begin by looking at how the term consciousness is used within the scientific community. We struggle through the verbal pitfalls of "mind-talk" as a construct separate from "brain-talk." Finally, we show how the brain's interactions with its environment (physical, biological, social) construct a world order of potentialities, and how from these potentialities a world order of appearances emerges, appearances that gradually seem to become "real."

THE HIERARCHICAL NATURE OF INQUIRY

All inquiry begins with our personal conscious experience. As children, we observe that contrary to most of our experience, some entities are detached from the ground and move gracefully above it; these are flying objects, and we inquire of our mother or father what they might be. Two hundred years ago, these flying objects would have been identified as birds. Fifty years ago, the flying objects might first be identified as airplanes and only later distinguished from birds. Perhaps in the future, parents will reply to a child's question in such a situation by stating that the flying objects are UFOs.

The initial process of identification looks upward in a hierarchy of queries. One such query might be, can birds land on remote objects such as the moon, the planets, and the stars? No, birds cannot, but rocket ships can. How is it that birds can't and rockets can? Because of gravity, which is a relationship between entities that acts on them despite a distance that separates them. Gravity has a name but the relationship did not always have one. Newton baptized "it" and "it" became "real," an entity in its own right.

Why does it get dark at night? Because during the day the sun gives us light and warmth, and then the sun sets. Where does the sun go when it sets? It goes underneath the horizon. But it doesn't really "set." Actually the earth is a ball and turns so that sometimes we are facing the sun and at other times the ball comes between where we are and where the sun is. These happenings are fairly regular and laws describe the regularities.

How does the sun bring us light and warmth? We call this experience radiation. The radiation allows plants and animals to grow, to do the work of growing and what other work we do. We measure the amount of work and give the radiation that made it possible a name. We call it energy.

How does the sun bring us light and warmth? Rapidly. In his imagination, Albert Einstein sat himself on a beam of light and showed that for almost all situations the speed with which he was traveling was as fast as anyone or anything could go in the universe. (The exceptions began to come when, at the other end of the hierarchy of inquiry, velocities faster than the speed of light were apparently necessary to explain observations in quantum physics.) Of course Einstein was not really traveling on a beam of light, because to experience light and warmth we need to have the radiant energy fall upon the sensors of the body, the eyes for light and the thermal receptor capacity of the skin for warmth. At that point radiant energy is converted into chemical and electrical signals that inform the brain of what has happened at the receptor surface. What Einstein was doing was expressing his attunement with radiant energy as he experienced it in terms of light.

Note that in all these inquiries we are looking *upward* toward a more encompassing understanding of our conscious experiences. We devise apparatus, do experiments, make observations, and use our imaginations to pin down the assumptions underlying the experiences. We often give these assumptions a name. "It" becomes an entity and thus "real."

The opposite route of inquiry is to analyze the conscious experience *downward* into component parts. The bird has feathers. What are feathers made of? The plane has engines. What are engines made of? Among other things, of metal. What metal is used? Might there be a better metal for the purpose of flying? Metals are chemicals. What is the chemistry of an airplane engine's metal? Could we improve the strength to lightness ratio by changing the chemistry of the metal? A career in chemistry, metallurgy, and solid state physics is launched. And so on down to the constituents of atoms.

These examples illustrate the course of inquiry: The fact that beginning with our conscious experience, the path of inquiry takes two rather different procedural approaches. In one case, we look upward in a hierarchy of experiences, and by refining our observations (often with the invention of better tools) our attunement with a more encompassing cosmos, with the "bigger picture," becomes better, more specified. In the downward procedure we are analyzing, taking apart the conscious experience to look at its components, again by making further observations and often inventing and using special tools to do so.

These two procedural paths are from time to time used in conjunction with each other. This is especially true when we reach a dead end using one method or the other. But often, as well, the shift in the direction of the path of inquiry is due to the inclinations of the person making the inquiry.

CONSCIOUSNESS CATEGORIZED

As we analyze the study of consciousness downward through the hierarchy of inquiry, three categories can be distinguished. First there is the medical meaning: You are deemed fully conscious if you respond specifically and appropriately to verbal or physical probing, such as, Hello! What day is it? Where are we? This definition comes close to the original Latin, *conscire*, to know together. Physicians and surgeons would classify your response in one of several ways: as fully conscious; as asleep (needs a few moments to awaken);

as stuporous (gives a nonspecific response such as a groan); or as comatose (indicates no response). We can refer to these descriptions as states of consciousness.

The dictionary, reflecting the common usage of the term, emphasizes a different meaning of consciousness: perceptions and feelings. Mostly we refer to *what* we are conscious of, what we feel. Consciousness in this sense refers to the *contents* of our conscious experience: I see the color red; I feel pain. Psychologists study the contents of conscious experience under the heading "perception" and philosophers refer to them as qualia. Some of these experiences refer to our bodies and are called egocentric (centered on one's self); others refer to the world outside our bodies and are called allocentric (centered on others). For pain and pleasure and related experiences, this distinction between self and other becomes blurred; we feel that our bodies have been violated or restored in some way by someone or something. The experience is neither egocentric nor allocentric but a fusion of both.

Finally, philosophers, psychoanalysts, and the esoteric community view consciousness in still a different way. The crux of this last use of the term consciousness is that it refers to *paying attention*, and we can refer to this category as the *processes* of consciousness. There is an important distinction to be made here between those processes to which we do attend and those that are almost automatic, to which we do not attend. For example, in popular parlance there is a hue and cry that we must expand our consciousness regarding the ecology of our planet; that is, we must pay attention to ecology. Or, a psychiatrist notes that experience is driven by unconscious processes, processes that we do not attend to. Another example is driving an automobile: A person who is just learning to drive must attend closely to his or her driving, while an experienced driver can attend to a heated conversation with a passenger because the process of driving has become nearly automatic for him or her.

Closely related to the concept of attention are the processes of intention and thought. When we *attend* to something, we consciously experience sensory input; when we *intend*, we consciously anticipate a motor output; and when we *think*, we ruminate our memories.

Understanding the process of consciousness is the key to exploring state and content. Conscious processes relate the state we are in to the contents of our experience and relate the contents of our experience to our state. For example:

1. One evening, walking home from work, my *state* of hunger prompts me to *pay attention* to the *content* of my environment that may relate to my hunger—for instance, restaurant signs.

2. I am walking to work the next morning and pass by the corner bakery. Odors which are a part of the *content* of my conscious experience catch my *attention* and induce a sudden *state* of craving for a donut.

3. The next morning is Saturday, and on awakening, the content of my conscious experience seems centered around the *contents* of a list of errands I need to accomplish. So I *thoughtfully* plan what I *intend* to do. By the end of the day, my *state* is task-incomplete, because I have not attended to all of the things on my list.

THE 21ST CENTURY—COGNITIVE PSYCHOLOGY

Cognitive psychology evolved in the 1950s and the 1960s. This approach differs from the more traditional behaviorist approach in that it takes subjects' verbal reports seriously. From the behaviorist tradition were taken changes in instrumental behavior, especially in reaction time. From the tradition of mathematical modeling of stimulus-response relations, computational programming models were invoked. These models fell into two classes: There were those that emulated the computational *software* and were therefore fairly insensitive to the hardware employed for their implementation; and there were those that looked to the interface between the programs and the specific hardware using *machine language* or, in the case of the brain, the "language" addressing the *wetware*. The software emulators are called *functionalists*; those whose interest is in the *wetware* are *neuropsychologists* and *cognitive neuroscientists*.

The functionalist approach to cognitive psychology is making a contribution to our understanding of conscious experience, primarily in the area of the processing involved in constructing conscious experience. If indeed there are patterns that are relatively independent of the hardware and *wetware* through which they work, how restricted is conscious experience to humans? How far away from the human experience can an embodied pattern, a *program* conveying information, be consciously experienced? That is, which animals have conscious experiences similar to ours? Which animals experience pain and joy as we do? The issue is not a trivial one or an easy one to resolve.

In an earlier paper (Pribram 1976), I expressed the view in terms of a "cuddliness criterion." The more cuddly the creature, the more we are likely to attribute to it conscious experiences similar to ours. John Searle (1984) took the attribution approach a step further: He stated that the material substrate of the behaving organism must be composed in a manner similar to us—of blood and guts, in other words. There are now researchers who have had computer chips implanted into their bodies. At what point are such implants extensive enough that we fail to identify these "hybrid humans" as capable of conscious experience similar to our own?

The "cuddliness criterion" should not be taken lightly. Remember R2D2 in Star Wars? She/he (the authors disagree as to the gender) makes us readily attribute something like conscious experience to her/him on the basis of her/his abilities to think through problems (via computer algorithms) and to be there for us when we need her/him. What if, a century from now there was a servant class of cuddly robots that met Searle's compositional criterion to some extent? When would some of us humans feel sufficiently guilty about taxation (not in terms of money but labor) without representation to consider giving these androids the vote? And what then?

The cognitive neuroscientists analyze the relation between brain systems and the various aspects of consciousness. Two very different ways in which we organize our conscious experiences have so far been established: The first organizing principle is the "me" and the second is the "I."

THE "ME"

The "me" is a body self-distinct from the outside shell that surrounds it. The "me" has the ability to locate itself in space and time. Locating is akin to, although more primitive than, a four-dimensional space-time coordinate dimensionality. In order to locate one has to distinguish oneself from the surrounding shell of the environment. In addition, once one has achieved this distinction, one can also distinguish a sensory perception based on input from that environment from an imagined image. For instance, one can vividly imagine a unicorn walking through the house, yet maintain the ability to distinguish between the unicorn (a part of our self-process) and a "real" horse (a part of processing the outside world). These processing distinctions are similar to those that allow us to distinguish between our intentions (which pave the road to Hell) and our acts. Franz Brentano, the Viennese philosopher who trained Freud, called this intentional inexistence, which has since been shortened to intentionality.

The construction of the intentional "me" takes place in systems of the brain's convexity, its top and middle region. Damage to these systems disrupts the body "me." A patient with such brain damage has what is called a neglect syndrome. I recall one such patient who would want to sit up, but couldn't do so because her arm was stuck in the bedclothes.

When her arm was pulled free and we would point out to her, "This is your arm," she would respond, "Yes, it is an arm." When told emphatically, "This is YOUR arm; it's attached to you right here. Do you see?", her response was, "Yes it is. But it doesn't feel like my arm." This damage to this woman's brain's convexity had disrupted a portion of her ability to constitute her "self"; in other words, her "me."

Probably the closest most of us come to understanding what this sort of disruption feels like is after we have a tooth cavity filled under local anesthesia. Until the novocaine wears off, the cheek and half the tongue seem swollen and dislocated from the normal "me."

THE "I"

While the "me" locates us and our bodies in the world, the "I" is concerned with sequencing and monitoring our experience. Sequencing does not relate us to clock time. Rather the relation is among episodes of experience, episodes that need to be made accessible in the future.

Episodic processing involves the amygdala of the brain. The amygdala is closely related to the hippocampus, which essentially deals with the events that make up an episode. The amygdala and the hippocampus are part of the limbic system, which is located on the front internal surface of the brain. Damage or irritation to the amygdala gives rise to a disruption of episodic processing.

An anecdote illustrates this well. While I had my lab at Stanford University, I also used to teach at Napa State Hospital. There was a staff member at Napa who would attend my lectures. I'll call her

"Joan." One day while we were walking out to the parking lot after my lecture, I said, "I hope you have a nice weekend." She said, "I hope so. We're going to a party tonight, and I'm really looking forward to it." The next Friday, after my talk, I again walked back to the parking lot with Joan and some of her friends. By way of conversation I asked, "Well, how was the party? How was last weekend?" She replied, "Oh, I never got to the party. I must have fallen asleep. I was feeling strange that night, and I don't remember falling asleep. But I must have gone to sleep." Her friends were surprised. "What do you mean?" they asked. "You were at the party. You seemed to have had a little too much to drink. You were sort of spaced out. But you were there."

So we know that Joan was at the party because her friends told us so. She was there and behaving in a party-like way. But that episode in her life was not integrated into the rest of her conscious life; an epileptic seizure in the vicinity of the amygdala had blanked out the episodic process.

By themselves, episodes still do not make an "I." Episodes must be ordered into a coherent story, that is, one's life. Thus, in contrast to the body "me," the storied "I" consists of a narrative or screenplay, Shakespeare's "all the world's a stage." It is the most forward part of the brain. It is the frontal lobes that integrate the functions of the amygdala and hippocampus to monitor what is happening in the brain systems of the convexity (at the top and back of the brain). Evidence indicates that the frontal lobes serve as the brain's executive.

THE DISTRIBUTED NATURE OF BRAIN PROCESSES

Cognitive neuroscience deals for the most part with the relationships between faculties of mind and the brain systems that organize these faculties. For instance, as noted, weaving events into episodes and juxtaposing these, in turn, into a personal narrative that identifies one's "I" involves the hippocampus, amygdala, and the frontal lobes of the brain respectively.

A different sort of brain organization accounts for the way the brain becomes modified by experience, and how it codes that experience in such a way that it can be used subsequently in a variety of ways. Paradoxically, this type of brain organization—which is distributed over systems and therefore is in many respects suprasystemic—has been tracked down by microelectrodes that allow the experimenter to map what is going on in the branches of single nerve cells.

The research that initiated the discovery of distributed systems resulted from neuropsychological observations of patients who had sustained brain injuries from accidents or strokes. Such patients often cannot recognize ordinary objects by using a particular sensory mode—for instance, vision—but have no difficulty recognizing the objects by using another sense—for instance, touch. An example would be a woman who, after a stroke, did not recognize a sweater she was in the process of knitting for her grandchild when the stroke occurred. As the doctor held the knitting before her face, she struggled to recognize and name it and finally gave up. Then the doctor handed the knitting to the woman. As she held the knitting needles in her hands and touched the soft, pink yarn, she suddenly said, "Linda's sweater!" The difficulties are called agnosias (not-knowings); the woman in our example had a visual agnosia. When parts of the brains of animals were removed in an experiment, similar findings resulted. These observations led to the idea that memory operated at two levels, a deep distributed coded "store" and a localized surface "program"—often sensory-specific or verbal— that organized elements of the store for current use.

While the surface "program" is made up of circuits located in the larger branches of connecting nerve cells, the deep distributed memory is located in the teledendrons and dendrites, the finer branches of nerve cells, and the synapses that connect them to one another. These distributions have been surveyed by using micro-electrodes and mapped as fields composed by oscillating electrical potential changes. The fields can be described mathematically by vectors (directional lines) or by contours of fields outlining the magnitudes of the potential differences at each location. In aggregate the distributions form a web that, together with the surface circuits that make up the surface stimulus, makes communication between systems of the brain possible. Communication by web is different from communication via brain circuits made up of larger branches of nerve cells connecting with each other.

The situation is much the same as our communication systems today: We have telephone circuits and we have the world wide web operating on the Internet. For distance communication, the web uses the circuits, but the possibility exists that communication over the web will, one day, be possible using radiant energy such as that used in radio and television broadcasts.

THE RESONANCE: TRANSCENDING SPACE AND TIME

The deep processing structure of the brain is composed of electrical oscillations, which can be described somewhat as broadcasts. Broadcasts encode information by enfolding space and time into frequency modulations of wave forms. Your TV or radio receivers decode these enfolded patterns. In a similar fashion the surface circuitry of the brain unfolds—decodes—the communication web's distributed processes into our ordinary space-time realm of experience.

Such encoding and decoding constitutes image processing in hospitals by positron emission tomography, or PET scans, and magnetic resonance imaging, or MRI. Maps are made by sending radiant energy (such as composes X rays and visible radiation) through the body part being examined. Each "shot" is then added to and/or multiplied with (the technical term is convolved) the rest and then transformed into a three-dimensional image of the body part.

The sensory and brain processes work in a similar fashion. Energy in the form of interference patterns stimulates our senses. The sensory receptors respond and relay the patterns to the brain, where they set up resonances with inborn or learned patterns of oscillations in the processing web. The process is much like that which takes place in a piano: The keys are the sensory receptors that are connected in an orderly fashion to the strings of the sounding board. The string vibrations (oscillations) resonate to the input from the keys. Beautiful music results. This model of the hearing functions of the brain was proposed over a hundred years ago by Georg Simon Ohm, the physicist responsible for Ohm's law of electricity, which relates current to voltage and resistance.

During the 1970s many laboratories ranging from Leningrad to Cambridge, Berkeley, and Stanford to Canberra, Australia, showed that the evidence from their microelectrode experiments explaining the brain processes that organize form vision (not only color vision) could be modeled in the same fashion. In other words, the eye behaved much as the ear did, except that the patterns of resonance were essentially four-dimensional (not including color) rather than two-dimensional.

Our everyday experience with stereoscopic sound gives an idea of the power of such a resonating system. Even a two-speaker stereo system will project the sound to a region between and in front of the speakers. The location of the perceived sound can be changed by changing the phase of the oscillations, the vibrations of the speakers.

This is much as the auditory brain system works. Georg von Bekesey was studying the cochlea, the auditory receptor in the inner ear that is the scene of the auditory input to the brain. A cochlea is *very* small, so when Bekesey heard that I was removing brains from beached dead porpoises and whales, he asked to be given their cochleas.

But even these proved hard to work with, so Bekesey built a model of a cochlea by lining up five vibrating mechanisms, or tuning forks, on a membrane. By placing the membrane on the forearm, Bekesey demonstrated how, when the phase relationships between the vibrators were adjusted, only a single spot was felt. By further adjustment of phases, the spot moved up or down the arm.

Next, Bekesey produced another such model and strapped one on each forearm. Once again, he adjusted the phase relationships and now, the single spot would jump back and forth from one arm to the other, even though I could clearly see five vibrators moving at the same time on both arms. This was interesting all by itself, but Bekesey asked, "Do you feel anything else?" I said no, and he told me to sit down for a while. So I sat and read some reprints he had sitting around his office. About fifteen minutes later I asked him, "What did you do?" He asked me what I meant; he had been off in another part of the lab working on something else. I said, "The spot stopped jumping!" He asked, "Where is it?" I answered, "IT'S OUT THERE!" By this I meant that I could "feel" the spot, not on either of my arms but in the space in front of me. "What in the world is going on?" I asked Bekesey. "How could it be OUT THERE?"

Bekesey explained the phenomenon. When surgeons do surgery they "feel" the tissue they are working with in their fingertips, even though there is an instrument (forceps, scalpel) between their fingers and the tissue. When someone writes with a pen, they "feel" the paper through their fingertips, even though the paper is below the pen. Bekesey had shown how tactile sensations could be projected, and how this sense, as well as hearing, operates by resonance among oscillatory processes.

Yes, the skin is like the ear, and not surprisingly, since the cochlea of the ear is derived from the lateral line system of fishes—a tactile sense organ that responds to vibrations. Hearing, touching, and seeing thus share similar sensory and brain processes that depend on resonance between a source and a receiver. The processes work by way of interference patterns among oscillating fields, fields initiated in Bekesey's membranes or in the connection web as surface distributions of varying spectral densities (frequencies).

A momentary slice through such a process yields a hologram. To convert a hologram into an ordinary perceived image, the transformation used in image processing (PET and MRI) was shown during the 1970s to operate in the sensory-brain systems described above as well. This transformation is accomplished by relative movement between the sensory receptor and the input to it.

While neuroscientists were discovering the distributed holographic-like organization of the brain's processing web, quantum physicists became aware that a similar organization characterized radiant energy in the cosmos. David Bohm, professor of physics at the University of London, described this organization as "implicate" because it enfolded (Latin *plicatus*: to fold) time and space. When the transformation is performed as in image processing in hospitals, time and space become unfolded into our ordinary "explicate" experience. Bohm pointed out that we need lenses to perform the transformation.

Bohm and I began a long-term collaboration. Essentially an old saying was proving true: "As above, so below." The deep structure of the brain's processing web and the quantum organization of cosmic radiation were kin. The formation of material objects in the cosmos and the biological development of sensory surfaces such as lenses to perceive these objects went hand in hand.

Theoretical insights obtained during the 1970s indicated that the brain's holographic processing was indeed quantum-like, a quantum holographic or holonomic (*holos*, whole, and *nomos*, rule-governed). The transactions taking place among the membranes and microtubules of the teledendrons, synapses, and dendrites were either taking place at the quantum level or quantum laws were operating on a larger scale as in superliquidity and superconductivity.

The importance of these experimental and theoretical advances indicated that the established world view that guided explanation in cognitive neuroscience was inadequate to explain the relation between minding and brain processing. A more encompassing panorama was being provided by physicists, a panorama which opens new vistas for research in the brain sciences. The next section of this chapter describes the origins of this perspective and its import in taking us beyond the current concern with the mind–brain issue.

THE MIND-BRAIN RELATION:
ANSWERING THE FIRST QUESTION

A topic critical to the study of consciousness has teased mankind for centuries: the mind–brain relation. Much popular attention has been focused during the last fifty years on answering such questions as, What is mind? What is brain? Are they the same? Are they different? In what way(s) do they differ?

Experimental inquiry into mind–brain issues has almost exclusively taken an analytical approach, looking downward in our hierarchy of inquiry. This analytical approach to mind has reduced mental processes to *material* brain processes and thus widened the chasm between science and the humanistic and spiritual aspirations of mankind. The separation of scientific from spiritual pursuits is artificial and harmful. C. Judson Herrick noted the consequences of such dualism most succinctly (bold ours):

> In our own culture the cleavage of the "spiritual" from the "natural," which is a survival from the most ancient mythologies, has fostered popular ideologies of religious fanaticism, class rivalries,

and political antagonisms that are biologically unfit and even suicidal because they result in social disintegration. **Our ultimate
survival is endangered as long as ideological fantasies that are
incompatible with things as they are control individual and
national patterns of behavior.** We must somehow manage to heal
this artificial dismemberment of the human personality before we
can hope for a permanent cure of the present disorder.[1]

The time is ripe for looking upward in the hierarchy of inquiry
in search of ways to fill this gap.

THE LANGUAGE GAME:
A DOWNWARD INQUIRY

In analyzing consciousness we come to an old argument which
debates whether brain and mind are two different *substances*. This
is referred to as the dualism issue.

The first task in coming to terms with dualism is to identify the
difference between mind and brain. Brain is perhaps the easier of
the two: In a simple definition, we can think of brain as a biological
organ housed within the skull.

For the most part, the scientific community has been able to dis-
pense with the issue of mind by accepting Gilbert Ryle's definition:
Mind comes from minding, paying attention.[2] With the accepted
definition of mind being a *process* rather than a *substance*, there
seem to be very few dualists left within the field of brain science.

However, the dualism issue still exists within the casual conversations of English-speaking laymen. Often brain talk and mind talk
are substituted for each other. This is because in English, the term
"mind" is a noun—a *thing*. In mind talk, the concept of mind as an
entity certainly exists in common parlance. Consider the following
examples:

> Person A: Do you *mind* taking the children with you when you go to the grocery store?
>
> Person B: I would take the children, but they won't *mind* me when I tell them not to run in the store.

In the first example, mind implies a process of evaluating desire. In the second example, mind clearly refers to paying attention. However, we might continue the conversation:

> Person A: I'm going to lose my mind if I don't get some quiet time to myself.
>
> Person B: I've changed my mind; I will take the children.

Here, the "mind" is referred to as a thing. The process implied here can be easily identified: In both examples, mind refers to the process of *reasoning*. But when speaking in casual conversation, does the English-speaking person recognize that mind is a process? And if not, why?

We humans have a tendency to reify, that is, to name every *thing*, even abstractions and processes, as though they were materialistic entities. To illustrate this, consider the origins of language. Language began with utterances called holophrases. These holophrases were more akin to concepts than words and were subsequently separated into nouns and verbs (and nouns further categorized as subjects and objects) with the consequence that there was an increased precision in understanding. Imagine the word "be" and try to imagine a holophrase that incorporates the subject form (a being) with the verb form (to be) and the object form (other beings). Consider the implications of such a holophrase. If all humans BE, then they are all integral, a whole.

Such is the case with the Hebrew word for being, which was originally Yahweh. Yahweh was converted to a *subject* (a being) who *acted* upon the *objects* (other beings) by throwing them out of the

Garden of Eden. The Old Testament or Hebrew Bible separated human from deity using language as a tool. It is easy to forget that the word BEING meant existence and "existence is us."

The following quotation describes this human tendency to reify and its powerful consequences (italics ours):

"In the beginning was the Verb," i.e., words originally referred to a flow of experience; early communication was "verbal"! The word *word* appears closely related to the word *verb*. At a recent conference on philosophy, during a presentation of the work of Benedict de Spinoza we were apprised of the fact that initially Hebrew words were verbs denoting being, action, and process. Similar forms are said to exist in preclassical Sanskrit. Be that as it may, there is every evidence that human thought, including scientific thought, begins by nominalizing, reifying what at first are sensed as processes. Piaget has documented this development in children; biochemists routinely operate in this fashion when [for example] they isolate first a function of…the pituitary gland, reify that function by giving it a name…ACTH, and then search for "it" until the name is substantiated, that is, found to be a chemical substance.

The power of nominalization can be gleaned not only from its use in science but from such observations as those of Helen Keller, whose world came to life [and whose ethical sense awakened] once she could name (objectify) items previously experienced only as processes:

I knew then that w-a-t-e-r meant that wonderful cool something that was flowing over my hand. That living word awakened my soul, gave it light, hope, joy, set it free! There were barriers still, it is true, but barriers that could in time, be swept away. I left the well-house eager to learn. Everything had a name, and each name gave birth to a new thought. As we returned to the house, every object that I touched seemed to quiver with life. That was because I saw everything with a strange new sight that had come to me. On entering the door, I remembered the doll I had broken. I felt my way to the hearth and picked up the pieces. I tried vainly to put them together. Then my eyes filled with tears for I realized what I had done [she had earlier destroyed the doll in a fit of temper], and for the first time I felt repentance and sorrow. (Helen Keller, 1880–1968).

As Walker Percy [who quoted these observations] so clearly perceives (Coles, 1978),

Here...in a small space and a short time something extremely important and mysterious had happened. Seven-year-old Helen made her breakthrough from the good responding animal which behaviorists study so successfully to the strange name-giving and sentence-uttering creature which is Homo Sapiens.

[Seven-year-old Helen] did not make the mistake of the radical behaviorists; subject as well as object were attended. Note also that in doing so, propositions were formed, and remembrances, repentances, and sorrows could be entertained. Subject could be responsible for object, cause could lead to effect.

Irrespective of whether process descriptions in terms of verbs preceded or arose coterminally with nominalization and whether nominalization preceded or arose coterminally with propositional utterances, the entire set of linguistic operations described above did occur in human prehistory and do occur in the development of every human being. Thus the mind–brain issue is joined at the very inception of what makes us human—our ability to make propositions; in other words, to conceptualize processes [in terms of duals such as] subjects acting on objects [mind acting on brain, or vice-versa]. In order to nominalize a process into a proposition made up of a subject, verb, and object, we must first categorize and then hierarchically arrange categories into logical relationships. We thus become logical animals—the word *logical* being derived from *logos*, Greek for "word." (701–702).[3]

We have been concerned here with the origin of *linguistic* duality. Its relation to the mind-brain duality is obvious whether we view mind as being organized by brain or vice versa.

The mind-brain duality becomes even more intriguing when we speak of spirituality. For example, an aspect of "mind," which is termed "soul," is often treated as a "thing" in the English language. This is not surprising since the German word for social science, *Seelenwissenschaft* (as opposed to *Naturwissenschaft*, the word for natural science) translates as "science of the soul." The French term *conscience* means both conscious and *conscience* (another English noun standing for a process, the capacity to determine right from wrong).

No one today denies that minding exists. As we noted earlier, minding is attending, the process that integrates conscious states with conscious contents. But are we being misled by our universal tendency to reify, which doesn't always work? Perhaps reifying minding into a *thing*, a material mind which has mass and therefore extension in time and space, is leading us astray. Is there perhaps another way to understand "mind"?

HOLOFORMS: AN UPWARD INQUIRY

At least since the time of Newton and Leibniz three hundred years ago, two rather different conceptual schemes have dominated thinking with respect to the mind–brain relation. Both are concerned with the relation between observed events. But the Newtonians express these relations in terms of the relations among *entities*, whereas the Leibnizians explain them in terms of the constructive effect of *waves* (oscillations).

1. Newtonian View: Looking downward in the hierarchy of inquiry, brain, by the process of organizing the input from the physical and social environment as obtained through the senses, constructs mental phenomena. That is, brain constructs mental processes.

2. The Leibnizian view: Looking upward in the hierarchy of inquiry, the pervasive organizing principle of the universe is a hierarchy of related structures.* Mental processes discern the pattern of the cosmos by virtue of the brain's attunement (albeit imperfect) to these forms inherent in the universe.† In other words, brain *enables* mental processes.

Almost all behavioral scientists and neuroscientists would today subscribe to some form of the Newtonian view. By contrast, the Leibnizian view reflects the beliefs of many theoretical physicists such as Albert Einstein, P.A.M. Dirac, Wolfgang Pauli, Erwin Schroedinger, and Eugene Wigner.‡

Those whose conceptualization operates primarily in the *space-time* domain (that is, bound by such concepts as space and time, as much of our ordinary human experience is) and who are consequently rooted in a materialistic perspective find the Newtonian emergentist view of mind most compatible, while those who are sensitive to the *spectral* domain (interference among waves produced by oscillations) are comfortable with the Leibnizian view.

---

*Leibniz formulates his view in terms of monads. Monads are structures that encompass one another, are interpenetrating and "windowless" and culminate in a "super-monad" that includes all others. Translated into current terminology, if we substitute "lensless" for windowless, we have the structure described in this essay.

†Or, as C.S. Peirce (1990) so poetically stated it: "Every single truth of science is due to the affinity of the human soul to the soul of the universe, imperfect as that affinity no doubt is.

‡For instance, Pauli, in a letter to Fierz (26 November 1926) stated that the individual systems of quantum mechanics (e.g. wave and particle) are windowless monads and there is, nevertheless, always the right fraction which reacts according to calculations.

As noted, some aspects of brain science, which have rarely until now looked upward in the hierarchy of inquiry, indicate that certain critical aspects of brain function take place in the spectral domain. This development gives considerable credence to the Leibnizian view, a view that is thus worth exploring further.

The mind–brain ontology developed in this chapter is monadic (in the spirit of Leibnizian monads) and therefore *monistic* in the sense of transcending a duality between mind-talk and brain-talk. Rather, another class of orders lies behind the level of organization we ordinarily describe in terms of space and time.

The *ordinary* order of *appearances* can, for the most part, be described in space-time coordinates. The enfolded class of orders is constituted of fine-grain *distributed* '*holoformic*' *organizations* (interference among patterns of waves) which can be thought of as *potential* because only after radical transformation is their palpability in experienced space-time terms realized. When the potential is manifested, the holoformic information (the form within) becomes *unfolded* into its ordinary space-time configurations. In the other (upward) direction, that is moving from space-time to enfolded order, the transformation *enfolds* and distributes the information much as this is done by interfering wave forms, in the holographic process. Because work is involved in transforming, descriptions in terms of energy (measured in quantum theory as wave lengths multiplied by Planck's constant) are suitable. And as the *form* of energy is what is transformed, descriptions in terms of the structure of information, that is, entropy (and negentropy) are also suitable. Thus, on the one hand, there are *enfolded* potential holoforms; on the other, there are *unfolded* orders manifested in space-time.

When one looks upward in the process of inquiry, one reaches a level where superficial manifestations transformable into one another are separable from more fundamental *invariant* (unchanging) structures, such as those embodied in DNA which in-form transformations (Pribram 1996). For instance, **A**, A, a are instantiations of the A design which is universal. Instantiations,[*] that is embodiments, of Beethoven's Sonata (Opus 111) are an initial composition (a mental operation completed while Beethoven was already totally deaf!); a score (a material embodiment); a performance mentally organized by a conductor, mentally envisioned by each player, and mentally audited by each listener, but coordinated by the score (material); a recording on compact disc (more material but with a mentally produced organization); and the sensory and brain processes (material) that make for appreciative listening (mental). But in the transitions from one instantiation to the next, a certain relation-structure remains *invariant* (the same). This invariant structure is unaffected by the centuries of "performances, recordings and listenings;" It is the *essence* of Beethoven's Opus 111. (For a detailed and sophisticated development of this thesis, see Arturo Rosenblueth's *Mind and Brain*, MIT Press 1970, Chapter 6; and Pribram 1986.)

What remains *invariant* across all instantiations is abstract structure, "in-formation," the form within. Thus, according to this analysis, it is Platonic "ideals," interpreted as informational structures, that motivate the enterprise dialogue spawned by the information revolution (for example, *"information processing"* approaches in *computational and cognitive science*). This enterprise differs from the current exchanges dialogue between (1) mind-brain dualists such as Karl Popper and John Eccles (1977); (2) materialists such as Dan Dennett (1991) and Patrick and Patricia Churchland (1986); and (3) mentalists such as John Searle (1992) and Roger Sperry (1980). The current exchange appears to be a vestige of the now waning industrial revolution.

---

[*] By instantiation of a universal (form or organization) is meant one of its reifications, i.e. embodiments (see Pribram 1971; 1991).

Platonic ideals are limits of ideas spawned, according to Aristotle, by human acts and precepts. In-formation conceived as negentropy structured rather than dissipated energy, is neither material nor mental. Thus a scientific pragmaticism akin to that suggested by Peirce and practiced by Pythagoreans and early Ionians* will most likely displace mentalism and dualism as well as materialism as a central concern of philosophy. Guides to this future have already been given by Bertrand Russell in his insights on relationship structures and Alfred North Whitehead in his process philosophy. Both the ideal mathematical structures, which are essentially mental, and the material structures in which they are instantiated are "real." By temperament, some of us need to be grounded in the nitty gritty of experimental and observational results as much as we are moved by the beauty of theoretical formulations expressed mathematically. Thus, the tension between (the potential) *idealism* and (the appearance) *realism* which characterized the dialogue between Plato and Aristotle will replace that between mentalism (*mind*) and materialism (matter, or *brain*). This change in tension will lead to a new surge of experimentation, observation, and theory construction in the spirit of a Pythagorean and Peircian pragmaticism.

In summary, an answer to the question as to how mind and brain become coordinate rests on looking upward in the hierarchy of inquiry. This direction of inquiry leads into understanding a holoform, which in today's terms is represented by the spectral domain. Although engineers daily use the enfolded order in radar, crystallography, and tomography—wherever image processing is important—cognitive neuroscientists are, as yet, only barely acquainted with this pervasive distributed order of nature. It is now necessary to make accessible, both by experiment and by theory, the rules for "tuning in"

---

*"The claim of the early Ionians that nature was intelligible was based on their view that the practical arts were intelligent efforts of men to cooperate with nature for their own good." (B. Farrington, 1961, p. 46.) This view was shared by Charles S. Peirce and Norbert Wiener.

on the universal order cognized by Leibniz through his co-invention (with Newton) of the differential and integral calculus—an order that we are apt to call spiritual.

HOW REAL IS OUR EXPERIENCE?
AN ANSWER TO THE SECOND QUESTION

What do we decide to call "real"? Is gravity real? An electron or a photon? Philosophers have argued the point for centuries. When we bump our shins against the edge of the bed when we are tired and ready to get into it, we are apt to dismiss the philosophers' worries. The pain is real and so is the something against which we bumped. But is it a bed just because we have agreed to call it that? With the advent of techniques that can mimic reality by appropriate sensory stimulation (virtual reality), the issue is again thrust upon us. Is a virtual bed real or is only our experience of it real, and how can we tell the difference between these experiences? We can if we know enough about the world order that produced the experience.

Knowing enough is an everyday enterprise in which we engage through inquiry in both downward and upward directions. The answer to our question as to how real is our conscious experience comes from upward-looking inquiry. As a baby we hear, see, touch, smell, and taste our environment. None of these sensations is remotely similar to any other. Think of it: The sight of mother's breast, her odor, the feel of the nipple, and the taste of the milk, all accompanied by a tranquilizing melody—what do these sensations have in common? Only by repeated juxtaposition as in classical conditioning do we come to "realize" these sensations into a common experience. This realization is composed by consensual validation.

Thus we construct our conscious experiences by consensual validation from a world order that includes potentialities that occur both outside ourselves and those that are a part of our biological makeup, our unconscious archetypical (Carl Jung's term) processes. There are constant interpenetrations among these orders (interpenetrations that Piaget called assimilation and accommodation). By applying the various procedures that compose the hierarchies, consensually validated *appearances gradually become "real" to us.*

It is more important to deconstruct this *appearance* of reality than to muse as to whether it is truly real. As Charles Peirce noted, the meanings of experiences are what we mean to *do* about them. Thus, if we are to make any further progress in understanding our conscious experiences, we need to inquire just *how* they have come to be composed. More formally stated, the important procedure to further understanding is an examination of the axioms that underlie it. Whatever logical edifice we build on current knowledge is only as good as the axioms upon which it is constructed. As Gödel showed, one cannot prove the verity of a logical (mathematical) structure by recourse only to that structure.

The premise here is that we are curious to know more. The children's questions mentioned earlier as to whether birds could land on the planets and the stars represent children's universal curiosity and drive to know more. History indicates that the scholarly community also continues in the search. And recent social experience indicates that when people are given the chance to freely enjoy inquiry they flock to lectures, to courses, and to the media for deeper understanding. Only when this appetite for learning is blunted by, for example, inappropriate teaching methods, does the search stagnate. But this is another story that needs to be addressed on another occasion.

In summary: In upward-looking inquiry, knowledge is gained by consensual validation. We are apt to label this knowledge and the experience that led to it as real. But all knowledge is based on apparent coincident sensory experience, on appearance.

Thus a fundamental clue to how science and spirituality can become reconciled lies in the concept of faith, in the validity of appearance. Scientists are constantly aware that they walk a high, narrow beam when it comes to aspects that are unknown and which they cannot measure. On the one side, while they acknowledge that there *are* unknowns (why else would they continue to experiment and measure?), they cannot be distracted by unknowns, lest they fall into undue speculation. On the other side, scientists must not forget that the current logical reality based on measured data will most likely, through future data (or the rediscovered past) become altered. The stabilizing device of this balancing act is what might be called the judicious suspension of disbelief.

CONCLUSION

Life is a process. The answers to our original questions lie embedded in the fact that human life is characterized, at its best, as a continuing process of inquiry: that is, gaining understanding of the world order through remembering what has been learned and then utilizing this gain to improve that world order. Thus, in response to Question 1, our perceptions of reality are virtual in that they are constructions that are continually modified. As for Question 2, modification occurs through the brain's processing of experiences not only in terms of current input but also in terms of memory.

This self-organizing process was called *entelechy* by Aristotle. Humans are able to accomplish such self-organization because of the inordinate processing capability of their brains. Processing does not take place helter-skelter, however. There are two hierarchies of inquiry that are routinely pursued, one reaching upward from conscious experience into evermore *encompassing* appreciation; the other reaching downward through analysis into the *components* of an experience to understand it. These hierarchies are interleaved from time to time, as are the pages of a book, especially when an impasse has been reached in the pursuit of one or the other path. When plateaus seem to be reached in the continuing inquiry, a new generation of inquirers comes along and *entelechy* begins anew.

Afterword

by Karen Shanor, Ph.D.

When I wrote my introductory remarks, I tried to convey the excitement that is sparking research into the connection between mind, brain, and our experience of reality. Now, as I prepare my concluding remarks, I find myself once again wondering at the myriad possibilities that emerge every day. And I am not alone; many examples of richness and surprise are energizing an enthusiastic throng of scientists from a variety of disciplines. These scientists are starting to talk to one another and learn from one another—engineers, computer scientists, psychologists, neuroscientists, mathematicians, physicists, and biologists, to name a few.

Emergence theory, a new concept in physics, has appeared and captured many people's imaginations, including mine. This theory proposes that there are numerous layers of different forms of energy, each with its own frequency, similar to frequency bands on the radio. While these frequencies superimpose upon one another, each frequency is separated from the others by a distinct border or gap, as it is called. It is thought that to bridge the gap from one layer to the next, a kind of holographic process is involved.

And, in what I like to think of as a coincidence, emergence theory—which I think may help to explain the levels of the mind—sounds very similar to the title of this book, although my editor suggested the title more than a year before I met the originator of emergence theory, professor George Farre, director of the interdisciplinary program in cognitive science at Georgetown and an expert in quantum physics.

Can emergence theory help explain the many layers of our thinking, awareness, and communication? Might it account for the divergent energy systems in the brain, such as the electrical activity an EEG can pick up from nerve impulses, and the sources of energy in the holographic, distributed, and nonlinear functions of the brain; or even subtle energy forces such as prana and chi? Can it explain how our thoughts and intentions might affect certain energy frequencies and interact with other levels of energy? How many levels of energy will we find, and in what domains?

Equally fascinating and reminiscent of the Star Trek catchphrase "Beam me up, Scotty," is what is referred to in science as "quantum teleportation" where a subatomic bit of information appears, disappears, and then reappears in a different and surprising way. Can such a phenomenon help explain how our thoughts might be communicated or could affect others at a distance? Research in many areas of quantum physics is beginning to help us better understand our mental powers.

As we learn more about the mind and the universe, it is as if we have fitted together the pieces of a jigsaw puzzle and expected to produce a beautiful picture, flat on a tabletop. But as we fit the pieces together, an exquisite three- (or even four-) dimensional form has emerged, much grander and more complex than the sum of its parts, and more majestic than anything we might have anticipated. It is as if, after years of not being able to see the forest for the trees, we are struck dumb with awe at the miracle of every single oak while standing immersed in the pungent shadows and earthy, leafy, living realm that we experience as forest.

While walking through the magnificent woods near my home yesterday, a squirrel skittered through the twigs at my feet and brought to mind the animals that have made their ways into the pages of this book. I began with seven blind mice exploring the elephant of consciousness, and now conclude with the memory of the tiny ant raising its head to the wondrous expanse above. With the image of that ant firmly in mind, I thank you for joining me on this journey, and urge you—don't forget to look up.

Notes

INTRODUCTION

1. Dr. Marilyn Schlitz and her colleagues at Stanford are continuing the research she originated with Dr. William Braud that shows that one person, through his or her thoughts, can change some part of the physiology—such as heart rate, blood pressure, or electrical conduction on the skin—of a person in another location.

   William Braud and Marilyn Schlitz, "Consciousness Interactions with Remote Biological Systems: Anomalous Intentionality Effects," *Subtle Energies*, 1992.

2. In February 1994, at a Smithsonian seminar developed by a scientist at the National Institutes of Health, participants were stunned to hear research results reported by Dr. Roger Nelson

of Princeton University's Engineering Anomalies Research Laboratory or PEAR Lab. Subjects in that study were able to communicate complex information such as images of very different types of buildings and sculptures to other subjects thousand of miles away. The proof that such information could be communicated mentally from one person to another was interesting enough, but what really astounded the Smithsonian audience was that in a large number of cases, receivers got the information up to three days *before* it was sent.

Dean Radin and Roger Nelson, "Consciousness-Related Effects in Random Physical Systems," *Foundations of Physics*.

Robert G. Jahn and Brenda J. Dunne, *The Margins of Reality*, New York: Harcourt Brace Jovanovich, 1987.

3. Interestingly, Dr. Lene Vestergaard Hau, her students at Harvard, and Dr. Steve E. Harris of Stanford, reported in the February 18, 1999, scientific journal *Nature* that they were able to slow a beam of laser light to 38 miles an hour. (Light usually travels about 186,000 miles per second.)

4. Ed Young, *Seven Blind Mice*, New York: Philomel Books, 1992.

CHAPTER ONE

1. Gerald D. Fischbach, *Mind and Brain, Readings from Scientific American*, New York: W. H. Freeman & Co., 1993.

2. Sir David Brewster, *Memoirs of the Life, Writings, and Discoveries of Sir Isaac Newton*, Edinburgh: T. Constable & Co., 1855. (As a sidenote, Sir David Brewster is credited with inventing the kaliedoscope in 1815.)

3. Francis Crick, *The Astonishing Hypothesis*, New York: Charles Scribner's Sons, 1994.

4. March 13, 1999, conversation with Professor of Philosophy Roger Paden of George Mason University.

5. Gerald D. Fischbach, *Mind and Brain, Readings from Scientific American*, New York: W. H. Freeman & Co., 1993; and March 13, 1999, conversation with Professor of Philosophy Roger Paden of George Mason University.

6. David Blask, a pioneering researcher in this area, writes of one way that melatonin thwarts cancer in our body:

> Recent work from our laboratory strongly indicates that both pharmacological and physiological levels of melatonin inhibit cancer growth by blocking the tumor uptake of the long chain essential fatty acid, linoleic acid, and its metabolism to a potentially important growth signal transduction molecule, 13-hydroxy octadecadienoic acid.

D. E. Blask, "Melatonin: The Pineal Gland's Anticancer Molecule," presented June 1997, Bolonga, Italy.

7. *New York Times*, November 19, 1989.

8. Jane Clark and Michael Cohen, "Interview: Roger Penrose about Consciousness and Science," *Beshara*.

9. Subash C. Kak, "The Three Languages of the Brain: Quantum, Reorganizational, and Associative," in Karl Pribram and Joseph King, eds., *Learning as Self-Organization*, New Jersey: Lawrence Erlbaum Associates, 1996.

10. Margaret Wheatley, *Leadership and the New Sciences*, San Franscico: Berrett-Koehler Publishers, Inc., 1992.

11. Quote from Dr. Robert Gottesman in Candace B. Pert, *Molecules of Emotion*, New York: Scribner, 1997.

12. Candace B. Pert, *Molecules of Emotion*, New York: Scribner, 1997.

13. John Beahrs, *Unity and Multiplicity*, New York: Bruner/Mazel, 1982.

14. E. R. Hilgard and J. R. Hilgard, *Hypnosis in the Relief of Pain*, Los Altos, California: William Kaufman, Inc., 1975.

E. R. Hilgard, *Divided Consciousness: Multiple Controls in Human Thought and Action*, New York: Wiley and Sons, 1977.

15. Lawrence Weiskrantz, *Blindsight*, New York: Oxford University Press.

CHAPTER TWO

1. Jacobo Grinberg-Zylberbaum, *Creation of Experience*, Mexico City: Instituto National, 1988.

2. Joseph LeDoux, *Barnes and Noble New American Encyclopedia*, "B," p. 449, USA: Grolier, 1991.

    Norman Geschwind and A. M. Galabunda, eds., *Cerebral Dominance*, 1988.

    Franco Lepore, et al. eds., *Two Hemispheres—One Brain: Functions of the Corpus Callosum*, 1986.

    S. P. Springer and Georg Deutsch, *Left Brain, Right Brain*, 2nd ed., 1985.

3. William Dement, *The Promise of Sleep*, New York: Delacorte Press, 1999.

4. Richard Restak, *The Brain: The Last Frontier*, Garden City, New York: Doubleday & Co., 1979.

5. Karen Shanor was the intern.

6. Based on Karen Shanor's 1981 radio interview with James Prescott.

7. Alvin Poussaint to Karen Shanor, November 1983.

8. In his eighties at the time, Carl Rogers said this as a guest on Karen Shanor's radio program in 1979.

9. D. P. Wolf, "Being of Several Minds: Voices and Versions of the Self in Early Childhood," eds. D. Cicchetti and M. Beeghly, *The Self in Transition: Infancy to Childhood*, Chicago: University of Chicago Press, 1990.

10. As quoted in C. Alvarado, "Disassociation and State Specific

Physiology During the Nineteenth Century," Dissociation 2, 1989.

11. T. Field, "Attachment as Psychobiological Attunement: Being on the Same Wavelength," eds. M. Reite and T. Field, *The Psychobiology of Attachment and Separation*, New York: Academic Press, 1985.

SUGGESTED READING

Ainsworth, M.D.S., M. C. Blehar, E. Waters, and S. Wall, *Patterns of Attachment: A Psychological Study of the Strange Situation*, Hillsdale, New Jersey: Erlbaum, 1978.

J. Bowlby, *Attachment and Loss*, vols. 1 & 2, New York: Basic Books, 1973.

Leslie Brothers, *Friday's Footprints*, New York: Oxford University Press, 1997.

Paul Ekman and Erika Rosenberg eds., *What the Face Reveals*, New York: Oxford University Press, 1997.

Jeffrey L. Elman, et al. eds., *Rethinking Innateness*, Cambridge Massachusetts: Bradford Book, MIT Press, 1996.

Daniel Goleman, *Emotional Intelligence*, New York: Bantam Books, 1995.

Stanley I. Greenspan, *The Growth of the Mind*, New York: Addison-Wesley, 1997.

Frank W. Putnam, *Dissociation in Children and Adolescents: A Developmental Perspective*, New York: The Guilford Press, 1997.

CHAPTER THREE

SUGGESTED READING

C. Alexander, R. Boyer, and V. Alexander, "Higher States of Consciousness in the Vedic Psychology of Maharishi Mahesh Yogi: A Theoretical Introduction and Research Review," *Modern Science and Vedic Science*, 1987.

J. I. Gackenbach and S. P. LaBerge, eds., *Conscious Mind, Sleeping Brain: Perspectives on Lucid Dreaming*, New York: Plenum, 1988.

J. I. Gackenbach and J. Bosveld, *Control Your Dreams*, New York: Harper & Row, 1989.

J. I. Gackenbach and A. Sheikh, eds., *Dream Images: A Call to Mental Arms*, Farmingdale, New York: Baywood, 1991.

J. I. Gackenbach, "Reflections on Dreamwork with Central Alberta Cree: An Essay on an Unlikely Social Action Vehicle," K. Bulkeley, ed., *Among All These Dreamers: Essays on Dreaming and Modern Society*, New York: SUNY Press, 1995.

H. Hunt, *The Multiplicity of Dreams: A Cognitive Psychological Perspective*, New Haven: Yale University Press, 1989.

S. LaBerge, *Lucid Dreaming*, New York: Ballentine, 1989.

L. Mason, C. N. Alexander, F. Travis, J. Gackenbach, and D. Orme-Johnson, "EEG Correlates of 'Higher States of Consciousness' During Sleep," *Sleep Research*, 24, 1995.

CHAPTER FOUR

SUGGESTED READING

Robert Ader, David Felton, and Nicholas Cohen, *Psychoneuroim-*

munology, 2nd ed., San Diego: Academic Press, 1991.

Deepak Chopra, M.D., *Ageless Body, Timeless Mind: The Quantum Alternative to Growing Old*, New York: Harmony Books, 1993.

_____. *Perfect Health: The Complete Mind/Body Guide*, New York: Harmony Books, 1991.

_____. *Quantum Healing: Exploring the Frontiers of Mind/Body Medicine*, New York: Bantam Books, 1989.

Jon Franklin, *Molecules of the Mind*, New York: Antheneum, 1987.

Stephen M. Hawking, A *Brief History of Time*, New York: Bantam Books, 1988.

Michio Kaku, Ph.D., and Jennifer Trainer, *Beyond Einstein*, New York: Bantam Books, 1987.

Stephen Locke, M.D., and Douglas Colligan, *The Healer Within*, New York: Dutton, 1986.

Guy Murchie, *The Seven Mysteries of Life*, Boston: Houghton Mifflin, 1978.

Heinz R. Pagles, *The Cosmic Code: Quantum Physics as the Language of Nature*, New York: Simon & Schuster, 1982.

Candace B. Pert, Ph.D., *Molecules of Emotion: Why You Feel the Way You Feel*, New York: Scribner, 1997.

Anthony Smith, *The Body*, New York: Viking, 1986.

Ken Wilber, ed., *Quantum Questions*, Boston: Shambhala, 1984.

CHAPTER FIVE

1. Kenneth R. Pelletier, "Between Mind and Body: Stress, Emotions, and Health," in Daniel Goleman, Ph.D., and Joel Gurin,

eds., *Mind/Body Medicine*, Yonkers, New York: Consumer Reports Books, 1993.

2. Blair Justice, *Who Gets Sick?: Thinking and Health*, Houston: Peak Press, 1987.

   Sandra Blakeslee, "Placebos Prove So Powerful Even Experts Are Surprised," *New York Times* Science Times section, October 13, 1998.

3. Bienenfeld, et al., "The Placebo Effect in Cardiovascular Disease," *Am Heart J.*, 1996.

4. B. J. Hansen, et al., "Placebo Effects in the Pharmacological Treatment of Uncomplicated Benign Prostatic Hyperplasia," *Scand J Urol Nephrol*, 1996.

5. Sandra Blakeslee, "Placebos Prove So Powerful Even Experts Are Surprised," *New York Times* Science Times section, October 13, 1998.

6. Ibid.

7. Ibid.

8. Epstein, M.D., "The Placebo Effect, a Neglected Asset in the Care of Patients," *JAMA*, 1975.

   H. Benson, *The Relaxation Response*, New York: William Morrow, 1975.

9. H. Benson, *The Relaxation Response*, New York: William Morrow, 1975.

10. Blair Justice, *Who Gets Sick?: Thinking and Health*, Houston: Peak Press, 1987.

11. Ibid.

12. Ibid.

13. S. C. Thompson, "Will It Hurt Less If I Can Control It? A Complex Answer to a Simple Question," *Psychological Bulletin*, 1981.

14. Blair Justice, *Who Gets Sick?: Thinking and Health*, Houston: Peak Press, 1987.

15. S. Cohen, D. A. J. Tyrell, and A. P. Smith, "Psychological Stress and Susceptibility to the Common Cold," *New England Journal of Medicine*, 1991.

16. Daniel Goleman and Joel Gurin, eds., *Mind-Body Medicine*, Yonkers, New York: Consumer Reports Books, 1993, p. 40.

17. James Gordon, *Manifesto for a New Medicine*, New York: Addison-Wesley.

18. Richard S. Surwit, "Diabetes: Mind Over Metabolism," in Daniel Goleman and Joel Gurin, eds., *Mind-Body Medicine*, Yonkers, New York: Consumer Reports Books, 1993.

19. A. McGrady and J. Horner, "Complementary/Alternative Therapies in General Medicine: Diabetes Mellitus," in J. Spencer and J. Jacobs, eds., *Complementary/Alternative Medicine: An Evidence Based Approach*, St. Louis: Mosby, 1998.

20. M. F. Scheier and C. S. Carver, "Optimism, Coping, and Health: Assessment and Implications of Generalized Outcome Expectancies," *Health Psychology*, 4, 1985. Cited in S. F. Taylor, *Health Psychology*, 2nd ed., New York: McGraw-Hill, 1991.

21. C. Peterson, M. E. P. Seligman, and G. E. Vaillant, "Pessimistic Explanatory Style Is a Risk Factor For Physical Illness: A Thirty-Five-Year Longitudinal Study," *Journal of Personality and Social Psychology*, 1988.

22. S. Tan and C. A. Leucht, "Cognitive-Behavioral Therapy for Clinical Pain Control: A 15-Year Update and Its Relationship to Hypnosis," *Int J. Clin Exp Hypnosis*, 1997.

23. B. D. Kinrnan, et al., "Hypnoanalgesia Reduces R-III Nociceptive Neflex. Further Evidence Concerning the Multifactorial Nature of Hypnotic Analgesia," *Pain*, 1995.

24. O. C. Simonton, et al., *Getting Well Again*, Los Angeles: Tarcher-St. Martins, 1978.

O. C. Simonton, et al., "Psychological Intervention in the Treatment of Cancer," *Psychosomatics*, 1980.

25. Karen Olness, "Hypnosis: The Power of Attention," in Daniel Goleman and Joel Gurin, eds., *Mind-Body Medicine*, Yonkers, New York: Consumer Reports Books, 1993.

26. D. A. Shannahoff-Khalsa, L. R. Beckett, "Clinical Case Report: Efficacy of Yogic Techniques in the Treatment of Obsessive-Compulsive Disorders," *Int J. Neurosci*, March 1996.

27. James Gordon, *Manifesto for a New Medicine*, New York: Addison-Wesley, 1996.

28. Yosio Kawakita, Shizu Sakai, Yasuo Otsuka, and Ishiyaku, eds., *The Comparison Between Concepts of Life-Breath in East and West: Proceedings of the 15th International Symposium on the Comparative History of Medicine—East and West*, Tokyo/St Louis: Euro-America, Inc., 1990.

29. Delthia Ricks, "Mystery Cancer," *Newsday*, May 1998.

30. John Christy, "Prayer as Medicine," *Forbes*, March 1998.

31. A. Ai, et al., "Psychological Recovery Following Coronary Artery Bypass Graft Surgery in the Use of Complementary Therapies," *J Alternat Complement Med Res Paradigm and Pract. Policy*, 1997.

32. Randolph C. Byrd, "Positive Therapeutic Effects of Intercessory Prayer in a Coronary Care Unit Population," *Southern Medical Journal*, July 1988.

33. 1995 study at Dartmouth-Hitchcock Medical Center.

34. D. B. Larson and M. G. Milano, "Religion and Mental Health: Should They Work Together?" *Alternative and Complementary Therapies*, March/April 1996.

35. Rene Spitz's research on orphans in northern European vs. Mexican foundling homes as discussed in James Gordon, *Manifesto for a New Medicine*.

36. University of Wisconsin psychologist Harry Harlow's research with baby monkeys in the 1950s in James Gordon, *Manifesto for a New Medicine*.

37. Carol Krucoff, *Washington Post*, Health Magazine, November 1998.

38. Norman Cousins, *Human Options*, New York: W. W. Norton and Co., 1981.

REFERENCES

A. Ai, et al., "Psychological Recovery Following Coronary Artery Bypass Graft Surgery in the Use of Complementary Therapies," *J Alternat Complement Med Res.Res Paradigm and Pract. Policy*, 1997.

D. B. Amav, et al. eds., *Standards and Guidelines For Biofeedback Applications in Psychophysiological Self Regulation*, Wheat Ridge, Colorado, 1992.

J. J. Ashby and R .S. Lenhart, "Prayer as a Coping Strategy for Chronic Pain Patients," *Rehabil Psychol*, 1994.

R. V. August, "Obstetrical Hypnoanaesthesi," *Am J. Obstet Gynecol*, 1960.

Adriane Berman-Fugh, *Alternative Medicine: What Works*, Tucson, Arizona: Odonian Press, 1996.

Epstein H. Benson, M.D., "The Placebo Effect, a Neglected Asset in the Care of Patients," *JAMA*, 1975.

H. Benson, *The Relaxation Response*, New York: William Morrow, 1975.

Bienenfeld, et al., "The Placebo Effect in Cardiovascular Disease," *American Heart J.*, 1996.

A. W. Braam, et al., "Reliogiosity as a Protector or Prognostic Factor of Depression in Later Life: Results from a Community Survey in the Netherlands," *Acta Psychiatr Scan*, 1997.

J. Chaves and S. F. Dworkin, "Hypnotic Control of Pain: Historical Perspectives and Future Prospects," *Int J. Clin Exp Hypn*, 1997.

De Craen, et al., "Effect of Colour of Drugs. Systematic Review of Perceived Effect of Drugs and of Their Effectiveness," *Brit Med J*, 1996.

L. Dossey, *Healing Words: The Power of Prayer and the Practice of Medicine*, San Francisco: Harper-Row, 1993.

M. S. Garfinkel, et al., *J. Rheumatol*, 1994.

James Gordon, *Manifesto for a New Medicine*, New York: Addison-Wesley, 1996.

B. J. Hansen, et al., "Placebo Effects in the Pharmacological Treatment of Uncomplicated Benign Prostatic Hyperplasia," *Scand J Urol Nephrol*, 1996.

W. L. Haskell, et al., "Complementary/Alternative Therapies in General Medicine: Cardiovascular Disease," in J. Spencer and J. Jacobs, eds., *Complementary/Alternative Medicine: An Evidence Based Approach*, St. Louis: Mosby, 1998.

J. K. Kiecolt, et al., "Psychosocial Enhancement of Immunocompetence in a Geriatric Population," *Health Psychol*, 1985.

B. D. Kinrnan, et al., "Hypnoanalgesia Reduces R-III Nociceptive Reflex. Further Evidence Concerning the Multifactorial Nature of Hypnotic Analgesia," *Pain*.

H. G. Koenig, "Attendance at Religious Service, Interkeukin 6 and Other Biolobical Parameters of Immune Function in Older Adults," *International Journal of Psychiat*, 1997.

D. B. Larson and M. G. Milano, "Religion and Mental Health: Should They Work Together?" *Alternative and Complementary Therapies*, March/April 1996.

M. Levitan, "Use of Hypnosis with Cancer Patients," *Psychiatr Medicine*, 1992.

May Loo, "Complementary/Alternative Therapies in Select Populations: Children," in J. Spencer and J. Jacobs, eds., *Complementary/Alternative Medicine: An Evidence Based Approach*, St. Louis: Mosby, 1998.

A. McGrady and J. Horner, "Complementary/Alternative Therapies in General Medicine: Diabetes," in J. Spencer and J. Jacobs, eds., *Complementary/Alternative Medicine: An Evidence Based Approach*, Mosby, St. Louis, 1998.

K. Morris, *The Lancet*, April 1998.

K. R. Pelletier, et al., "Current Trends in the Integration and Reimbursement of Complementary and Alternative Medicine by Managed Care, Insurance Carriers and Hospital Providers," *American Journal of Health Promotion*, 1997.

Candice Pert, *Molecules of Emotion*, New York: Scriber, 1997.

M. A. Piercy, et al, "Placebo Response in Anxiety Disorders," *Ann Pharmacother.*

C. L. Rossi and D. B. Cheek, *Mind-Body Therapy: Ideodynamic Healing in Hypnosis*, New York: Norton, 1988.

R. Schneider, et al., "A Randomizied Controlled Trial of Stress Reduction for Hypertension in Older African Americans," *Hypertension*, 1995.

T. Schmidt, et al., "Changes in Cardiovascular Risk Factors and Hormones During a Comprehensive Residential Three Month Kriya Yoga Training and Vegetarian Nutrition," *Acta Physiol Scan*, 1997.

Khalsa Shannahoff, D.A. and L. R. Beckett, "Clinical Case Report:

Efficacy of Yogic Techniques in the Treatment of Obsessive-Compulsive Disorders," *International Journal of Neuroscience*, March 1996.

O. C. Simonton, et al., *Getting Well Again*, Los Angeles: Tarcher-St. Martins, 1978.

O. C. Simonton, et al., "Psychological Intervention in the Treatment of Cancer," *Psychosomatics*, 1980.

J. Spencer, "Maximization of Biofeed Following Cognitive Stress Preselection in Generalized Anxiety," *Perception Mot Skills*, 1986.

J. Spencer and J. Jacobs, eds., *Complementary/Alternative Medicine: An Evidence Based Approach*, St. Louis: Mosby, 1998.

J. Spencer, "Essentials of Complementary/Alternative Medicine," in J. Spencer and J. Jacobs, eds., *Complementary/Alternative Medicine: An Evidence Based Approach*, St. Louis: Mosby, 1998.

S. Steggles, "Hypnosis for Children and Adolescents with Cancer: An Annotated Bibliography, 1985–1995," *Journal of Pediatric Oncol Nurs*, 1997.

S. Tan and C. A. Leucht, "Cognitive-Behavioral Therapy for Clinical Pain Control: A 15-Year Update and Its Relationship to Hypnosis, *International Journal Clin Exp Hypnosis*, 1997.

Ann Gill Taylor, "Complementary/Alternative Therapies in the Treatment of Pain," in J. Spencer and J. Jacobs, eds., *Complementary/Alternative Medicine: An Evidence Based Approach*, Mosby, St. Louis, 1998.

J. A. Turner, et al., "The Importance of Placebo Effects in Pain Treatment and Research," *JAMA*, 1994.

A. J. Weaver, "A Systematic Review of Research on Religion in Four

Major Psychiatric Journals, 1991-1995," *Journal of Nervous and Mental Disease*, 1998.

CHAPTER SIX

1. Quoted from Frank J. Sulloway, *Freud: Biologist of the Mind*, New York: Basic Books. Original quote from Freud's autobiography.
2. From Dr. David Spiegel's May 26, 1994, lecture at the Smithsonian's eight week series, "The Brain and Consciousness: Frontier of the 21st Century."
3. Ibid.
4. J. R. Hilgard, *Personality and Hypnosis: A Study of Imaginative Involvement*, Chicago: University of Chicago Press, 1970.
   Helen Crawford, *Cognitive Flexibility, Dissociation and Hypnosis*, presidential address to the meeting of the Hypnosis Division of the American Psychological Association, Los Angeles, 1985.
5. E. R. Hilgard, *Hypnotic Susceptibility*, New York: Harcourt Brace Jovanovich, 1965.
6. Milton Erickson, *Healing in Hypnosis*, Ernest Rossi, Margaret Ryan, and Florence Sharp, eds., New York: Irvington, 1983.
7. Ibid.
8. Martin T. Orne, *Barnes and Noble New American Encyclopedia*, "H," Grolier, 1991.
9. From Dr. David Spiegel's May 26, 1994, lecture at the Smithsonian's eight week series, "The Brain and Consciousness: Frontier of the 21st Century."
10. Ibid.
11. Ibid.
12. Ibid.
13. Ibid.
14. Milton Erickson, *Healing in Hypnosis*, Ernest Rossi, Margaret

Ryan, and Florence Sharp, eds., Irvington, New York, 1983.
Milton Erickson, *Life Reframing in Hypnosis*, Ernest Rossi,
Margaret Ryan, and Florence Sharp, eds., Irvington, New York,
1983.

15. Milton Erickson, *Healing in Hypnosis*, Ernest Rossi, Margaret
Ryan, and Florence Sharp, eds., Irvington, New York, 1983.

16. Milton Erickson, *Mind-Body Communication in Hypnosis*, Ernest
Rossi, Margaret Ryan, and Florence Sharp, eds., Irvington, New
York, 1986.

17. Milton Erickson and Ernest Rossi, *Hypnotherapy: An Exploratory
Casebook*, New York: Irvington, 1979.

18. Ibid.

19. Ibid.

CHAPTER SEVEN

SUGGESTED READING

D. C. Dennett, *Consciousness Explained*, Boston: Little, Brown and
Co, 1991.

C. S. Peirce, *Collected Papers*, C. Hartshorne, P. Weiss, and A.
Burks, eds., Cambridge, Massachusetts: Harvard University Press,
1990.

K. R. Popper and J. C. Eccles, *The Self and Its Brain*, New York-
Berlin: Springer-Verlag, 1977.

K. H. Pribram, "Quantum Information Processing in Brain Systems
and the Spiritual Nature of Mankind," *Science and Culture: A Common Path for the Future*, 1996.

Final Report of the UNESCO/UNU Tokyo Symposium held Sep-
tember 1995.

K. H. Pribram, "Mind and Brain, Psychology and Neuroscience, the Eternal Verities," in S. Koch and D. E. Leary, eds., *A Century of Psychology as a Science*, New York: McGraw-Hill, 1985.

K. H. Pribram, "Problems Concerning the Structure of Consciousness," in G. Globus, G. Maxwell, and I. Savodnik, eds., *Consciousness and Brain: A Scientific and Philosophical Inquiry*, New York: Plenum, 1976.

K. H. Pribram, *Languages of the Brain: Experimental Paradoxes and Principles in Neuropsychology*, Englewood Cliffs, New Jersey: Prentice-Hall, 1971; Monterey, California: Brooks/Cole, 1977; New York: Brandon House, 1982.

B. Russell, *Human Knowledge, Its Scope and Limits*, New York: Simon & Schuster, 1948.

J. R. Searle, *The Rediscovery of Mind*, Cambridge, Massachusetts: MIT Press, 1992.

J. R. Searle, *Minds, Brains & Science*, Cambridge, Massachusetts: Harvard University Press, 1984.

R. W. Sperry, "Mind/Brain Interaction—Mentalism, Yes—Dualism, No," *Neuroscience*, 1980.

AFTERWORD

1. Scientists at the University of Innsbruck in Austria demonstrated a form of teleportation by causing something to vanish at one location and to instantaneously reappear elsewhere in the lab, although there was no physical connection or known form of communication between the two locations. Innsbruck researcher Anton Zeilinger was quoted as saying, "There is no limit to how far the process can send something."

(The team had reported a physical condition in which a photon—a particle of light—was destroyed in one place and simultaneously reappeared in another.) In the journal *Nature*, December 11, 1997.

Bibliography

Ader, Robert, David Felton, and Nicholas Cohen, *Psychoneuroim-munology*, 2nd ed., San Diego: Academic Press, 1991.

Ainsworth, M. D. S., M. C. Blehar, E. Waters, and S. Wall, *Patterns of Attachment: A Psychological Study of the Strange Situation*, Hillsdale, New Jersey: Erlbaum, 1978.

Beahrs, John, *Unity and Multiplicity*, New York: Bruner/Mazel, 1982.

Benson, Herbert, *The Relaxation Response*, New York: William Morrow, 1975.

Bowlby, J., *Attachment and Loss*, vols. 1 & 2, New York: Basic Books, 1973.

Brothers, Leslie, *Friday's Footprints*, New York: Oxford University Press, 1997.

Bruner, J., *Child's Talk: Learning to Use Language,* New York: W. W. Norton and Co., 1982.

_____. *Actual Minds, Possible Worlds,* Cambridge, Massachusetts: Harvard University Press, 1986.

_____. *Acts of Meaning,* Cambridge, Massachusetts: Harvard University Press, 1990.

Chopra, Deepak, M.D., *Ageless Body, Timeless Mind: The Quantum Alternative to Growing Old,* New York: Harmony Books, 1993.

_____. *Perfect Health: The Complete Mind/Body Guide,* New York: Harmony Books, 1991.

_____. *Quantum Healing: Exploring the Frontiers of Mind/Body Medicine,* New York: Bantam Books, 1989.

Cousins, Norman, *Human Options,* New York: W. W. Norton and Co., 1981.

Crick, Francis, *The Astonishing Hypothesis,* New York: Charles Scribner's Sons, 1994.

Dement, William C., *The Promise of Sleep,* New York: Delacorte Press, 1999.

Dennett, D. C., *Consciousness Explained,* Boston: Little, Brown and Co., 1991.

Damasio, Antonio R., *Descartes' Error: Emotion, Reason, and the Laws of Physics,* New York: Avon Books, 1994.

Dossey, L., *Healing Words: The Power of Prayer and the Practice of Medicine,* San Francisco: Harper-Row, 1993.

Ekman, Paul, and Erika Rosenberg, eds., *What the Face Reveals,* New York: Oxford University Press, 1997.

Elman, Jeffrey L., et al. eds., *Rethinking Innateness,* Cambridge, Massachusetts: Bradford Book, MIT Press, 1996.

Erickson, Milton, *Healing in Hypnosis,* eds. Ernest Rossi, Margaret Ryan, and Florence Sharp, New York: Irvington, 1983.

_____. *Life Reframing in Hypnosis,* eds. Ernest Rossi, Margaret Ryan, and Florence Sharp, New York: Irvington, 1985.

_____. *Mind-Body Communication in Hypnosis*, eds. Ernest Rossi, Margaret Ryan, and Florence Sharp, New York: Irvington, 1986.

Erickson, Milton, and Ernest Rossi, *Hypnotherapy: An Exploratory Casebook*, New York: Irvington, 1979.

Field, T., "Attachment as Psychobiological Attunement: Being on the Same Wavelength," in M. Reite and T. Field eds., *The Psychobiology of Attachment and Separation*, New York: Academic Press, 1985.

Fischbach, Gerald D., *Mind and Brain, Readings from Scientific American*, W. H. Freeman & Co., New York, 1993.

Franklin, Jon, *Molecules of the Mind*, New York: Antheneum, 1987.

Gackenbach, J. I., and S. P. LaBerge, eds., *Conscious Mind, Sleeping Brain: Perspectives on Lucid Dreaming*, New York: Plenum, 1988.

Gackenbach, J. I., and J. Bosveld, *Control Your Dreams*, New York: Harper & Row, 1989.

Gackenbach, J. I., and A. Sheikh, eds., *Dream Images: A Call to Mental Arms*, Farmingdale, New York: Baywood, 1991.

Gackenbach, J. I., "Reflections on Dreamwork with Central Alberta Cree: An Essay on an Unlikely Social Action Vehicle," in K. Bulkeley, ed., *Among All These Dreamers: Essays on Dreaming and Modern Society*, New York: SUNY Press, 1995.

Goleman, Daniel, *Emotional Intelligence*, New York: Bantam Books, 1995.

_____. *Vital Lies, Simple Truths*, New York: Simon & Schuster, 1985.

Goleman, Daniel, and Joel Gurin, eds., *Mind/Body Medicine*, Yonkers, New York: Consumer Reports Books, 1993.

Gordon, James, *Manifesto for a New Medicine*, New York: Addison-Wesley, 1996.

Grinberg-Zylberbaum, Jacobo, *Creation of Experience*, Mexico City: Instituto National, 1988.

Greenspan, Stanley, *The Growth of the Mind*, New York: Addison-Wesley, 1997.

Harman, Willis W., *Global Mind Change*, San Francisco: IONS and Berrett-Koehler, 1998.

Hawking, Stephen M., *A Brief History of Time*, New York: Bantam Books, 1988.

Hilgard, E. R., *Divided Consciousness: Multiple Controls in Human Thought and Action*, New York: Wiley and Sons, 1977.

Hilgard, E. R., and J. R. Hilgard, *Hypnosis in the Relief of Pain*, Los Altos, California: William Kaufman, Inc., 1975.

Hilgard, J. R., *Personality and Hypnosis: A Study Of Imaginative Involvement*, Chicago: University of Chicago Press, 1970.

Hunt, H., *The Multiplicity of Dreams: A Cognitive Psychological Perspective*, Connecticut: Yale University Press, 1989.

Jahn, Robert G., and Brenda J. Dunne, *Margins of Reality*, New York: Harcourt Brace Jovanovich, 1987.

Jung, Carl G., *Man and His Symbols*, Garden City, New York: Doubleday, 1964.

Justice, Blair, *Who Gets Sick?: Thinking and Health*, Houston: Peak Press, 1985.

Kak, Subash C., "The Three Languages of the Brain: Quantum, Reorganizational, and Associative," in Karl Pribram and Joseph King, eds., *Learning as Self-Organization*, New Jersey: Erlbaum, 1996.

Kaku, Michio, Ph.D., and Jennifer Trainer, *Beyond Einstein*, New York: Bantam Books, 1987.

Kawakita, Yosio, Shizu Sakai, and Yasuo Otsuka, eds., *The Comparison Between Concepts of Life-Breath in East and West: Proceedings of the 15th International Symposium on the Comparative History of Medicine—East and West*, Tokyo/St. Louis: Ishiyaku Euro-America, Inc., 1990.

LaBerge, S., *Lucid Dreaming*, New York: Ballentine, 1985.

Locke, Stephen, and Douglas Colligan, *The Healer Within*, New York: Dutton, 1986.

Mason, L., C. N. Alexander, F. Travis, J. Gackenbach, and D. Orme-Johnson, "EEG Correlates of 'Higher States of Consciousness' During Sleep," *Sleep Research,* 24, 152 (1995).

Masterson, James F., *Search for the Real Self,* New York: Free Press, 1988.

Murchie, Guy, *The Seven Mysteries of Life,* Boston: Houghton Mifflin, 1978.

Pagles, Heinz R., *The Cosmic Code: Quantum Physics as the Language of Nature,* New York: Simon and Schuster, 1982.

Pert, Candace B., *Molecules of Emotion: Why You Feel the Way You Feel,* New York: Scribner, 1997.

Penrose, Roger, *The Emperor's New Mind,* New York: Oxford University Press, 1989.

_____. *The Large, the Small, and the Human Mind,* Cambridge: Cambridge University Press, 1997.

Pinker, Steven, *How the Mind Works,* New York: W. W. Norton and Co., 1997.

Popper, K. R., and J. C. Eccles, *The Self and Its Brain,* New York/Berlin: Springer-Verlag, 1977.

Pribram, K. H., *Languages of the Brain: Experimental Paradoxes and Principles in Neuropsychology,* Englewood Cliffs, New Jersey: Prentice-Hall, 1971; Monterey, California: Brooks/Cole, 1977; New York: Brandon House, 1982. (Translations in Russian, Japanese, Italian, and Spanish.)

_____. *Brain and Perception,* New Jersey: Erlbaum, 1991.

Putnam, Frank W., *Dissociation in Children and Adolescents: A Developmental Perspective,* New York: The Guilford Press, 1997.

Restak, Richard, *The Brain: The Last Frontier,* Garden City, New York: Doubleday & Co, 1979.

_____. *Brainscapes,* New York: Hyperion, 1995.

Rossi, Ernest L., *The Psychobiology of Mind-Body Healing,* New York: Norton, 1986.

Russell, B., *Human Knowledge, Its Scope and Limits*, New York: Simon & Schuster, 1948.

Searle, J. R., *The Rediscovery of Mind*, Cambridge, Massachusetts: MIT Press, 1992.

_____. *Minds, Brains & Science*, Cambridge, Massachusetts: Harvard University Press, 1984.

_____. *The Mystery of Consciousness*, New York: New York Review, 1997.

Simonton, O. C., et al., *Getting Well Again*, Los Angeles: Tarcher-St. Martins, 1978.

Siu, R. G. H., *Ch'i: A Neo-Taoist Approach to Life*, Cambridge, Massachusetts: MIT Press, 1974.

Smith, Anthony, *The Body*, New York: Viking, 1986.

Spencer, John, Joseph Jacobs, eds., *Complementary/Alternative Medicine: An Evidence Based Approach*, St. Louis: Mosby, 1999.

Spiegel, David, *Living Beyond Limits*, New York: Times, 1993.

Spiegel, H., and D. Spiegel, *Trance and Treatment*, New York: Basic Books, 1978.

Trefil, James, *Are We Unique?*, New York: John Wiley & Sons, 1997.

Weiskrantz, Lawrence, *Blindsight*, New York: Oxford University Press, 1986.

Wheatley, Margaret, *Leadership and the New Science*, San Francisco: Berrett-Koehler, 1992.

Wilber, Ken, ed., *Quantum Questions*, Boston: Shambhala, 1984.

Wolf, D. P., "Being of Several Minds: Voices and Versions of the Self in Early Childhood," in D. Cicchetti and M. Beeghly, eds., *The Self in Transition: Infancy to Childhood*, Chicago: University of Chicago Press, 1990, pp. 183–212.

Zukav, Gary, *The Dancing Wu Li Masters*, New York: Bantam, 1979.

Dr. Karen Nesbitt Shanor is a clinical psychologist in private practice in Washington, D.C. She has consulted for the White House and a number of leading corporations. She is the successful author of *The Shanor Study: The Sexual Sensitivity of the American Male, The Fantasy Files: The Sexual Fantasies of Contemporary Women,* and *How to Stay Together When You Have to Be Apart,* and has written for magazines such as *Ladies Home Journal, Cosmopolitan, Today's Health,* and *Esquire.* She has also hosted her own radio and television programs on psychology and appears regularly on national television.